The
Reference Shelf®

U.S. National Debate Topic: 2021-2022

Water Resources

The Reference Shelf
Volume 93 • Number 3
H.W. Wilson
A Division of EBSCO Information Services, Inc.

Published by
GREY HOUSE PUBLISHING
Amenia, New York
2021

The Reference Shelf

The books in this series contain reprints of articles, excerpts from books, addresses on current issues, and studies of social trends in the United States and other countries. There are six separately bound numbers in each volume, all of which are usually published in the same calendar year. Numbers one through five are each devoted to a single subject, providing background information and discussion from various points of view and concluding with an index and comprehensive bibliography that lists books, pamphlets, and articles on the subject. The final number of each volume is a collection of recent speeches. Books in the series may be purchased individually or on subscription.

Publisher's Cataloging-In-Publication Data
(Prepared by The Donohue Group, Inc.)

Names: Grey House Publishing, Inc., compiler.
Title: U.S. national debate topic, 2021-2022. Water resources / [compiled by Grey House Publishing].
Other Titles: US national debate topic, 2021-2022. Water resources | United States national debate topic, 2021-2022. Water resources | Water resources | Reference shelf ; v. 93, no. 3.
Description: Amenia, New York : Grey House Publishing, 2021. | Includes bibliographical references and index.
Identifiers: ISBN 9781642657913 (v. 93, no. 3) | ISBN 9781642657883 (volume set)
Subjects: LCSH: Water quality--United States--21st century--Sources. | Water conservation--United States--21st century--Sources. | Water-supply--United States--21st century--Sources. | Water--Government policy--United States--21st century--Sources.
Classification: LCC TD223 .U8 2021 | DDC 363.610973--dc23

Printed in Canada

Contents

5

Policy Issues

Preface

A Limited Resource

The most current estimate on total water consumption comes from 2015, at which time America consumed a collective 322 billion gallons of water each day. The biggest drain on water resources comes from the use of water for thermoelectric power generation and to irrigate farmland.[1] The average American household uses 300 gallons a day. Nearly a quarter of this is from flushing toilets, while another 20 percent is used by people taking showers. Clothes washing accounts for another 17 percent and 19 percent more comes out of kitchen and bathroom faucets.[2]

This tremendous demand on the world's water resources must be considered in light of the fact that only 1 percent of all water on the earth is safe for human use. The majority of the planet's water is toxic without processing, and processing water to make it potable is a wasteful and often pollution-heavy process. The supply of fresh water will remain relatively the same even as the human population, and therefore demand for water, increases. With each passing year, there is less and less water available for human use. The limited supply of water means it is essential to preserve remaining water resources before the loss of water resources proves disastrous in the uncomfortably near future.

The Water Resources Crisis

As in many other parts of the world, America's water resources are under threat from a variety of sources. One of the great challenges when trying to protect water resources is that the water systems of the world are interlinked. Rivers and streams eventually connect to the ocean, and oceanic systems contribute water to climate cycles that return rain to the land. What this means is that water resource issues often extend beyond geographical or political boundaries. Protecting water resources is therefore often an international or at least regional issue. Success in the effort to protect water resources often depends on intergovernmental cooperation. This is also true of the fight to protect water resources within the United States, where reservoirs of water frequently pass through multiple states or territories. This makes it next to impossible for a single government to effectively manage water resources independently and requires at least some level of cooperation to achieve any meaningful success.

It is difficult to combat any individual threat without taking into account other kinds of threats that also endanger the nation's water supplies and resources. That being said, it is possible to identify several major categories within the broader debate over the nation's water resources.

1. Pollution is the primary threat to much of the water currently available to American communities for drinking and hygiene. Pollution is sometimes directly deposited by individuals, communities, and corporations, into natural bodies of water. There is also the threat of pollution that indirectly impacts water systems after being deposited elsewhere. Pollution spilled into watersheds, which are terrestrial areas that drain into natural bodies of water, indirectly ends up polluting lakes, rivers, and streams. Ultimately, this pollution ends up in the ocean where it creates toxic algal blooms, kills sea creatures, and threatens the welfare of all Americans.

2. Waste and wastewater management is a subcategory of the pollution threat focusing specifically on the way that America's communities manage and dispose of wastewater from homes and businesses. Wastewater and sewage is one of the most important contributors to water pollution worldwide, and it is a problem that it intensifying in America. In part, this is because in many states sewage infrastructure is aging and insecure. Addressing this problem is difficult because the cost to repair or upgrade sewage systems is prohibitive, especially in states facing other budgetary problems. In some regions, especially where flooding is frequent, sewage system pollution has developed into a major crisis, threatening supplies of drinking water, agricultural land, and contributing to health issues within communities.[3]

3. A challenge related to both pollution and the looming sewage crisis is the issue of federal and state policy with regards to water conservation. The Clean Water Act (CWA) has been one of the nation's most successful efforts at environmental legislation, and studies show that the CWA greatly helped to reduce direct pollution into the nation's water reserves. However, the threats to America's water supplies are changing and intensifying, and many feel that the CWA must be updated to address these changes. Enacting stronger legislation, at either the federal or the state level, is difficult because such efforts are opposed by lobbyists for industries that profit by exploiting natural resources. Politicians allied with these corporate interests have weakened regulations on pollution. The Donald Trump administration, for instance, used a rewritten U.S. Environmental Protection Agency (EPA) regulation to greatly weaken the CWA, allowing companies to more freely pollute and reducing the capacity for communities or environmental protection organizations to hold corporations responsible for releasing hazardous waste into the nation's water supplies.[4]

4. There is another dimension to the water resources debate involving the ways in which water resources are essential for national security. On the global scale, water insecurity and the decline in availability of fresh, clean water creates humanitarian crises and contributes to political and military conflict. American interests are therefore threatened both directly and indirectly as more and more countries around the world face water resource issues. Within the United States, water shortages, flooding and pollution issues represent a major challenge to national security. Any of these factors can contribute to civil

unrest, lead to outbreaks of disease, and destabilize communities. In addition, America's military and national security agencies also face a direct threat from pollution, and some military facilities and installations are located in areas that face water shortages.[5]

America's water resources face a variety of threats that exist within a complex economic and sociological landscape. Political conflict and the struggle to balance corporate productivity and profit against public welfare is the greatest challenge to protecting water resources. In many cases, it is impossible to address issues involving water scarcity, water pollution, or natural resource conservation without addressing concerns that further environmental and anti-pollution legislation will increase costs to businesses. However, it is not true that environmental legislation is always bad for businesses. In fact, in the 2020s sustainable development produces more profit and more employment opportunities than industrial agriculture, fossil fuels, or any of the industries most directly related to water pollution and other environmental threats. It is possible, therefore, for states and nations to invest more heavily in sustainable development without a loss of economic growth or stability, though doing so will still require challenging the political influence of those companies and industries that most contribute to water resource depletion and pollution.

The Warming Earth

All of the many challenges facing America's effort to preserve water resources for future generations are also complicated by the threat of climate change and how this phenomenon will change the global environment and life on earth.

Human activity, especially the harvesting and burning of fossil fuels, is creating a global environmental crisis. The production of greenhouse gases is warming the planet and, as the climate warms, once-reliable resources supplies are becoming unstable. Rivers, streams, creeks, and lakes will lose water as rainfall patterns change and as increasing heat leads to longer periods of more intense drought. As this occurs, many communities will begin to experience more frequent and more extended water shortages. The loss of freshwater systems will also mean a loss of biodiversity. This will mean fewer fish for recreational use and for aquaculture. The loss of biodiversity will filter into the oceanic environment, precipitating a drop in oceanic productivity. The seafood industry will therefore decline, as will communities dependent on this resource.

Climate change will also bring more intense and longer-lasting severe weather systems. Tornadoes, hurricanes, and tropical storms will all become more frequent and more destructive. Flooding will become a common problem in many parts of the world that now only experience periodic flooding. Floods will pollute remaining bodies of freshwater, and this pollution will filter into the ocean, where pollutants coupled with intense seasonal heat will create massive oceanic algae blooms that are toxic to both human and animal life. Sewage systems will more often overflow and fail, leading to polluted communities, farmland, and natural water reservoirs.[6]

The proof of climate change is inescapable, and scientists around the world have contributed to our understanding of this very real and dangerous phenomenon. It has also been definitively proven that humanity is responsible for the rapidly chang-ing climate and that the fossil fuel industry is the primary agent of this change.[7]

The earth's environment is not a stable, static system but is constantly in flux. One change is a process called "desertification," whereby arid territory becomes desert. Currently, around 30 to35 percent of the earth is covered in semiarid land. At least 30 percent of the land in the United States falls into this category. Land that is semiarid or arid will eventually become desert. Mass agriculture and unsustain-able agricultural practices contribute to this process by removing vegetative growth and eroding soil quality. This leaves territories that might once have been prairie or grassland vulnerable to desertification. Climate change is accelerating the rate at which desertification is occurring. Studies indicate that 40 percent of the United States is at risk for desertification, meaning that many communities now struggling with water shortages could in the near future face a near total loss of available wa-ter. If this problem is allowed to continue unabated, many Americans communities might no longer be sustainable. This is one of the ways that climate change poses a direct threat to human lives, livelihoods, and cultures.[8]

Opportunities Amidst the Problems?

The threats to America's water infrastructure and resources are dire, and experts in public welfare and environmental conservation warn that America is facing multiple water crises at once, with few clear answers with regard to how the nation might best address and meet these challenges. However, where challenges exist, there are also opportunities for innovation and for growth and even profit. Over the last half century, investment in green infrastructure has accelerated rapidly, and economic experts predict that sustainable development will continue to command significant economic potential in the future. Many challenges facing Americans might also pro-vide new opportunities to address some of the nation's economic challenges while helping to blunt the impact of the environmental threats facing the nation. How the nation proceeds will therefore depend on how public opinion shifts and on what percentage of Americans embrace environmental conservation as an important na-tional goal. Public opinion is likely to change, however, as the impact of climate change and water resource shortages becomes more widespread. More Americans may find their opportunities in emerging industries meant to enhance sustainability and to protect resources for future generations.

Works Used

Harrington, Samantha. "Causes of Global Warming: How Scientists Know That Humans Are Responsible." *Yale Climate Connections*. Mar 27, 2020. https://yaleclimateconnections.org/2020/03/causes-of-global-warming/.

"How Sewage Pollution Ends Up in Rivers." *American Rivers*. 2019. https://www.americanrivers.org/threats-solutions/clean-water/sewage-pollution/.

"How We Use Water." *EPA*. https://www.epa.gov/watersense/how-we-use-water.

Kenney, Carolyn. "Climate Change, Water Security, and U.S. National Security."

Center for American Progress. Mar 22, 2017. https://www.americanprogress.org/issues/security/reports/2017/03/22/428918/climate-change-water-security-u-s-national-security/.

McSweeney, Robert. "Explainer: 'Desertification' and the Role of Climate Change." *Carbon Brief.* Aug 6, 2019. https://www.carbonbrief.org/explainer-desertification-and-the-role-of-climate-change.

Pimental, David, et al. "Water Resources: Agricultural and Environmental Issues." *BioScience.* Vol. 54, No. 10. Oct 2004.

Richards, Ryan. "Debunking the Trump Administration's New Water Rule." *Center for American Progress.* Mar 27, 2019. https://www.americanprogress.org/issues/green/news/2019/03/27/467697/debunking-trump-administrations-new-water-rule/.

"Total Water Use in the United States." *USGS.* https://www.usgs.gov/special-topic/water-science-school/science/total-water-use-united-states?qt-science_center_objects=0#qt-science_center_objects.

Notes

1. "Total Water Use in the United States," *USGS.*
2. "How We Use Water," *EPA.*
3. "How Sewage Pollution Ends Up in Rivers," *American Rivers.*
4. Richards, "Debunking the Trump Administration's New Water Rule."
5. Kenney, "Climate Change, Water Security, and U.S. National Security."
6. Pimentel, et al. "Water Resources: Agricultural and Environmental Issues."
7. Harrington, "Causes of Global Warming: How Scientists Know That Humans Are Responsible."
8. McSweeney, "Explainer: 'Desertification' and the Role of Climate Change."

1
The Right to Drink

By Pete Souza, Obama White House, via Wikimedia.

President Barack Obama visited Flint, Michigan, for a roundtable on the city's water crisis in 2016. Above, roundtable participants drink filtered Flint water.

The U.S. Drinking Water Crisis

Lack of access to water is a problem with many dimensions. Around the world, 1 in 9 people lack access to safe drinking water, and roughly a third of the global population lack access to toilets and water for sanitation. For 40 percent of the global population, water scarcity is a primary issue, with drought becoming more and more common and leaving at least 700 million at risk for being displaced from their communities.[1] For others, lack of water isn't the problem, but rather a lack of infrastructure and the long-term impact of pollution. Even in areas with plentiful water, there may be precious little clean water for people to drink or to use in cleaning. According to *Water.org*, a child dies every two minutes from water-related illness.[2] Experts in public health have been drawing attention to this global water crisis, but awareness remains elusive. For many Americans with plentiful access to relatively clean water, the crisis over clean water may not be immediately evident. But recent events have brought America's water problems into sharp focus and have helped to raise awareness that the water crisis is a truly global issue.

The American Water Crisis

In the 2010s, media coverage of the water crisis in Flint, Michigan, brought America's water crisis to national attention. In 2014, the city of Flint, in an effort to save revenues, began obtaining drinking water from the Flint River rather than from the municipal water system in nearby Detroit. Unfortunately for the residents of Flint, the city did not invest in water treatment and testing, and physicians noticed a sharp increase in health issues related to unclean water. Critics allege that the local government ignored complaints from residents and denied that there was a systemic problem. Residents using the city's new water supply suffered from a variety of problems, including skin rashes and hair loss. It wasn't until considerably later that water testing revealed that the city's water was contaminated with lead, leading to lead-related illness, especially in the city's children. Testing also found high levels *E. coli* and other bacteria. In 2015, testing determined that the city of Flint had violated the Safe Drinking Water Act because of high levels of TTHM (total trihalomethanes) in the water supply.[3]

Investigations determined that the city had not only been neglectful in addressing resident complaints and reports, but that city officials had conspired to hide information about lead contamination and other pollutants. A coalition of residents filed suit against two companies: Veolia, a French company that consulted with the city for water-quality control, and Lockwood, Andrews & Newman, who were hired in 2011 to operate a water treatment plant on the Flint River. In 2016, criminal charges were filed against six government officials, including those in the city's

Department of Health and Human Services, an epidemiologist hired by the city, and several others involved in city management.[4]

By 2019, scientists announced that the Flint drinking water problem had been solved, with clean water running to every home in Flint where the water was tested. Addressing the problem turned out to be extremely complex, requiring years of cleanup and rebuilding to create a safe infrastructure to deliver drinking water to the city's inhabitants. However, for those who lived through the crisis, there was an unforeseen problem; a loss of trust. Even after remediation had proven successful, many Flint residents remained skeptical of their government's ability to keep them safe.[5]

The Flint water crisis serves as a microcosm of problems that exist in many locations across America. Ageing infrastructure, insufficient testing and water quality controls, and governmental failures have left many American communities vulnerable to water-quality-related health issues. This issue remains in the background in part because newsworthy water-quality crises rarely occur or receive wide spread media attention. With nearly half a million residents, Flint was a large enough metropolitan area that the city's lead crisis gained widespread media traction. In addition, the investigation into the Flint crisis uncovered such high levels of governmental incompetence and corruption that media agencies followed the Flint crisis consistently over several months. By contrast, there are many rural communities in the United States struggling with water quality issues, areas where residents have limited access to sufficient supplies of clean water but where little attention has been paid to the issue.

According to the U.S. Water Alliance, more than 2 million Americans lack access to running water or basic indoor plumbing. There are many communities, especially rural communities, in which local drinking water contains unacceptable levels of pollutants, constituting a major health concern. In many cases, water quality issues are the result of ageing infrastructure or insufficient investment from cities and towns to maintain their water infrastructure. In many cases, lack of resources is key to this issue, with towns and communities that struggle monetarily much more likely to face serious challenges in terms of water quality or availability.[6]

The Social Justice Angle

America's water crisis is a problem plaguing Americans in every region and across many states, but studies have shown, also, that people of color and the poor are far more likely to suffer from a lack of access to clean water. An investigative report published in *Time Magazine* found many examples of poor communities in which water quality is a major problem. For instance, in Denmark, South Carolina, which residents described as being like a "third-world country," untested chemicals added to drinking water to combat rusty pipes resulted in an outbreak of illness and skin conditions. In Inez, Kentucky, residents have been in a decades-long effort to remove toxic chemicals leached into the water supply by industries that once occupied the region, leading to high levels of mercury and arsenic that have seen residents face high levels of kidney damage and disease and certain cancers. The report noted that many of the communities in which water quality issues have been identified but not remedied are communities of color or are home to the state's poorest residents. One example can be found in territory stretching through the states of Mexico, Arizona, and Utah where at least 300,000 members of the Navajo Nation live; here, environmentally irresponsible mining practices have resulted in uranium pollution, leading to generations suffering from developmental difficulties, cancers, and a number of other ailments.

Time Magazine journalist Matt Black wrote,

> "For those without it, water amounts to an ongoing crisis. But no great urgency is felt in Washington, D.C., or in state capitals. Laws may be out of data, and existing rules ignored, but as an 'issue,' water seems to sprout up only when a seemingly one-off event like the Flint water crisis captures public attention."[7]

In Flint and elsewhere around the country, access to clean water has a distinct racial dimension. Studies have found that households of color are many times more likely to lack access to drinking water, or water for sanitation, than white households. Researchers have noted that state and federal investment in infrastructure is a major part of the problem. Historically poor communities, many of which are also home to America's minority residents, have been neglected. In Flint, where more than half of the city's residents are black, the state failed to provide resources for adequate improvements to the water infrastructure. In California, Native American reservations have been ignored when the state allocates funding for water system updates.

When the federal government passed the Safe Drinking Water Act in 1974, billions were allocated to update drinking water systems across the country. At the time overt racial prejudice meant that some legislators neglected to expand these infrastructural improvements to minority neighborhoods. In the town of Zanesville, Ohio, for instance, the entire city's water system was upgraded to conform to the Safe Drinking Water Act, except the portion of the city that housed most of the city's African American neighborhoods. Similar systems have been uncovered around the country, in which cities and towns neglected to improve water systems in their poorest neighborhoods, or those housing the city's minorities.[8] There is now significant evidence indicating that investment in infrastructure has not been equitable and that minority communities have been neglected. One of the problems, however, is that state budget deficits have made it difficult for some states to commit to significant infrastructural investment.

Another way in which access to water has become a social welfare issue is because the cost of water has increased faster than compensation levels in many communities. During the Coronavirus crisis of 2019 and 2020, as unemployment rates rose sharply and many individuals and families lacked sufficient resources, many Americans were unable to afford access to clean water, which contributes to a number of health issues and increases the risk of disease. Social scientists have described this problem as a "water gap," wherein an increasingly large share of Americans have been priced out of access to water. This problem is more acute in areas where water systems are managed by private corporations and where access to water is governed by corporate profit margins. The price of water and sewer access increased by an estimated 80 percent between 2010 and 2018, but average wages did not increase at the same rate. As a result, a 2020 report found that nearly two-fifths of residents in some states had difficulty affording access to water for drinking and/or sanitation.[9]

The Right to Drink

It might seem surprising that many Americans struggle to obtain access to clean water, a problem often associated primarily with developing nations. While it is true that access to safe, clean water is a more severe problem in many developing nations, historical patterns of neglect and uneven distribution of revenues means that there are areas within even the most developed societies where access to basic resources remains problematic.

In 2010, the United Nations General Assembly passed resolution 64/292, which formally recognizes the "right to safe and clean drinking water and sanitation as a human right that is essential for the full enjoyment of life and all human rights."[10] Further publications under the UN-Water Decade Programme on Advocacy and Communication explain that the 2010 resolution means that, under international law, member states are responsible for implementing water resources according to a "human rights based approach (HRBA)." Further, this means that states implementing changes to enhance water access should engage in these activities in a way that is fair and equitable and that does not further violate basic human rights. The UN further recognizes five separate dimensions to the right to water:

1. **Availability**—The supply of water should be sufficient for personal/domestic purposes, including drinking, food preparation, hygiene, clothes washing, and cleaning. According to the UN, this means that individuals and families should have between 50 and 100 liters of water per person each day.

2. **Accessibility**—Water and sanitation facilities must be accessible to all residents (regardless of gender, race, or creed), at all times and should be provided in such a way that individuals do not risk their lives or safety to obtain access. The UN specifies that access to water should be no further than 1,000 meters from a person's home. Further, collecting water for daily needs should take no longer than 30 minutes.

3. **Quality and Safety**—Water should meet basic standards for consumption and hygiene, and should be free of pollutants and microorganisms that pose a threat to public health.

4. **Acceptability**—Facilities for distributing or accessing water should be created to conform to the cultural or social norms, but only as far as these norms align with other human rights principles. For instance, states should provide gender-specific water access in cultures where there are strong existent cultural norms in place with regard to gender roles, but should not provide access in a way that exacerbates gender prejudice or other kinds of prejudicial treatment.

5. **Affordability**—Water must be provided affordably, with total costs not exceeding 3 percent of a family's income. The cost of accessing water resources

should not rise to a level where citizens are forced to accept unsafe alternatives or where the cost of water limits the capability to acquire other basic goods.[11]

Though UN member nations have agreed to recognize water as a human right, this does not mean that the United States or other nation are legally bound to adopt measures or reforms so as to conform with this resolution. It does, however, mean that the United States and other nations in which citizens lack basic access to clean and safe water could be sanctioned by the United Nations for violating human rights standards. In the United States, persistent problems in the distribution of resources have left many communities vulnerable to water safety and access issues, but the problem is difficult to fix because the investment needed is substantial and political factions disagree about the distribution of resources to cover the cost or about the importance of investing in certain communities. Whether or not societies successfully expand access to water to previously underserved areas also depends on whether or not local and national authorities are able to fairly distribute resources without prejudice. When decisions made on the allocation of resources are shaped by prejudice and classism, disenfranchised populations develop and may continue to be neglected at least until some major catastrophe, as witnessed in the Flint water crisis, brings widespread attention to the issue.

Works Used

Black, Matt. "America's Clean Water Crisis Goes Far Beyond Flint: There's No Relief in Sight." *Time*. Feb 20, 2020. https://pulitzercenter.org/stories/americas-clean-water-crisis-goes-far-beyond-flint-theres-no-relief-sight.

Borja-Vega, Christian, and Eva Kloeve. "Why a Human Rights Based Approach to Water and Sanitation Is Essential for the Poor." *World Bank*. Sep 28, 2018. https://blogs.worldbank.org/water/why-human-rights-based-approach-water-and-sanitation-essential-poor.

Denchak, Melissa. "Flint Water Crisis: Everything You Need to Know." *NRDC*. Nov 8, 2018. https://www.nrdc.org/stories/flint-water-crisis-everything-you-need-know.

"Drought." *World Health Organization*. 2021. https://www.who.int/health-topics/drought#tab=tab_1.

Kennedy, Merrit. "Lead-Laced Water in Flint: A Step-By-Step Look at the Makings of a Crisis." *NPR*. Apr 20, 2016. https://www.npr.org/sections/thetwo-way/2016/04/20/465545378/lead-laced-water-in-flint-a-step-by-step-look-at-the-makings-of-a-crisis.

Lakhani, Nina. "Revealed: Millions of Americans Can't Afford Water as Bills Rise 80% in a Decade." *The Guardian*. Jun 23, 2020. https://www.theguardian.com/us-news/2020/jun/23/millions-of-americans-cant-afford-water-bills-rise.

McGraw, George, and Radhika Fox. "Closing the Water Access Gap in the United States." *US Water Alliance*. 2019. http://uswateralliance.org/sites/uswateralliance.org/files/publications/Closing%20the%20Water%20Access%20Gap%20in%20the%20United%20States_DIGITAL.pdf.

"Resolution Adopted by the General Assembly on 28 July 2010." *United Nations*.

Sixty Fourth Session. Aug 3, 2010. https://documents-dds-ny.un.org/doc/UN-DOC/GEN/N09/479/35/PDF/N0947935.pdf?OpenElement.

Robertson, Derek. "Flint Has Clean Water Now: Why Won't People Drink It?" *Politico*. Dec 23, 2020. https://www.politico.com/news/magazine/2020/12/23/flint-water-crisis-2020-post-coronavirus-america-445459.

"The Water Crisis." *Water.org*. 2021. https://water.org/our-impact/water-crisis/.

Willis, Jay. "The Hidden Racial Inequities of Access to Water in America." *GQ*. Nov 25, 2019. https://www.gq.com/story/hidden-racial-inequities-water-access.

Notes

1. "Drought," *WHO*.
2. "The Water Crisis," *Water.org*.
3. Denchak, "Flint Water Crisis: Everything You Need to Know."
4. Kennedy, "Lead-Laced Water in Flint: A Step-By-Step Look at the Makings of a Crisis."
5. Robertson, "Flint Has Clean Water Now: Why Won't People Drink It?"
6. McGraw and Fox, "Closing the Water Access Gap in the United States."
7. Black, "America's Clean Water Crisis Goes Far Beyond Flint: There's No Relief in Sight."
8. Willis, "The Hidden Racial Inequities of Access to Water in America."
9. Lakhani, "Reveales: Millions of Americans Can't Afford Water as Bills Rise 80% in a Decade."
10. "Resolution Adopted by the General Assembly on 28 July 2010," *United Nations General Assembly*.
11. Borja-Vega and Kloeve, "Why a Human Rights Based Approach to Water and Sanitation is Essential for the Poor."

The US Drinking Water Supply Is Mostly Safe, but That's Not Good Enough

By Joan Rose

The Conversation, May 29, 2019

Most Americans take clean drinking water for granted as a convenience of modern life. The United States has one of the world's safest drinking water supplies, but new challenges constantly emerge.

For example, on May 6 researchers at the nonprofit Environmental Working Group and Northeastern University reported that 43 states have sites where water is contaminated with toxic fluorinated compounds known as PFAS. And many farm workers in California's Central Valley have to buy bottled water because their tap water contains unsafe levels of arsenic and agricultural chemicals that have been linked to elevated risks of infant death and cancer in adults.

As a scientist specializing in water quality, I believe water providers and regulators can't afford to be complacent. So I was distressed to hear EPA Administrator Andrew Wheeler tout the quality of drinking water in the U.S. in an interview on March 20, 2019. "I want to make sure the American public understands 92 percent of the water everyday meets all the EPA requirements for safe drinking water," Wheeler said.

Let's do the math on that. Nationwide, 327 million Americans each drink two to eight glasses of water on average every day. If 8% of that supply doesn't meet EPA standards, that's up to 209 million unsafe glasses of water per day, or 2.3 billion gallons of water–enough to fill a quarter of a million bathtubs. In short, high compliance numbers do not mean everything is fine.

Aging and Underfunded

For more than 40 years the Safe Drinking Water Act has provided a consistent set of national standards for monitoring and managing contaminants to ensure the safety of water. The Environmental Protection Agency develops these standards and works with states and water utilities to ensure that drinking water supplies conform to them. Thanks to rules implemented under the Safe Drinking Water Act in the 1980s waterborne disease declined in the United States but in recent decades has crept back up.

> **Researchers have estimated that as many as 32 million cases of waterborne disease occur nationwide every year.**

The EPA also provides funding to states and communities to monitor and test water supplies. This support is essential as the agency develops new standards and monitoring approaches for emerging contaminants, such as PFAS. However, the EPA's annual appropriations budget for water infrastructure has been virtually flat since 2000.

There are more than 151,000 public water systems in the United States serving residential communities, schools, office buildings, hospitals and other sites. It is especially challenging for small communities to fund infrastructure upgrades and monitor water quality. The American Society of Civil Engineers gave the U.S. drinking water delivery system a D on its most recent infrastructure report card, based on the high number of leaks and the presence of both legacy contaminants like lead and new threats like PFAS.

Millions of Violations Every Year

Nationwide, the fraction of all water systems in compliance with health standards has hovered between 90% and 93% since 2013. However, some key sources are doing less well. For example, at schools and daycare facilities compliance was only 90% on average from 2014 to 2019, and appears to have declined in the past several years.

And some regions are better-served than others. EPA data for the first quarter of 2019 show that the percentage of water systems in compliance ranged from 84% to 95%. The fractions of populations with access to water that met all national standards varied even more, ranging from 60% to 95%. EPA Regions 2 (New York and New Jersey) and 6 (New Mexico, Texas, Oklahoma, Louisiana and Arkansas) had the poorest compliance records. In Region 2, nearly 12 million people were served by a system in violation of at least one federal regulation.

Sickened by Tap Water

What are the most common violations? Of the 10,083 systems that were in violation of a federal standard in 2015, 72% were based on the Total Coliform Rule or other microbial violations. This means that bacteria were found in the water, and that there was a potential for waterborne disease due to fecal contamination or inadequate treatment.

Researchers have estimated that as many as 32 million cases of waterborne disease occur nationwide every year. The most recent summary from the Centers for Disease Control of actual reported problems in community water systems found 42 outbreaks in 2013 and 2014, with 1,006 cases of illness, 124 hospitalizations and 13 deaths. For the water industry these events represent failures to fulfill its core mission, much like plane crashes for the aviation industry.

Climate change is producing more intense storms and flooding, which is significantly affecting water quality. Extreme precipitation and floods wash contaminants from sewage and animal manure into water supplies. It is clear that rainfall is associated with widespread transport of fecal contamination from humans and animals into rivers and lakes.

Grade: Incomplete

No other industry would accept an 8% failure rate, and I do not believe U.S. water professionals see that figure as acceptable. In my view, the first step is to put more resources into water supply monitoring and diagnostics that can detect emerging pathogens, such as protozoa and viruses.

Early work on the occurrence in water supplies of *Cryptosporidium*, a microscopic parasite that can cause gastrointestinal illness, eventually led to new rules for drinking water monitoring and treatment. Today, water utilities could identify whether fecal pollution was coming from humans or animals using new technologies and this would allow them to target impaired waterways before outbreaks occurred.

Another valuable step would be funding pilot and demonstration plants that could demonstrate new treatment systems' potential to reduce waterborne disease risks. For example, in Ohio a consortium of cities, consulting engineers and universities is assessing new treatment systems for combined sewer and stormwater discharges. Creating more such facilities would support innovation and adoption of promising new strategies.

Finally, I believe water providers and regulators should reaffirm their commitment to providing safe water whenever Americans turn on a tap or take a shower. A perfect score may be unattainable today, but even a 1% rise in compliance would make numerous Americans' lives safer and healthier. And investments in new water infrastructure can make 99.999% compliance achievable.

Print Citations

CMS: Rose, Joan. "The US Drinking Water Supply Is Mostly Safe, but That's Not Good Enough." In *The Reference Shelf: National Debate 2021-2022: Water Resources,* edited by Micah L. Issitt, 9-11. Amenia, NY: Grey House Publishing, 2021.

MLA: Rose, Joan. "The US Drinking Water Supply Is Mostly Safe, but That's Not Good Enough." *The Reference Shelf: The Reference Shelf: National Debate 2021-2022: Water Resources,* edited by Micah L. Issitt, Grey House Publishing, 2021, pp. 9-11.

APA: Rose, J. (2021). The US drinking water supply is mostly safe, but that's not good enough. In Micah L. Issitt (Ed.), *The reference shelf: National debate 2021-2022: Water resources* (pp. 9-11). Amenia, NY: Grey House Publishing.

Millions of Americans Drink Potentially Unsafe Tap Water: How Does Your County Stack Up?

By Katie Langin
Science Magazine, **February 12, 2018**

Tainted tap water isn't just a problem in Flint, Michigan. In any given year from 1982 to 2015, somewhere between 9 million and 45 million Americans got their drinking water from a source that was in violation of the Safe Drinking Water Act, according to a new study. Most at risk: people who live in rural, low-income areas.

In general, "the U.S. has really safe water," says Maura Allaire, a water economist at the University of California, Irvine, and lead author of the new study. Still, problems with drinking water crop up every year, and in some municipalities, year after year. The contaminants in the water can cause stomach flu or "more chronic conditions including a variety of cancers and neurological disorders," she says.

Allaire lived near Flint in 2015, when the city's water crisis captured the nation's attention. That made her wonder: "How widespread a problem is this across the country?" She couldn't find a satisfying answer. For more than 3 decades, the U.S. Environmental Protection Agency (EPA) had been compiling information about water quality violations across the country—but no one had published a national assessment looking at long-term trends in those data. So, she took it on herself.

Allaire and her colleagues downloaded EPA's data and looked at the number of health-related water quality violations for 17,900 community water systems in the continental United States over a 34-year period. Some were for elevated lead levels, the problem in Flint, but the data set also included violations for coliform bacteria—a group of microbes that is easy to detect and serves as an indicator of bacterial contamination in general—nitrates, arsenic, and other contaminants. The researchers combined those data with information from the U.S. census such as housing density and average household income, to figure out which communities were most vulnerable.

> **They found that during the Flint water crisis in 2015, nearly 21 million Americans—about 6%—were getting water from systems that violated health standards.**

They found that during the Flint water crisis in 2015, nearly 21 million Americans—about 6%—were getting water from systems that violated health standards. And looking back over time, the number of violations generally increased from 1982 to 2015—spiking in the years following the addition of a new regulation, the team reports today in the *Proceedings of the National Academy of Sciences*. For instance, after a rule about coliform bacteria was enacted in 1990, the number of violations doubled within 5 years. Such spikes don't mean that the water suddenly got worse, Allaire says, just that previously accepted levels of a contaminant were now considered too high.

At the bottom of the pack were Washington, D.C., Oklahoma, Idaho, and Nebraska. In the latter three, more than a third of water systems had violations in multiple years. And when the researchers looked at what counties were most vulnerable, they found that low-income, rural counties were the hardest hit, especially in Oklahoma and in parts of Texas and Idaho. Small water systems can't afford the latest and best treatment technology, and sometimes they can't even afford a full-time operator, Allaire says. "So, they're struggling." But there was a silver lining: Small communities that purchased treated water from larger utilities—especially privately owned ones—had fewer violations. (EPA declined to comment on the new study.)

When treating water, some communities are dealt a bad hand to start with because of dirty source water—especially in southern states such as Oklahoma and Texas, where hot summer temperatures create an ideal breeding ground for bacteria. That's why it's important to prevent contaminants from getting into the source water in the first place, for instance by installing wood chip bioreactors on farms to reduce nitrates in runoff water, says Michelle Soupir, a water quality engineer at Iowa State University in Ames. We'd "have a better, safer drinking water supply and take some of the burden off the water treatment."

Another idea is to merge "teeny water systems" with larger systems, says Erik Olson, a policy expert at the Natural Resources Defense Council in Washington, D.C. We can't have these rural providers "continuing to serve bad water," he says.

Print Citations

CMS: Langin, Katie. "Millions of Americans Drink Potentially Unsafe Tap Water: How Does Your County Stack Up?" In *The Reference Shelf: National Debate 2021-2022: Water Resources*, edited by Micah L. Issitt, 12-13. Amenia, NY: Grey House Publishing, 2021.

MLA: Langin, Katie. "Millions of Americans Drink Potentially Unsafe Tap Water: How Does Your County Stack Up?" *The Reference Shelf: National Debate 2021-2022: Water Resources*, edited by Micah L. Issitt, Grey House Publishing, 2021, pp. 12-13.

APA: Langin, K. (2021). Millions of Americans drink potentially unsafe tape water: How does your county stack up? In Micah L. Issitt (Ed.), *The reference shelf: National debate 2021-2022: Water resources* (pp. 12-13). Amenia, NY: Grey House Publishing.

Flint Has Clean Water Now: Why Won't People Drink It?

By Derek Robertson
Politico, December 23, 2020

FLINT, Mich.—In a city synonymous for half a decade with disaster, something remarkable happened in February 2019. A team of researchers reported that Flint's homes—even the ones at the highest risk for undrinkable, lead-poisoned tap water—finally had clean water running through their pipes.

After years of painstaking cleanup and rebuilding, the study's results were a sparkling capstone. Earlier tests already hinted at good news, and this one confirmed it: In the vast majority of such homes, lead levels were 5 parts per billion or better—far below even the strictest regulations in the country. Local news outlet MLive trumpeted the news, and Michigan's Department of Environmental Quality tacked it to their ongoing list of promising signs that indicated the city's potable present and future.

But a few weeks later, another, equally remarkable thing happened. As part of a United Nations-sponsored "World Water Day" celebration, the City of Flint parked 12 semitrailers stacked with pallets of bottled water on the city's street corners, offering them to any city resident who could show an ID. People flocked to the pickup locations. They lined up their cars and popped their trunks to collect cases of water to use in their homes—water in bottles, from somewhere else, that they actually trusted.

The wariness wasn't out of ignorance. Equally wary was Jim Ananich, a lifelong Flint resident and outgoing leader of the Democratic minority in the Michigan State Senate. Ananich wasn't in line that day, but he understands why people were.

"I can't tell somebody they should trust [claims that the water is safe], because *I* don't trust them—and I have more information than most people," said Ananich. "Science and logic would tell me that it should be OK, but people have lied to me."

For Americans who stopped following the Flint water crisis after its first few gritty chapters, it might come as a surprise how far the city has come: Today, after nearly $400 million in state and federal spending, Flint has secured a clean water source, distributed filters to all residents who want them, and laid modern, safe copper pipes to nearly every home in the city that needed them. Its water is as good as any city's in Michigan. And to compensate its just under 95,000 people for the damage they've suffered—economically, medically and psychologically—the city and state reached a settlement in August that will pay nearly $650 million to Flint residents.

From an outside perspective, it sounds like a happy ending. For people who live in Flint, the story looks very different. After six years of lies, deliberate or not, a revolving door in a disempowered City Hall, and the dysfunction wrought by a high-profile, high-stakes recovery process, they find themselves still unable to trust either their water or the people telling them to drink it.

"The anger, the lack of trust, it's all justified," Ananich says.

The breakdown in trust is rooted not only in the water crisis itself, but its domino effect on state and local politics over the following years: a halting pipe-replacement program marked by accusations of graft; a criminal investigation into those responsible for the crisis that mysteriously "rebooted" and dropped charges against state officials; a city government still decimated by post-Great Recession, state-imposed austerity measures; a basic inability to believe what should be neutral facts.

Providing water and appropriating settlement funds are simple compared with the task the city now faces: convincing its residents not only that they have a future, but that they can trust their government to provide for their most basic of needs.

"We just want to live normally, and actually be able to drink the water that comes out of our tap safely, with no concerns," said Melissa Mays, a vocal Flint water activist. "Like normal people."

In the nation outside Flint, with the coronavirus vaccine at hand, the eyes of "normal people" are eagerly turning toward a post-pandemic world. Optimists and institutionalists hope that new leaders in Washington can deliver the return to normalcy they've been promised, and maybe rebuild some of that easily burned-off trust.

But there's another possibility at play, not as laden with excitement or relief: that after a certain point, the destruction of that trust is the story, as much as any material deprivation Flint's people could have suffered. And with the gravity of that loss comes the possibility that no number of promises kept, and no amount of empirically-provable repair, can bring it back.

In that scenario, Americans might not take the Covid-19 vaccine, failing to trust in its efficacy and that it won't severely harm them or their children. They might not trust their criminal justice system, with no incentive to respect a system that allows elites to break the law with impunity. They might not trust the results of a presidential election, behaving as if they live in a banana republic and not a robust, if flawed, democracy.

In that scenario, the future of American politics looks a little less like the nation before Covid or before Trump, and a little more like Flint in 2020.

Even before its pipes started leaching lead, Flint was deeply in trouble, as badly off as any other Rust Belt city—or worse. Since the slow-motion collapse of the American auto manufacturing industry, its population had shrunk by 50 percent from its postwar peak to just under 100,000 residents. Roughly an hour's drive north of Detroit, freezing in the diminished warmth of that city's own economic sun, Flint struggled to pay its legacy pension obligations, flirting with bankruptcy as its tallest building was imploded after decades of neglect.

Adding to its economic woes, much like its larger cousin down the road, Flint has a vexed political relationship with the state. The city's population is 54 percent Black, compared with the state's overall Black population of 14 percent. And while Flint's political tug of war with a majority-white state government isn't unique, that dynamic gave an extra sting to the city's repeated financial takeovers by state-appointed emergency managers, culminating in the austerity-driven call to switch its water supply to the contaminated Flint River.

There are plenty of ways to tell the story of what went wrong in Flint leading to that moment. If you spend enough time there, you'll find someone eager to tell each of them—but the most convenient place to start is April 25, 2014. After the city entered a state of financial emergency during the Great Recession, state, city and county officials collectively decided to save money by switching to a new water source. Instead of partnering with the Detroit Water and Sewerage Department as they had in the past, they'd utilize a new pipeline being built by the Karegnondi Water Authority to draw less expensive water from Lake Huron. As a temporary fix to start saving money while that pipeline was completed, the city began drawing its water from the Flint River, something it hadn't done since the 1960s.

On that day in April, the plan came to fruition. Mayor Dayne Walling, then a 40-year-old Flint native who had won a Rhodes Scholarship before coming back to serve his hometown, raised a glass of that river's water, toasted a jolly "Here's to Flint!," and downed it in one swig, surrounded by his fellow bureaucrats who dutifully followed suit. Just moments before, captured on video now for eternity, Walling had pushed a button on a panel at the city's water treatment plant that turned an ominous, glowing red. Though nobody knew it at the time, that red glow signified the end of the clean water that flowed from Detroit, and the beginning of a saga that would change the course of Flint's history.

Not long after, residents started to complain about strange odors and brackish, brown water coming out of their pipes. In August 2014, the city issued a boil water advisory after fecal bacteria were identified in the water. By the time the U.S. Environmental Protection Agency notified Michigan in early 2015 that there were dangerous levels of lead in Flint's water, its residents had complained for months of mysterious illnesses.

When scientists analyzed that water, they discovered to their horror that the city's treatment of it was woefully inadequate to reduce its levels of harmful bacteria and acid—and that the latter had begun to corrode Flint's antiquated pipes from the inside, delivering tiny bits of lead through people's faucets. For months, it turned out, Flint had had been exposing its residents to that lead at levels that could cause lifelong damage to the health of its children. The levels of bacteria likely caused an outbreak of Legionnaires' disease that also followed the switch, killing at least a dozen people.

Although Walling literally pressed the button, the decision to use Flint River water had much deeper roots. After a panel appointed by Michigan's Republican then-governor, Rick Snyder, declared the city in a state of financial emergency—taking its finances, and therefore most major decisions, out of the hands of City Hall and putting them under the control of a hand-picked emergency manager, Walling and Flint's other elected officials became effectively ornamental.

The city's financial emergency was the result of years of mismanagement by former Mayor Don Williamson, a brash, proto-Trumpian businessman who oversaw year after year of multimillion-dollar deficits during the 2000s—a large portion of which were due in part to his fending off various lawsuits from city employees.

Walling was elected in 2009 to succeed Williamson, after the latter resigned rather than face a recall election. The new mayor's voters viewed him as exactly the kind of good-government technocrat capable of reversing the city's slide. As well as being a Rhodes Scholar, he was an aide to the former U.S. Representative and titan of Flint-area politics Dale Kildee, and Flint residents viewed him as a welcome technocratic contrast with Williamson's unique governing style. Urbane where his predecessor was crass, credentialed where Williamson had only a rap sheet, brainy instead of flexing his political brawn, Walling was exactly the kind of homegrown talent a troubled, once-proud city needed.

But his efforts to repair the damage his predecessor wrought weren't fast enough for the state's liking. Snyder installed Michael Brown as the first in a line of emergency managers—stingingly, on the same day as Walling's 2011 reelection.

I met Walling at Café Rhema, a small coffee shop in downtown Flint that seeks to do its part in revitalizing the city by invoking the better days of the Jazz Age. Walling is now a consultant and occasional college adjunct, imparting hard-earned wisdom from his time in office to the would-be technocrats of tomorrow. Since he first took office, there have been no fewer than two subsequent mayors and four emergency managers (one serving two nonconsecutive terms), giving Flint residents a leadership that goes far beyond the "revolving door" to approach a whirlwind.

"I get elected in 2009," he said. "I get reelected in 2011, and then we get the sequence of [four] emergency managers, who under state law effectively become the mayor and the city council, even though they don't take that title," Walling told me. "Then the emergency manager leaves, and I'm back [in charge] at the end of April 2015. I lose reelection [that November,] and Mayor [Karen] Weaver gets sworn in. ... It's been an incredible cast of characters who have been in charge at City Hall."

Walling attempted a political comeback in 2018, running to represent a Flint-area district in the Michigan House of Representatives, and losing in the Democratic primary to John Cherry III, the son of the state's former lieutenant governor. When he looks back at his time in office, Walling remembers it the same way that many of his constituents probably do: as a time of being caught flat-footed, without recourse or relief.

"There's the Great Recession, then the Tea Party takeover, and then the rewrite of the emergency manager law, where the state now says, 'We will take over absolutely everything' ... and then I didn't see the water crisis coming out of out of that," Walling told me. "That sequence was extraordinarily difficult. ... Hopefully, the scope of those challenges will at some point begin to narrow, but I don't think we're at that point."

Benjamin Pauli, a professor of social sciences at Flint's Kettering University and author of *Flint Fights Back: Environmental Justice and Democracy in the Flint Water Crisis*, draws a direct connection between the state takeover and the groundswell of anger and mistrust around the water crisis, describing how even before the water switch Flint's activist community was "interested in democracy, and it just so happened that water and democracy were starting to come together."

That intersection resulted in one of the water crisis' most unique political consequences: Walling's succession by Karen Weaver, a local booster, business owner and child psychologist, to replace Walling in 2015. In contrast with Walling, whom her campaign painted as an out-of-touch bureaucrat gladly carrying out the state's bidding, Weaver was sharply attuned to the demands of Flint activists—and, significantly, became the majority-Black city's first Black mayor in more than a decade, defeating Walling by 10 points in his second reelection bid as the crisis raged.

One of Weaver's campaign promises was that she would declare a state of emergency in the city, out of a belief that the city needed to fan the media flames more aggressively in order to draw the national attention and resources necessary to remedy the crisis. She did so in December 2015, a month after her election, and President Barack Obama then declared a federal emergency in January 2016, freeing up $5 million in aid.

Despite what some see as the shortcomings of Weaver's administration, her emergency declaration is viewed as a key moment in transforming a story of local mismanagement into one with nationwide repercussions. In a city with a long legacy of dysfunction, it's the rare action that can be matched to a clear and obvious positive outcome.

"The emergency declaration we will be forever thankful for," said Nayyirah Shariff, a longtime activist and the director of the nonprofit Flint Rising. "She had a press conference, it was on the ticker at CNN by 4:00, and she was on 'Rachel Maddow' by 9:00. Regardless of how people may feel about her administration, if she had not done that emergency declaration, Flint would not have been international news."

Weaver was elected as an outsider, someone who would give voice to Flint's common man and upend the sclerotic status quo through sheer force of personality. But her tenure in office revealed the difficulties faced by all outsiders once they get inside.

"One of the things about Karen is that she's a regular person, and not a politician, and so there were some issues with that, mostly from some of the people she listened to," said Mays, the activist. "I can't say I agree with everything she said and did, but she stood with us, and she pushed for us, and she understood the urgency we felt."

Activists heralded her election, but during her four years in office, Weaver frequently stumbled. She became mired not only in controversies over the water crisis' complicated infrastructural fix, but accusations she used her office to reward friends and family and boost her own profile.

Weaver was narrowly defeated in her 2019 re-election bid by Sheldon Neeley, a state representative and former city council member who relentlessly needled the mayor

> **"People are weary... They wanted all of this to be fixed a long time ago, and they still don't trust the institutions that are supposed to be protecting them."**

for her mismanagement of the arduous project to replace the city's lead pipes, calling her a "ceremonial mayor" who basked in the media spotlight.

When I spoke to Mayor Neeley, he acknowledged the difficulties Flint faces—public safety, sanitation and managing the city's teetering pension system—and that the ability of residents to trust that the government can meet those needs was at an all-time low.

"People just want a government that works," Neeley said. When I asked him about his evaluation of Weaver, he was guarded in his response, but invoked an oft-repeated campaign slogan—one that's hints at Flint's desperate need to believe in something beyond its own ongoing diminishment.

"The majority of voters thought I could deliver better things for them. And for the other half, I will serve them equally; I believe that over the last few months, we're winning them over," Neeley said. "We're a community of victors, not a community of victims."

In the past 12 years, then, Flint has had four different mayors. It's also had four state-appointed emergency managers who are fully unaccountable to voters. Its water source was switched from a Detroit-owned plant on Lake Huron to the Flint River, and back again. On a deep level, it's been drilled into Flint residents' heads that they can't trust their local officials to get the job done when it comes to even the most basic necessities, exemplified by the installment of the city's emergency managers. And then they failed, too.

"There would not have been a water crisis if we had democracy in the city," Shariff told me, pointing to how the city abandoned Detroit's water source only at the behest of its austerity-minded, unelected state officials.

"We didn't have the chance for residents to weigh in. Once things started to look hinky, local elected officials could have made a different decision."

If you're one of those residents, the water crisis isn't just a story about lead leaching from corroded pipes, or the dizzying, Altmanesque cast of characters promising to fix it. The repair effort itself became an unending nightmare, marked by the orange flags and construction backfill that have endlessly dotted the city's landscape since 2016, markers of the long, arduous process of replacing corroded lead pipes.

One of the city's primary goals during its recovery has been very straightforward: Replace all of its lead and galvanized steel pipes with safer, more modern copper lines. But after that, nothing was simple. Like many older cities, Flint had no clear record of which pipes were outdated or dangerous; such information was scrawled on more than 100,000 note cards that languished in a city basement, some more than a century old. The information they provided was, to be generous, incomplete.

To remedy that and determine which homes were most likely to have harmful lead pipes in need of replacement, in 2016 a team of computer scientists at the University of Michigan developed a machine-learning model. Making its predictions based on homes' ages and additional input from the state about which areas and residents might be at the highest risk, it had a 70 percent success rate, a rare spot of good news in a brutal half-decade.

"They were using this system to go to the homes that were most likely to have lead or galvanized [pipes], and they had a lot of success," Mays told me. "Then AECOM took over."

In late 2017, Weaver's administration gave AECOM, a national infrastructure firm that boasts on its website of being one of Fortune's "Most Admired Companies," a $5 million contract meant to speed up the program. Instead, the city's success rate in finding the pipes in question plummeted from 70 percent to 15—worse than would be expected if homes had been chosen completely at random.

The reason: AECOM had completely abandoned the University of Michigan computer scientists' system, opening the door for Weaver to direct pipe excavations based on political considerations. Alan Wong, then AECOM's project manager, told *The Atlantic* in early 2019 that her administration "did not want to have to explain to a councilperson why there was no work in their district."

AECOM no longer oversees the program, having been replaced last year by ROWE Engineering, a local firm that conducted the initial phase of pipe replacement. (AECOM defends its work, telling *Politico* in a statement that the company is "very satisfied with the results delivered," and noting it "exceeded expectations" set by the city's pipe replacement program.)

Weaver, who did not respond to a request for comment for this story, was roundly criticized in Flint and throughout the state for her handling of the pipe replacement program. She does, however, have an unlikely defender: Dayne Walling, the man she defeated to become mayor.

"In fairness to Mayor Weaver, I do think the citizens of the city deserved to see [pipe excavation] done in different parts of the city," Walling said. "There could have been a combination of approaches, where the most capacity was focused on the highest-risk areas, and some could have been dedicated to, you know, complaints from someone who the model may not show is in a high-risk place. ... I think you can do 75 percent of one and 25 percent of the other, but what actually happened was that it went totally the other way."

Jim Ananich, the state senator and Flint politics lifer who has represented the city at the local and state level for 15 years, is equally sympathetic, saying the issues with pipe replacement speak to how the water crisis touches everything from public health to good governance and infrastructure.

"I'm not making excuses for anybody, but when you have a major program that no one's ever done before, there's going to be bumps," Ananich said. "But you fix bumps, right? You don't just keep them there. There was no question that the program was not the most efficient at times, and I think there were a lot of contractors that had never done this kind of work before. ... Lansing [Michigan's capital city] did this, and it took them 12 years to do it. We were trying to do it in two, and now we're in our third or fourth year."

Like nearly everyone I interviewed for this story, Ananich has his own personal story about dissatisfaction with the pipe-replacement program. In his case, tired of waiting for the city, he hired a crew to swap out the pipes on his own dime. But he acknowledges that many others are not as fortunate.

Chandra Walker-Smith is among them. "We had to have our yard torn up, and it took months for them to replace what they damaged, with no commitment to replace any of the landscaping we had there," Walker-Smith told me. Walker-Smith conducts outreach for the National Resources Defense Council, contacting Flint residents who haven't yet had their pipes replaced. She said that, in her experience, a majority of the people she encounters cite the high level of disruption to daily life as a major reason why they don't want their pipes replaced.

Still, the city's work has continued apace. Its most recent official update, from early October, shows that lead and galvanized steel pipes have been replaced in 9,769 homes. Fewer than 500 remain to be inspected. But even with that project finally reaching its completion after years of strife, and EPA administrators saying Flint's water is "better than it's ever been," most of the Flint residents I interviewed said they're still wary of what comes out of their tap.

"I don't have detected lead anymore, and I still don't trust it," Ananich told me. "I'll drink out of the tap on occasion, or make the coffee with it, but my son doesn't."

Given the pain and distrust that followed the water crisis, and the potential health effects that still lurk in its aftermath, it's understandable that Flint is desperate to hold someone accountable—perhaps to hold a lot of people accountable.

From 2016 to 2019, this looked like a real possibility. Republican Former Attorney General Bill Schuette appointed special prosecutor Todd Flood to head a broad, aggressive criminal investigation into the water crisis. Flood charged more than a dozen officials, including charging both the head of the state's Department of Health and Human Services and its chief medical executive with felonies. But now Flint finds this form of resolution, too, possibly slipping out of reach.

In June 2019, around 100 Flint residents crowded into the city's UAW Local 659 meeting hall for an update on the investigation from the new investigators appointed by recently elected Democratic Attorney General Dana Nessel. In a shocking development that made national headlines, those prosecutors had recently dropped all pending charges in the investigation, something the Kettering professor Pauli said hit the city "like a punch to the gut." The people of Flint were upset. And after hearing the investigators' explanation, they were still upset.

The new investigators accused Flood of failing to adequately examine all the evidence available to him, saying that even his various felony charges may have been too lenient given the scope of the potential malfeasance. Michigan Solicitor General Fadwa Hammoud, one of the lead prosecutors appointed by Nessel, warned that those who made plea deals based on those charges would "walk away from this with nothing [on their record]" and promised a more robust investigation that would result in a higher level of accountability.

Perhaps she did intend to push harder, but Flint felt angry and betrayed. The new prosecutors said the town hall would offer more concrete answers after their vague initial statement that promised a "full and complete investigation" moving forward. Instead, they ended up spending most of the evening hearing from anguished Flint residents skeptical they would see further convictions or accountability at all. (I covered this meeting in my former role as a reporter for the *Michigan Advance*.)

By then, more than five years had passed since the switch flipped that began the crisis. Angry resident after angry resident stepped up to the podium to question the investigators about grievances new and old, physical and psychic. As the evening wore on, Flint resident Elizabeth Taylor needled them for their perceived eagerness to draw the proceedings to a close: "How can we trust you when you look at the clock and say you want to leave? You ended [the investigation]. We didn't. We're not finished with you all."

Many of the residents who lined up to speak did so through tears. Some, as the clock ran out on the evening, didn't even get that opportunity. And a year and a half later, no new charges have been filed. On April 25 of this year, the six-year anniversary of Walling's fateful photo op, the statute of limitations for misdemeanors and felony misconduct charges in Michigan expired.

The development drew little attention outside the state's borders, but the sense of abandonment and betrayal that followed it goes far beyond the grassroots.

"I don't think there's a chance in hell that all of those 15 people [charged in Flood's investigation] are going to get charged again," Pauli said. "Maybe they'll end up with one charge surviving, and they'll at least make a show of trying to hold a few people accountable with that charge, but ... the gap between that as an outcome and what residents were hoping for and expecting is huge."

"There's nothing. There's no information coming out, none," Mays said. "Instead of actually going after the people who poisoned us, they're just going after Todd Flood. All that was coming out [of] the attorney general's office [last summer] was bashing Todd Flood. Like, what the hell are you doing? He didn't poison us. At that town hall, what people walked away feeling is that the attorney general now feels like Todd Flood poisoned us all."

Nessel's communications director declined to comment for this article, citing the ongoing investigation.

This year, Ananich, the state senator, sponsored a bill that would have extended the statute of limitations, but it lost momentum just as the Covid-19 pandemic took hold. In April, he told Flint's local *East Village Magazine* that he was "certain there were other crimes," and that "there were plenty of opportunities for misconduct after April 25."

The people of Flint remain, understandably, skeptical.

"It's hard to maintain people's trust in institutions when you don't see justice being done with your own eyes," Pauli said. "I shudder to think what's going to happen if these cases just evaporate into thin air, because it's going to be yet another trauma inflicted upon the community, whether people intend it that way or not."

"For me, you can't have trust without truth-telling," Shariff said. "Or at least admitting you've done something wrong. Gov. Snyder has never come here to say he's sorry. So what's the trust level?"

Flint is now shifting its focus toward rebuilding and accountability, but our understanding of what happened there evolves every day, raising new and troubling questions about whether good government is feasible at all in America's hardest-struggling cities. Those questions touch on not only the crisis' far-reaching medical consequences but its roots in a decades-long divestment of power from the people the crisis hurt the most, as well as the extent to which government might endanger lives to evade blame or embarrassment for such a scandal.

As the Trump administration's nonresponse to Covid-19 allows the disease to tear unabated through America's most vulnerable populations, with unknown long-term health effects and serious questions on the horizon about equity in vaccine distribution, this might sound a little bit familiar. And if you listen to those have seen it all before, all too recently, in Flint, there's little reason to expect a new era of good feelings on the horizon.

Dr. Laura Sullivan, a Kettering scientist who has advised the city on water issues, described to me how the city's aging and inadequate infrastructure led to an outbreak of Legionnaires' disease that accompanied the water crisis. She believes the state vastly underplayed, and therefore worsened, that outbreak at the time.

"There were all kinds of efforts at the government level to quiet, and to disregard, and to discourage the idea that there were issues regarding bacteria [during the water crisis]," Sullivan said. "The state is well prepared to argue out any legal liability from lead poisoning, but you can't really argue out the bacteria if you can show that the bacteria is there because of the water switch, and there are researchers now who have shown that."

The fact that some residents still say they experience mysterious water issues doesn't inspire their confidence, either. "We still don't consume it," said Walker-Smith, whose tap water has tested negative for lead. "They tell us that the water's OK now, but I have excessive itching on my back right now. There's been hair loss; I could go on and on about the things I've heard."

But even amid all the pessimism, there's an important distinction to be made between a city's government and its people. Former Mayor Walling described to me the improbable hope and dedication he's seen in the community across his decade-plus working and campaigning in Flint politics.

"There are some people who say, you know, 'I'm looking for a ticket out of here.' But there's a much larger percentage of people who love this place," Walling said. "There's this deep attachment to the community, bordering on desperation. And it's a positive kind of desperation, in that it's a desperate desire for something better."

Whatever that "something better" is, it may explain why, despite her complaints, Walker-Smith hasn't left Flint, and doesn't plan to.

"People think we're just poor and have no means to leave. Some of us just don't *want* to leave. Both sides of my family are here. I own my home; it's paid for;

I don't have a mortgage. I don't want to leave my home," she said. "You just have to adjust."

For the time being, it's unclear what that adjustment may look like or exactly how it will arrive. Despite a parade of presidential contenders through the city in 2019 and 2020, eager to prove their bona fides on environmental and racial justice, Flint residents are skeptical that their salvation will come through the ballot box.

"People are weary," Pauli said. "They wanted all of this to be fixed a long time ago, and they still don't trust the institutions that are supposed to be protecting them, and they have some pretty good reasons for not doing so."

Flint has fought tooth and nail to reach something that even vaguely resembles normalcy. Its water quality has undeniably recovered, and despite concerns about equity, the new developments that dot the city's downtown are striking when compared with its trajectory just half a decade ago. Its people clearly take pride in the renovated Capitol Theatre, the bustling farmer's market and the Ferris Wheel, a gleaming, conspicuously modern startup incubator on the main drag of Saginaw Street. But that pride is matched—doubled, really—by a hard-bitten awareness that with the end of a crisis comes a new batch of problems, with less obvious solutions.

Those in Flint who choose to stick around and help find those solutions now face an improbable-seeming question, after nearly seven full years of crisis. It's a question that Americans throughout the country may find themselves asking when the dust settles from the chaos of 2020: Where, even, to begin?

Print Citations

CMS: Robertson, Derek. "Flint Has Clean Water Now: Why Won't People Drink It?" In *The Reference Shelf: National Debate 2021-2022: Water Resources,* edited by Micah L. Issitt, 14-24. Amenia, NY: Grey House Publishing, 2021.

MLA: Robertson, Derek. "Flint Has Clean Water Now: Why Won't People Drink It?" *The Reference Shelf: National Debate 2021-2022: Water Resources,* edited by Micah L. Issitt, Grey House Publishing, 2021, pp. 14-24.

APA: Robertson, D. (2021). Flint has clean water now: Why won't people drink it? In Micah L. Issitt (Ed.), *The reference shelf: National debate 2021-2022: Water resources* (pp. 14-24). Amenia, NY: Grey House Publishing.

The Pandemic Has Exposed America's Clean Water Crisis

By Khushbu Shah
Vox, April 17, 2020

Day after day, Deanna Miller Berry watches the requests pile up in her inbox.

"Please help me," a resident of Denmark, South Carolina, pleads. "I'm stuck in my house and don't want to drink the water."

"Just water," another resident writes in.

A third request for water comes in from a family of two who live in an apartment in the center of town on a block flanked by Baptist churches and not too far from the Piggly Wiggly. Miller Berry logs the responses to the dozen questions in an Excel sheet for the Denmark Citizens for Clean Water: Yes, someone in the home is directly impacted by Covid-19. Yes, someone has a disability. Yes, someone is elderly. No, neither one has access to their own transport.

Amid the coronavirus pandemic, Miller Berry's document keeps growing longer. As the founder of Denmark Citizens for Clean Water, she helps supply the community with clean water instead of the brown, smelly liquid that has been sloshing out of the taps in a number of homes for more than a decade. She delivers tanks and pays the monthly water costs—sometimes hundreds of dollars—for residents in the majority-black community.

The town's battle with drinking water—laced with HaloSan, a pesticide meant to kill bacteria—long precedes the pandemic, though. Residents told a local outlet 10 years ago, "The smell is terrible." More recently, former Democratic presidential candidate Tom Steyer mentioned the residents' concerns over their water system on the campaign trail.

Virginia Tech civil engineering professor Marc Edwards, who exposed the unsafe lead levels in the water in Flint, Michigan, and helped bring national attention to the issue, has also gone down to Denmark to test the town's well at the request of the community. In 2017, he collected dozens of samples from homes, Miller Berry says, but when Edwards asked the town's mayor if he could test a well for possible bacterial contamination after spotting a leaky sewage pipe, the mayor refused.

As for Flint, Mayor Sheldon Neely is still busy dealing with the community's access to clean drinking water six years after large amounts of lead were detected. And now there is the pandemic. When *Vox* spoke with Neely a few weeks ago, he had declared a state of emergency before the president of the United States had, and had ordered water that was shut off by the previous administration reconnected.

Meanwhile, miles away in Detroit, lawyers and activists are also fighting to turn water back on for the city's most vulnerable populations, after officials promised it would do so amid coronavirus concerns—yet hundreds still remain without access.

Having chemical- and lead-free water—or water at all—in the pandemic is vital: Hand-washing with soap is one of the most effective ways to fight off the virus. But millions of Americans across the country lack clean water—from small, rural towns in Kentucky to New Jersey's densely populated city of Newark. And while clean water access isn't only an issue for majority-black communities like Flint, Denmark, or Detroit, one study did find race to be the strongest correlative to lack of clean water. It is a crisis that is further exacerbated by the coronavirus, compounding years-long injustices in water-poor communities.

> While clean water access isn't only an issue for majority-black communities like Flint, Denmark, or Detroit, one study did find race to be the strongest correlative to lack of clean water.

"It's just a Catch-22," Edwards tells *Vox*. "If [these communities] don't engage in rigorous hygiene, they're endangering themselves to coronavirus, and if they do, they're fearful of the water."

Communities without Access to Clean Water Are in a "Constant State of Emergency"

Contaminated water isn't confined to a few communities or states, experts say. In any given year from 1982 to 2015, nearly 45 million Americans were accessing water that violated health standards, according to a 2018 study in the Proceedings of the National Academy of Sciences.

While that may be true, the lack of water access impacts low-income communities like Denmark, Flint, and Martin County, Kentucky, more aggressively.

"That is a reality for our poorest Americans," Edwards said, which "translates into a lot of problems. ... Cities that have a lot of water shutoffs. Others are living in fear of bathing and showering because of distrust in their water. And so even the basic functional water and quantity for hygiene isn't being delivered."

In Martin County, Kentucky, BarbiAnn Maynard, who has seen brown, milky water in her shower and kitchen for nearly two decades—when she does have water—waves off the collective panic around coronavirus.

"This is not anything unusual for us," Maynard, a member of the Martin County Water Warriors, tells *Vox*. "I used hand sanitizer rather than our water" before coronavirus. She has been afraid to wash her hands for a long time, and the pandemic has changed almost nothing, she says. When she takes a shower, she uses antibacterial hand-wash.

The Martin County Water District operates in a "constant state of emergency," the state's Public Service Commission noted. A 2019 report from the Appalachian Citizens Law Center noted nearly half of the county's residents couldn't afford to buy water regularly. (The water department did not return *Vox*'s request for comment.)

Now in the pandemic, many of the grocery stores in the county are out of water, Maynard says. Donors paying into a fund for residents to buy water are still making contributions, but the only grocery store allowing residents to buy water at market value limits it to two gallons per person per visit. It takes an average of four gallons to get through the day, Maynard says. Before the pandemic, residents could make a 45-minute drive to a spring in West Virginia, but now they're not allowed to cross state lines.

To work around the grocery stores' rules, Maynard went directly to the bottle distribution center in Elkhorn City, Kentucky, more than an hour drive from her home, to buy cases in bulk.

But even before the coronavirus, Martin County needed more bottled and distilled water than other places in the US. "It's just as bad inhaling it in the shower, so you have to get right back out," Maynard says.

The threat of dirty, lead-infused, or chemical-laced water—and, in some cases, no water at all — is not only a rural concern. Last year, more than 23,000 accounts had their water shut off in the city of Detroit, and 37 percent still hadn't had service restored as of mid-January. With the virus spreading, the city promised to restore water to residents, but as of March 31 had only done so for 1,050 of the 10,000 people who called with a water service problem (8,000 of those callers did not qualify for the Coronavirus Water Restart Plan, according to a city report).

Kristi Pullen Fedinick, the director of science and data at the environmental nonprofit Natural Resources Defense Council, attributes the overlooked water crises across the country to governmental "policies that have led to specific communities being disenfranchised and marginalized."

These dozens of communities across the United States, she says, have been facing not only water crises but many other issues because they have been systematically ignored for decades by those in charge. She ticks off the problems communities tend to face when they lack water: poor air quality, poor access to health care, and higher-than-average death rates. "The pandemic really exacerbated those issues they have been facing for a very, very, very long time."

In Newark, New Jersey, for example, the state's largest city, lead-contaminated water has impacted the health of its residents for years, with city officials denying there was a problem. In 2018, they abruptly changed course, however, and started handing out water filters to some residents after a new study confirmed that lead was indeed in the water at an alarmingly high rate, the *New York Times* reported. In August, the Environmental Protection Agency sent a letter to the mayor recommending the city advise residents "to use bottled water for drinking and cooking, until we can be assured of the reliable efficacy of filtration devices." At the same time, the Newark Water Coalition provided hundreds of gallons of water and filters at its distribution sites pre-pandemic, to fill in the void of just how much water residents need.

But with the stay-at-home mandates in a hot spot like New Jersey, the coalition's co-founder Sabre Bee says getting water out to those in need isn't always possible when keeping social distancing in mind.

"We were doing [distribution] at church, but of course, we can't gather in groups of five or more," Bee says. "And so we haven't been able to move distributions." Instead, she and other advocates for clean water deliver water to older and ill people, those who cannot get around in the middle of a pandemic.

People are telling Bee they're boiling water when they can't get clean water, which she knows works with bacteria. But with lead, she says, that only concentrates the amount in the water.

"I know this is serious," Bee says about the pandemic, "and I have to help my immune system during this time, but I'm drinking water that's poisoned. So now I'm just a ball of nerves and feeling helpless and hopeless."

Local Water Advocacy Groups Are Stepping in to Bring Water to Their Communities

In 2018, the NRDC found that more than 30 million Americans, nearly 10 percent of the country's population, drank from sources that violated the EPA's federal regulations. The issue, as the Centers for Disease Control and Prevention outlines on its website, is that even though the EPA puts out regulations—like setting legal limits on contaminants in drinking water and regularly updating water standards—they are just regulations. There is no national standard that mandates states implement the EPA's guidelines. This leaves a gap in local and state governments carrying out these guidelines, because in many cases, they may not have the financial resources to improve their drinking water.

As Edwards says, all the blame cannot be placed on small, local governments: "Many of our post-industrial cities and towns in America are losing population, and those who are left behind cannot afford to upgrade their infrastructure and maintain it to meet existing federal laws and standards. And so [those in charge] end up cutting corners because they have no choice."

This leaves those communities at risk to take it upon themselves to find—and many times buy—their own clean drinking water.

In Denmark, Miller Berry has taken on the burden of helping those in her community. "We've gotten zero help from the state of South Carolina. We've gotten zero help from our county, and we've gotten zero help from our city officials. We are being ignored by all three," Miller Berry says. (Multiple attempts by Vox to contact the mayor's office went unanswered.)

She has paid more than 20 residents' water bills over the past few months, according to her calculations, and word is spreading. These days, she gets more than 60 calls a day.

"I've been reaching out to the National Guard today to see if they could provide a water buffalo [tank]. But a [tank] cannot be provided to us until our county emergency management manager declares Denmark an emergency," Miller Berry says.

This is a stark contrast to local governments that have stepped up in the pandemic. In Newark, construction workers have replaced more than half of the nearly 19,000 lead-laden pipes since 2019, according to Kareem Adeem, the city's director of water and sewage. Filters that should last the better part of a year were passed out before the coronavirus outbreak to the residents who still have lead-contaminated water in their pipes, he said.

In Kentucky, Maynard can't even finish her sentence when she talks about how people are supporting her community. "Getting donations right now is, oh, my gosh," she says over the phone with relief. A state representative sent 60 gallons of distilled water for medical needs, while another Democratic state Senate candidate, Scott Sykes, sent 200 cases of water to residents, she said.

Even though it's a massive public health threat, coronavirus feels like a blip to communities struggling with water, Edwards says. "There [are] many dimensions to this problem and [coronavirus] is a minor dimension, but it's symptomatic of a frustrating situation that you can't even rely on to get water from your tap."

Print Citations

CMS: Shah, Khushbu. "The Pandemic Has Exposed America's Clean Water Crisis." In *The Reference Shelf: National Debate 2021-2022: Water Resources,* edited by Micah L. Issitt, 25-29. Amenia, NY: Grey House Publishing, 2021.

MLA: Shah, Khushbu. "The Pandemic Has Exposed America's Clean Water Crisis." *The Reference Shelf: National Debate 2021-2022: Water Resources,* edited by Micah L. Issitt, Grey House Publishing, 2021, pp. 25-29.

APA: Shah, K. (2021). The pandemic has exposed America's clean water crisis. In Micah L. Issitt (Ed.), *The reference shelf: National debate 2021-2022: Water resources* (pp. 25-29). Amenia, NY: Grey House Publishing.

Revealed: Millions of Americans Can't Afford Water as Bills Rise 80% in a Decade

By Nina Lakhani

The Guardian, June 23, 2020

Millions of ordinary Americans are facing rising and unaffordable bills for running water, and risk being disconnected or losing their homes if they cannot pay, a landmark *Guardian* investigation has found.

Exclusive analysis of 12 US cities shows the combined price of water and sewage increased by an average of 80% between 2010 and 2018, with more than two-fifths of residents in some cities living in neighbourhoods with unaffordable bills.

In the first nationwide research of its kind, our findings reveal the painful impact of America's expanding water poverty crisis as aging infrastructure, environmental clean-ups, changing demographics and the climate emergency fuel exponential price hikes in almost every corner of the US.

America's growing water affordability crisis comes as the Covid-19 pandemic underlines the importance of access to clean water. The research shows that rising bills are not just hurting the poorest but also, increasingly, working Americans.

"More people are in trouble, and the poorest of the poor are in big trouble," said Roger Colton, a leading utilities analyst, who was commissioned by the *Guardian* to analyse water poverty. "The data shows that we've got an affordability problem in an overwhelming number of cities nationwide that didn't exist a decade ago, or even two or three years ago in some cities."

Water bills exceeding 4% of household income are considered, for this analysis, unaffordable.

Colton's 88-page report is published today at the launch of a major project on America's water emergency by the *Guardian*, *Consumer Reports* and other partners.

Our research found that between 2010 and 2018 water bills rose by at least 27%, while the highest increase was a staggering 154% in Austin, Texas, where the average annual bill rose from $566 in 2010 to $1,435 in 2018–despite drought mitigation efforts leading to reduced water usage.

Meanwhile, federal aid to public water utilities, which serve around 87% of people, has plummeted while maintenance, environmental and health threats, climate shocks and other expenditures have skyrocketed.

"A water emergency threatens every corner of our country. The scale of this crisis demands nothing short of a fundamental transformation of our water systems. Water should never be treated as commodity or a luxury for the benefit of the wealthy," said water justice advocate Mary Grant from Food and Water Watch, reacting to the *Guardian's* research.

In Washington, 90 lawmakers from across the country–all Democrats–are pushing for comprehensive funding reforms to guarantee access to clean, affordable running water for every American.

The *Guardian's* investigation shows that the water poverty crisis is likely to get much worse, with bills in many cities becoming unaffordable for the majority of America's poor over the next decade.

In **Austin**, **Texas**, if prices in the city continue to go up at the current rate, more than four-fifthso low income residents–defined as people living under 200% of the federal poverty line (FPL)–could face unaffordable bills by 2030.

In **Tucson, Arizona,** another drought affected city, the number of low income residents facing unaffordable bills doubled to 46% between 2010 and 2018–as the average bill increased by 119% to $869.

Rising costs are disproportionately impacting poor Americans. In **New Orleans, Santa Fe and Cleveland**, about three-quarters of low income residents live in neighbourhoods where average water and sewage bills are unaffordable.

Amid rising costs and diminishing federal dollars, the use of punitive measures–shutoffs and liens (a legal claim on the house linked to a debt which can lead to foreclosure)–is widespread. Just like mortgage foreclosures, water shutoffs and liens can force affected households to abandon their homes.

Jarome Montgomery, 48, a truck driver from Warrensville Heights in Cleveland, has borrowed from his partner, mother, grandmother and sisters to repay more than $30,000 to the water department since 2013, and avoid his home being auctioned off at a tax sale. Despite this, he still owes more than $5,000 in water and sewer charges including penalties and interest.

"I've done two payment plans, but I'm still in foreclosure, it's like they're trying to make me homeless," said Montgomery. "There is no way I'm using the amount of water they're charging me for but I'm in a no-win situation, I don't want to lose my home so I have to keep finding the money."

In **San Diego,** the average bill was $1,416 in 2018: 62% of low income people live in neighbourhoods where the average bill was unaffordable, representing almost one in five of the city's total population. Among the poor, one in seven faced average water bills upward of 12% of the total household income in 2018.

Currently, tech hub Seattle has the lowest poverty rate of the cities analysed, and only 13% of Seattleites struggle to afford water–even though bills rose to $1,254 in 2018 in order to help fund earthquake and climate change resilience improvements. Nevertheless, by 2030, three-quarters of low income residents could be living in neighbourhoods with unaffordable bills.

Nationwide, water bills were almost universally unaffordable for the poorest poor in 2018. In 11 of the 12 cities, 100% of the population with incomes below 50% of the federal poverty level lived in neighbourhoods with unaffordable water bills, with the 12th city, Fresno, reaching 99.9%.

Federal Neglect

Federal funding for water systems has fallen by 77% in real terms since its peak in 1977–leaving local utilities to raise the money that is needed to upgrade infrastructure, comply with safety standards for toxic contaminants like PFAS, lead and algae blooms, and adapt to extreme weather conditions like drought and floods linked to global heating.

For years, maintenance and clean-up projects were deferred by utilities, which has contributed to the current infrastructure and toxic water crisis. This helps explain why more than $6bn worth of water is lost annually to leaks, according to industry analysts Bluefield Research.

"High-cost low-quality water is a national issue … the federal government is clearly not playing the role it needs to play," said Howard Neukrug, director of the water centre at the University of Pennsylvania and former head of Philadelphia's water department.

"The bottom line is that assuming there's no federal helicopter with $1tn, rates are going to go up dramatically to pay for infrastructure and quality issues," he added.

At least $35bn every year for 20 years–that's how much investment the Environmental Protection Agency (EPA) says is needed just to comply with federal safety regulations for water, sewage and storm water.

Part of the problem is that for years, maintenance and clean-up projects were deferred by utilities, without squirreling away money or planning for the climate crisis. It's led to a massive backlog, but putting off improvements is no longer an option, so cities must now borrow the money to invest in infrastructure programmes and/or hike up prices in order to deliver safe, clean water.

Nationwide, the rising cost of water has significantly outstripped the consumer price index over the past decade.

The US is the only country in the industrialized world without a regulatory system–like Ofwat in the UK–responsible for monitoring rates and performance, according to Stephen Gasteyer, professor of sociology at Michigan State University.

He said: "Water rates have gone up dramatically–mostly in places where

Our research found that between 2010 and 2018 water bills rose by at least 27%, while the highest increase was a staggering 145% in Austin, Texas.

people are also struggling with food, housing and other basic services. It's a symptom of the inequalities and segregation problems we have in the US, where poor people are agglomerated in particular places and local governments are shouldered with the responsibility for raising revenue for services."

There are federal programmes to help low income households afford energy and telecoms bills, but nothing for water. There is however, legislation proposed to fund the infrastructure shortfall and create a water affordability fund.

The water act was first introduced in 2016, and has gained momentum since it was reintroduced last year by Brenda Lawrence, Democratic congresswoman representing Michigan, and co-sponsored by Bernie Sanders in the Senate.

"Access to water has never been a priority in the country, because it's been a poor person's issue. We need to transform that mindset and make sure every American has clean running water," said Lawrence.

Punitive Measures

As many as one in 20 homes are disconnected for unpaid bills annually, according to the only national study. No one knows how many eventually catch up on payments or have to learn to survive without water to flush the toilet, shower and cook. There's no national watchdog and most census questions about water access and poverty have been eliminated since the 1980s.

The Covid-19 pandemic exposed the plight of people like Deborah O'Barr, 62, from **Goodspring**, **Tennessee**, and her husband, Bobby, 63, who've lived without running water since 2016 as they don't have the money or correct paperwork to get a new meter.

"It feels like nobody cares. We must be the lowest of the low as far as the water company is concerned. We just don't matter, not even during a pandemic," said O'Barr, who relies on a local spring, rainwater and her son to fill containers.

As the virus spread, leaving tens of thousand dead and millions jobless, **Detroit** became the first city to suspend shutoffs and pledge to reconnect households disconnected in the previous year. In 2014, shortly after filing the largest municipal bankruptcy in US history, the city launched a massive shutoff programme and has since disconnected at least 141,000 households, according to records obtained by news website Bridge.

The UN said the debt collection scheme violated human rights and condemned the disproportionate impact on African Americans, who account for about 80% of the city's population.

As the virus spread, hundreds of localities and 13 states eventually issued moratoriums, though only a fraction agreed to reconnect those without running water because of unpaid bills.

This included **New Orleans**, **Louisiana**, where the water department has one of the country's harshest shutoff programmes, disconnecting almost one in five households in 2016.

In New Orleans, our research found 79% of low income residents living in neighbourhoods with an unaffordable water burden—which could rise to 93% by 2030 if rates keep climbing. Bills have already doubled over the past decade, to $1,268 in 2018—in a city where many rely on bottled water due to concerns about toxins—which means the poorest simply cannot afford to pay.

In 2018, about 30% of poor residents lived in areas where the average bill cost more than 12% of household income.

In total, almost a third of all water customers in New Orleans are considered "delinquent" and together owe well over $50m.

"It is difficult to argue with a conclusion that New Orleans is in the worst shape of the 12 cities studied," according to Colton, when considering the depth and breadth of the water affordability crisis residents face.

Close behind are **Cleveland, Ohio,** and **Santa Fe, New Mexico.**

Santa Fe saw the smallest increase but the highest bill in 2018 at $1,845. By 2030, 99% of low income residents will live in neighbourhoods with unaffordable bills.

Nationwide, nobody knows how many Americans were without water at the start of the pandemic–nor how many were disconnected during. What is known is that financial aid to help families and utilities keep taps running was excluded from federal rescue packages.

Is affordable water possible?

In **Philadelphia**, advocates working in a predominantly low-income black and brown neighbourhood in 2014 came across people who had been without running water for decades–forced to use plastic bags for the toilet and bottled water to wash their hands. "It was widespread, and clearly a human rights issue," said Rachel Lopez, director of the west Philadelphia legal clinic. "A manmade drought disproportionately affecting low-income people of colour."

Some people were denied a water account because their names weren't on the deeds or lease–so-called tangled titles, which are fairly common among low income communities. Others were shutoff after accumulating large debts, sometimes inherited, often exacerbated by fines, and some simply couldn't afford to pay for a replacement pipe or meter.

Our research shows that between 2010 and 2018, the number of poor Philadelphians living in neighbourhoods where water is unaffordable doubled to 54% as bills topped $900. During the first three months of the pandemic, the city reconnected almost 9,000 homes.

Colton worked with the city to create the tiered assistance programme (TAP) after it emerged that in 2017 around 40% of water customers were behind on their bills–amounting to $242m in uncollected revenue.

The premise is pretty simple: the most effective way to improve compliance–and maximise revenue–is to make bills affordable, in other words based on a person's ability to pay, like the energy sector has been doing for years.

The programme has made an impact: about 15,000 people are currently enrolled, though this is still far short of the 60,000 households estimated to be eligible even before the current economic disaster.

But, the city continues to convert water debt into tax liens, and once a month, these properties are auctioned off at a sheriff's tax sale.

"Water debts are clustered in communities of colour which disproportionately devalue their homes and neighbourhoods," said attorney Robert Ballenger from Community Legal Services.

In a move welcomed by advocates, city officials recently agreed to introduce debt forgiveness, which should mean that TAP enrollees will see their water debts wiped–no matter how big–after two years of compliance.

This could be a game changer, as currently water debt is a burden passed down through generations.

Earlier this year, Cheryl Gregg, 50, returned from the hospital after being admitted with high blood pressure and respiratory problems, to find that the water had been disconnected–this time because of a leaking pipe. "I had to take an Uber to my daughter's house to wash and buy bottled water, it's expensive. I have no income," Greg said from her hospital bed, after being readmitted a few days later.

This was not the first time, according to daughter Amber, 28, who recalls months camped out at relatives' houses because they couldn't afford the water bill. "My mom and grandma had a lot of health problems and couldn't work, we got cut off so many times. We never knew what we'd find after school every day, no lights or no water, it was so stressful," she said.

The water debt, which includes interest and penalties, is over $26,000.

Greg is now on TAP and the family hope the debt will be forgiven. Amber, who works two jobs at a parking company and a burger joint, said: "I make sure my mom pays every month so we don't lose the house."

Water Industry Response

Water providers are aware of the rising burden on people from bills due to the costs of aging infrastructure and "want to find ways to assist them while being responsible stewards of the water system", according to Greg Kail, of the American Water Works Association (AWWA), whose members include water utilities.

Responding to the *Guardian's* research, Kail said there was no "silver bullet" to solve affordability but said "significant progress" had been made, citing the AWWA's research last year that more than 80% of large water utilities have a capital assistance program, up from 60% a year earlier.

Cleveland Water did not comment on Montgomery's case but said it was committed to building a "more equitable water future".

Print Citations

CMS: Lakhani, Nina. "Revealed: Millions of Americans Can't Afford Water as Bills Rise 80% in a Decade." In *The Reference Shelf: National Debate 2021-2022: Water Resources,* edited by Micah L. Issitt, 30-35. Amenia, NY: Grey House Publishing, 2021.

MLA: Lakhani, Nina. "Revealed: Millions of Americans Can't Afford Water as Bills Rise 80% in a Decade." *The Reference Shelf: National Debate 2021-2022: Water Resources,* edited by Micah L. Issitt, Grey House Publishing, 2021, pp. 30-35.

APA: Lakhani, N. (2021). Reveals: Millions of Americans can't afford water as bills rise 80% in a decade. In Micah L. Issitt (Ed.), *The reference shelf: National debate 2021-2022: Water resources* (pp. 30-35). Amenia, NY: Grey House Publishing.

The Hidden Racial Inequities of Access to Water in America

By Jay Willis
GQ, November 25, 2019

Most Americans do not give a second thought to what happens after they turn on a faucet handle or flush a toilet. This is because the result is always the same: Clean, potable water comes out, available to drink, wash hands, cook food, clean clothes, or tidily dispose of waste, whatever the case may be.

Yet in many places throughout the country, running water is a scarce resource, or even an unattainable luxury. A report released earlier this week sheds new light on the scope of this phenomenon, and its conclusions are startling. More than two million people in the world's most prosperous democracy live without running water or modern plumbing. And although socioeconomic status correlates with water and wastewater services access, race is the single strongest predictor: African-American and Latinx households are almost twice as likely as white households to not have full indoor plumbing, while Native American households are about *19 times* as likely, the report says. The researchers caution that given the challenges in obtaining accurate data from the groups most affected by the «water access gap,» these figures may be undercounts.

The water crisis in Flint, Michigan, is perhaps the most infamous recent example of racial inequities in water access, where local officials' failure to adequately treat tap water exposed the city's nearly 100,000 residents, more than half of whom are black, to dangerous levels of lead and other contaminants. The problem is also acute in more remote or rural areas, including certain majority-black communities in the Deep South, majority-Latinx communities in California's Central Valley, and Native American reservations in the Southwest, among others. Nationwide, 17 percent of people in rural areas have had trouble obtaining potable water, and 12 percent have experienced problems with their sewage systems, according to the report. In some places, conditions are getting worse, not better. "In six states and Puerto Rico, we're going backwards—fewer people will have running water next year than this year," says George McGraw, the founder and CEO of DigDeep, a nonprofit that co-authored the report.

These racial and socioeconomic disparities are not an accident. In an effort to cut down on the dangers posed by waterborne diseases, Congress passed the Safe Drinking Water Act (SDWA) in 1974, a landmark statute that empowers the

Environmental Protection Agency to set and enforce national standards for drinking-water-contaminant levels. And throughout most of the previous century, the federal government invested

African-Americans and Latinx households are almost twice as likely as white households to not have full indoor plumbing, while Native American households are about 19 times as likely.

heavily in infrastructure, making water and wastewater services available in some of the nation's previously far-flung corners. Especially in cities and towns with higher population densities, this was a no-brainer investment in public health and economic productivity, and allowed utilities to provide high-quality water to consumers at relatively low prices.

This infrastructure boom, however, was not equal-opportunity. Cities and towns building out their systems would not always do so in majority-minority areas nearby. As the report documents, in the 1950s, the town of Zanesville, Ohio, did not build water lines in its African-American neighborhoods, and the following decade Roanoke, Virginia, did not extend its infrastructure to Hollins, a neighboring majority-black town. Discriminatory local government law practices also played a role: In the Central Valley of California, predominantly Latinx communities were discouraged from formally incorporating, which prevented them from accessing construction financing available to cities and towns. As a result, no one bothered to install a water system in the first place. Even today, there are places in the country where homes lack running water, within walking distance of neighborhoods that enjoy the full spectrum of water and sanitation services, says Zoë Roller, senior program manager at the nonprofit U.S. Water Alliance, which also co-authored the report.

The Safe Water Drinking Act also doesn't apply to systems that include fewer than 15 connections, or that serve fewer than 25 people. This means anyone who isn't linked into a large grid is more or less on their own, and the facilities they have to build, install, and maintain are subject to little regulatory oversight. The report says that nearly 23 percent of private wells tested by the U.S. Geological Survey yielded evidence of arsenic, uranium, or other dangerous forms of contamination.

Meanwhile, federal investment has plummeted over the past several decades, from a 63 percent share of total capital spending on water and wastewater in 1977 to less than 9 percent today. Free grant money turned into expensive loans, forcing state and local governments to take on debt in order to make meaningful improvements. In lower-income, rural areas where subsidized construction hasn't already occurred, modest local budgets can't compensate for the shortfall, and the customer base isn't large or wealthy enough to independently finance the costs of improvements. Oftentimes, this doesn't just mean that tap water is unsafe; it means there is no tap water at all. "Communities without access now have to struggle to catch up to the rest of the country with both hands tied behind their backs," McGraw says.

Instead, residents rely on a patchwork system of solutions to meet their needs: using wells, collecting from springs, buying bottles, and occasionally building unsanctioned, jerry-rigged hookups to nearby mains. In majority-Latinx *colonias* near the U.S.-Mexico border, the report documents how residents haul water by car or on foot, or pay up to $250 a month to have it trucked in—and even then, they aren›t sure if it›s safe to drink. Problems like these affect lower-income areas that are predominatingly white, too; in parts of Appalachia, researchers found that some residents waited to shower until a rainstorm and then stood outside underneath overflowing gutters.

For sanitation, those without access to sewer systems use septic tanks, lagoons, and improvised systems of PVC pipe that drain untreated wastewater outside, sometimes into their own yards. In eastern Puerto Rico, researchers interviewed people who deal with daily flooding in their yards because the developer installed insufficient septic systems in their homes. People also cut way back on overall water usage: In Red Mesa, Arizona, a Navajo Nation town along the Utah border, researchers learned that residents use as little as two to three gallons of water per day. The average American uses 88. As documented by PBS last year, even in areas of Navajo Nation where a water main is accessible, hooking into it can take up to 15 years and cost more than $12,000.

This dependence on inefficient delivery systems, crumbling infrastructure, and obsolete technology entails a host of devastating consequences. Waterborne illnesses that are functionally nonexistent elsewhere remain a constant worry. Property values can plummet, since homes without running water are hard to sell, and economic growth can stall. "We talked to people in towns without sewer systems where businesses thought about locating there, and then didn't because they'd have to build their own wastewater system," Roller says. In areas with large undocumented populations, people can be reluctant to complain or seek help for fear of drawing the attention of immigration authorities. And the cost of obtaining water stretches the finances of already cashed-strapped households, preventing them from meeting other critical but not necessary-for-human-life needs. In Red Mesa, researchers met a resident whose water-gathering efforts cost $200 per month in gas money alone.

Going without running water carries a social stigma, too. Many people who collect their water outside the home do so at night, for example, in order to avoid being seen by their neighbors. The rationing process can be especially hard on children. "Imagine you haven't brushed your teeth or showered in a week, and everyone else in your school did so this morning," says McGraw. "We hear all the time from parents whose kids don't want to go to school because they're worried about how they smell."

The access gap is exacerbated by conditions like industrial runoff, pesticide contamination, and climate change, and the associated burdens are borne disproportionately by low-income people and people of color. In Navajo Nation, more than 80 percent of surface-water resources have disappeared in the past 25 years, says McGraw. Last year, the California Water Board declared dozens of water systems in rural Tulare County—"ground zero for contaminated groundwater," a Board scientist told the *Visalia Times-Delta*—to be out of compliance with state regulations, thanks to both naturally occurring arsenic and also the nitrate fertilizers in heavy rotation. When wells dry up during climate-change-induced droughts, families are left without their usual water source, and what little water they can get has a higher-than-usual concentration of contaminants. Roller adds that as extreme weather patterns become more common, periods of intense rainfall cause older septic systems to overflow, depositing raw sewage in front yards and inside homes.

The projected costs of addressing a public health crisis of this magnitude are staggering. According to a 2011 United Nations report, the Alabama Department of Public Health estimates that between 40 and 90 percent of households in Lowndes County, where 72.5 percent of residents are black, have either shoddy or no septic systems in place; of the homes that are equipped with septic systems, half are failing or will fail soon. Providing universal access to the homes in Navajo Nation, the Indian Health Service says, would cost around $200 million. Implementing fixes in lower-income white communities is expensive, too: Reporting from West Virginia Public Broadcasting earlier this year found that the state, which is more than 90 percent white, would need $17 *billion* to modernize hundreds of its decaying water and sewer systems. At the end of 2017, only $8.5 million had been allocated to do so.

But the returns on investment can be staggering, too: According to the Indian Health Service, every dollar it spent on sanitation facilities yields at least twenty dollars in health benefits. "Water sits at the base of everything we do," McGraw says. "Your ability to get enough clean running water to get through the day determines whether you can get an education, keep a job, or even just have time to play with your kids." For millions of people living in America, this world still remains beyond their reach.

Print Citations

CMS: Willis, Jay. "The Hidden Racial Inequities of Access to Water in America." In *The Reference Shelf: National Debate 2021-2022: Water Resources,* edited by Micah L. Issitt, 36-39. Amenia, NY: Grey House Publishing, 2021.

MLA: Willis, Jay. "The Hidden Racial Inequities of Access to Water in America." *The Reference Shelf: National Debate 2021-2022: Water Resources,* edited by Micah L. Issitt, Grey House Publishing, 2021, pp. 36-39.

APA: Willis, J. (2021). The hidden racial inequities of access to water in America. In Micah L. Issitt (Ed.), *The reference shelf: National debate 2021-2022: Water resources* (pp. 36-39). Amenia, NY: Grey House Publishing.

How Development of America's Water Infrastructure Has Lurched Through History

By David Sedlak

PEW Trend Magazine, March 3, 2019

Throughout history as cities grew, new water infrastructure was built to supply this vital resource to increasing numbers of people. Initially, urban dwellers carried water from hand-dug wells and lakes and streams that ran through the city. As cities advanced, engineers built aqueducts and canals to import water from great distances. Among the engineering marvels of the ancient world, the Roman water system of elevated aqueducts, underground piping, and the world's first sewer network is an iconic example of the ingenuity that made possible Europe's first city of a million people.

Modern water systems owe a lot to the Roman innovations from 2,000 years ago. But instead of celebrating the technology that has allowed millions of people to survive in places where the local water supply is limited, we hide our water infrastructure underground and go about our daily lives oblivious to these lifelines. Today, we talk about urban water systems only when they fail. And therein lies our current problem: Much of the water infrastructure in the United States, Western Europe, and many other places is aging and in serious need of replacement or upgrading, especially to address the effects of a changing climate and new generation of man-made contaminants.

Due to our complacency, only a serious crisis that could leave people without access to tap water is likely to free up the financial resources needed to bring water infrastructure—which in many places still includes pipes from the 1800s—into the 21st century. Absent an emergency, cash-strapped water utility managers will continue to deal with aging water systems by economizing on routine maintenance and deferring upgrades for as long as possible. This chronic funding shortage is so dire that the American Society of Civil Engineers has awarded the drinking water infrastructure of the United States grades of D-minus or D for over a decade.

Our reluctance to invest means that we allow our water systems to deteriorate until they nearly fail and invest in them only after the public decides that the status quo is unacceptable. Our water systems' shortcomings were brought to the public's attention by Flint, Michigan's, recent experience. But it doesn't end there: Water systems are teetering on the edge of viability in numerous cities. We have seen this pattern before—and the present-day warning for us all is that the past is often prologue.

As the United States grew during the 1800s, it transformed from an agrarian nation to an industrialized one as populations increased and built drinking water infrastructure on a grand scale. But these developments had less to do with real planning than with reacting to crises. The first crisis occurred when the rapid population growth overwhelmed the water infrastructure of the period—typically shallow wells or small reservoirs located within the city—leaving it unable to provide sufficient quantities of drinking water.

The clearest example of this was in New York, where the population more than tripled, from about 60,000 people to more than 200,000 people, between 1800 and 1830. After decades of denial by city leaders during which the wealthy drank water provided by the Manhattan Water Co. (the predecessor of Chase Bank) while the poor drank well water of dubious quality, New York's leaders invested $9 million (about $850 per person in today's dollars) to import water to the city using a system of canals, pipes, and reservoirs situated about 40 miles to the north.

Building upon this early success, New Yorkers spent another $177 million (about $500 per person today) to expand their water system out another 60 miles in search of more clean water as the city grew in the subsequent decades. This pattern of population growth outstripping the capacity of local water supplies, followed by investments of hundreds of dollars per person to import water from great distances, also took place in Boston, Washington, Philadelphia, and other cities during this period. The periodic crises of growing East Coast cities taught the young country some valuable lessons. The technological know-how gained from the construction of dams and reservoirs helped our nation's westward migration that began several decades later when leaders of Seattle, San Francisco, and Los Angeles were able to build massive imported water systems before their cities reached a state of crisis.

These solutions to the nation's first water crisis, though, spawned its second one. Once city dwellers had access to large quantities of water, per capita water consumption increased as they indulged in stay-at-home baths and replaced their outhouses with indoor toilets. The sewage produced by city dwellers flowed to the nearest rivers, which often served as the drinking water supply for the next downstream city. By the late 19th century, typhoid fever and other waterborne diseases had increased to epidemic levels.

The new challenge was to develop treatment plants that could make sewage-contaminated waters safe to drink. By the early 1900s, billions of dollars had been invested in the new technology of drinking water treatment. The corresponding decrease in waterborne disease and lengthened life spans resulting from these advances has been hailed as one of the top five technological achievements of the 20th century by the National Academy of Sciences. Thanks to water filtration and chlorination, the second water crisis was averted.

America's third water crisis occurred as cities again grew during the economic expansion that followed World War II. As people migrated to urban areas, the increased volume of wastewater they produced overwhelmed the assimilative capacity of the nation's rivers, lakes, and estuaries, which had purified the modest amount of pollution that they had received in the previous years. For the next 25 years, foul smells emanated from urban waterways, dead fish washed up on shorelines, and runaway algal blooms became the norm in lakes. Water pollution was a nuisance, but city leaders lacked the will to tax their constituents to build sewage treatment infrastructure that might benefit downstream communities more than their own—and the state of the nation's waterways further deteriorated until the early 1970s. It was only then that the nation, fed up with water pollution, came to support the Clean Water Act—a federal law that established requirements for sewage treatment. The federal government provided cities with grants and low-interest loans to upgrade their inadequate sewage infrastructure. During the two decades ending in 1992, the federal government invested over $60 billion (about $700 per person today) to again make America's waterways fishable and swimmable.

As these investments in sewage treatment improved the environment, cities continued their struggle to keep up with the demand of growing populations. In addition to building more imported water systems, they turned their attention to conservation and passed laws that required low-flow fixtures and less thirsty landscaping in new housing developments.

But as we soon enter the third decade of the 21st century, two potential crises are again poised to threaten our ability to keep up with thirsty American cities: continued demand and the growing perception by residents of some communities that their tap water is no longer safe to drink.

The availability of water has continued to be an issue as population growth has driven demand. But what is complicating things more than before are climate change-induced shifts in precipitation patterns and a greater recognition that taking too much water from rivers and streams damages aquatic ecosystems. This means that the old model of piping water in from long distances is no longer attractive. For example, the water level in the massive dams on the Colorado River, which supplies some of the drinking water to about 10 percent of the nation's population, has been falling since 2000 due to climactic shifts and increasing demand from cities and farmers. The imminent declaration by the Colorado River's managers of a shortage means that water is about to get more expensive, and water rights lawyers will become more plentiful in cities throughout the Southwest as legal disputes increase. Recent droughts of historic duration and intensity from Texas to California also have contributed to a sense that action is needed to enhance water security—that simple notion of having enough available, clean water to meet society's needs. Atlanta, Tampa, Florida, and Charlotte, North Carolina, are worrying about the security of their existing water supplies because their populations are approaching a point where local water sources will no longer be sufficient, especially during dry years.

Some communities facing water shortages have begun to think ahead by investing in new strategies for decreasing their reliance on imported water. This movement, which is sometimes referred to as water self-sufficiency, is furthest advanced in Southern California, where water has long been a scarce resource. The 2.5 million people of Orange County now recycle nearly all of their wastewater, passing it through an advanced treatment plant and returning it to the aquifer from which they draw their drinking water. The county currently satisfies 75 percent of its drinking water needs by combining water from wastewater recycling with groundwater recharged with rainwater that falls within the city and water from an effluent-laden stream that bisects the county. If the remaining 25 percent of the region's imported water supply becomes too expensive or unreliable, the county could meet its water needs by building seawater desalination plants, just as its neighbors to the south, in San Diego, and to the north, in Santa Barbara, did in response to their water scarcity concerns.

Elsewhere, the drive toward water self-sufficiency has taken a different form, shaped by local geography and geology. In California's Salinas Valley, technologies similar to those used to recycle wastewater in Orange County are being repurposed to create drinking water from a mixture of municipal wastewater effluent, runoff from city streets and farm fields, and wash water from food processing plants.

On the East Coast, in eastern Virginia, the local utility is treating wastewater with advanced technologies before using it to recharge the local drinking water aquifer. The project makes sense in that relatively wet part of the country because it eliminates the discharge of nutrient-rich wastewater to the ecologically sensitive Chesapeake Bay and counteracts land subsidence that has made the region increasingly vulnerable to flooding from rising sea levels.

The second potential water crisis is related to a growing public perception that tap water is no longer safe to drink. The failure of the municipal water system in Flint to properly manage its aging pipe network, which contaminated the water supply with lead and *Legionella* bacteria, was national news a few years ago. More recently, the discovery that chemicals used for firefighting and industrial manufacturing—the per- and polyfluoroalkyl substances referred to as PFAS—have contaminated water supplies for about a quarter of the nation has further highlighted the vulnerability of drinking water systems to man-made pollutants.

> **The drive toward water self-sufficiency has taken a different form, shaped by local geography and geology.**

Most important, this discovery raises a significant new issue: Can our old water filtration and disinfection plants protect public health? Simply retrofitting treatment plants in places where water supplies are known to be contaminated and banning difficult-to-treat chemicals like PFAS will not protect us from the coming quality challenges. Evidence of the systemic shortcomings of the existing drinking water system are apparent a short drive south of Flint, in Toledo, Ohio, where continued release of nutrients from farms, wastewater treatment plants, and city streets, coupled with warmer temperatures in the Great Lakes, resulted in blooms of toxic algae that made tap water unsafe for several days in 2014. The exact cause of more recent toxic algal blooms that have occurred in Florida, Oregon, Ohio, and other parts of the country is unclear, but most experts suspect that nutrients that are legally released from farms and cities are the main culprit. Simply put, our aging drinking water systems are not ready for the less forgiving future that will prevail in an era of climate change and inadequate pollution regulations.

Considering the way that change has come about in the past, it seems likely that the nation will have to weather a few more high-profile drinking water contamination incidents before public opinion forces action. When change does come about, it would be useful if the means of evolving our water systems were ready to be deployed. Using the water self-sufficiency movement as a starting point, it may be possible to rapidly adapt existing infrastructure. For example, the reverse osmosis technology used to make municipal wastewater effluent and seawater safe to drink by forcing water through a membrane that captures salts, microbes, and chemicals could be repurposed to remove PFAS and algal toxins from water supplies. With a little more development, emerging technologies that have yet to be deployed at scale, such as energy-efficient LED water disinfection lamps and treatment systems that use electricity instead of difficult-to-manage chemicals to decontaminate water, could provide new approaches for solving water-quality problems. Although advanced treatment technologies will not solve all of the problems related to decaying water pipes, aging dams, and inadequate treatment plants, they may create the means to move away from our historic reliance on massive infrastructure projects that have become too expensive to properly maintain.

For example, point-of-entry water filters that purify only the water that comes into the kitchen and building-scale water recycling systems that clean up any contaminants that entered the water within the underground pipe network could reduce costs by allowing water used outdoors for cleaning and irrigation to be treated less stringently than drinking water. Additional savings could be realized by investments in underutilized technologies that prevent treated water from escaping from aging water pipes between the treatment plant and the user.

Given these needs, our nation's water systems are on the cusp of a once-in-a-generation change involving costs that could reach $100 billion. Whether the change is preceded by crises that compromise public health and damage local economies will depend upon the investments that are made over the next few years. Federal agencies, including the National Science Foundation and the Department of Energy, along with water-stressed cities in Southern California and Texas, have begun to invest in the research and development needed to adapt urban water infrastructure to a future with greater water scarcity and increasing threats to water quality. Elected officials and community leaders now must recognize that they have an important role to play in reforming the institutions, regulations, and financial policies that impede systemic change. Our history of crisis and response will likely continue, but the more we can anticipate and plan, the better the chance that we'll have the safe water we all need in a less forgiving future.

Print Citations

CMS: Sedlak, David. "How Development of America's Water Infrastructure Has Lurched Through History." In *The Reference Shelf: National Debate 2021-2022: Water Resources*, edited by Micah L. Issitt, 40-45. Amenia, NY: Grey House Publishing, 2021.

MLA: Sedlak, David. "How Development of America's Water Infrastructure Has Lurched Through History." *The Reference Shelf: National Debate 2021-2022: Water Resources*, edited by Micah L. Issitt, Grey House Publishing, 2021, pp. 40-45.

APA: Sedlak, D. (2021). How development of America's water infrastructure has lurched through history. In Micah L. Issitt (Ed.), *The reference shelf: National debate 2021-2022: Water resources* (pp. 40-45). Amenia, NY: Grey House Publishing.

Why Scientists Should Shape Environmental Policy

By James Saiers
Foreign Policy, March 14, 2020

Solar power, wind energy, smart grids, and energy storage often command the current discourse on energy innovation. Yet none of these technologies has transformed the U.S. energy landscape to the degree of high-volume hydraulic fracturing, known as "fracking," which is unlocking previously inaccessible crude oil and natural gas from underground reservoirs. Thanks to fracking, the 40-year decline in U.S. domestic crude oil production has reversed, and the United States has recently become a net exporter of natural gas for the first time.

For many, this record-setting pace of oil and gas production is no cause for celebration, because it reflects a continued reliance on fossil fuels. Nevertheless, fracking has made oil and gas plentiful and cheap, making these energy resources hard to resist. Like it or not, we may depend on oil and gas—and the technologies that produce them—for the foreseeable future.

Fracking begins after a gas or oil well is drilled and involves injecting a mixture of water, sand, and chemical additives into rock. The high pressure causes the rock to fracture, providing conduits for the oil and gas to flow into the nearby wellbore. Public perceptions of fracking are shaped by controversies between an industry that has downplayed the risks of fracking and the citizens alleging that it has polluted air, contaminated drinking water, and scarred landscapes.

People within communities hosting fracking were scared, looking to experts to make sense of this issue. While experts were easy to find, definitive answers were in short supply. The deployment of fracking had raced ahead of the science needed to illuminate its potential impacts. As fracking activities evolve, uncertainties remain. We must advance a science-based approach to management of fracking activities—one that engages the fossil fuel industry, while drawing from the research of independent scientists.

The natural gas company Range Resources inaugurated Pennsylvania's shale gas rush in 2004, targeting the Marcellus Shale, which extends from West Virginia to the southern tier of New York State. The shale gas boom revitalized many of Pennsylvania's small towns. Still, not everyone was happy. Residents grew frustrated with the traffic to and from drilling sites, noise, bright lights, and dust. Tensions mounted between residents who held lucrative natural gas leases and those forced to endure the inconveniences without benefiting from the financial windfall. And the public was becoming increasingly concerned about its water.

Although water withdrawals for fracking were not imposing undue stress on Pennsylvania's streams and rivers, problems arose when industry tried to put this used water back. Fracking wastewater is exceptionally salty and may contain naturally occurring radioactive materials, such as radium, in addition to various hydrocarbon compounds. Much of this wastewater was discharged into streams and rivers after processing at treatment facilities.

The treatment plants were not equipped to handle the briny wastewater. Trouble sprouted in 2008, when monitoring of the Monongahela River in southwestern Pennsylvania—a source of drinking water for 1 million people—revealed that the waterway carried elevated loads of bromide, a precursor in the formation of cancer-causing brominated disinfection byproducts. Two years later, the Pittsburgh Water and Sewer Authority observed increases in those byproducts in its drinking water, linked to the discharge of Marcellus wastewater into the Allegheny River and its tributaries. Fears of contamination from intentional discharges were compounded by uncontrolled releases of fracking fluids, drilling fluids, and wastewater from leaks at fracking sites, trucking accidents, and illegal dumping.

Spills and stream salinization were not the only problems. Methane was detected in high levels in well waters of more than a dozen households in the small town of Dimock. The homeowners blamed nearby gas wells that were drilled and fracked by Cabot Oil and Gas. While not toxic, methane is flammable, and its release into the enclosed airspace at the top of a water well can lead to an explosion. Cabot Oil and Gas eventually reached a settlement, but, as part of the settlement terms, was not required to acknowledge responsibility for the contamination.

The first scientific study published after the Dimock incident received considerable public attention. By leveraging chemical fingerprinting techniques, the scientists attributed the source of methane present in a subset of 60 well-water samples to industry activities. Although methane does occur naturally in Pennsylvania's drinking-water aquifers, a recent analysis of environmental records revealed that 39 wells drilled into the Marcellus Shale between 2004 and 2015 allowed methane migration that impacted 108 drinking water supplies.

The problems encountered at the outset of the shale gas boom did not arise from a lack of regulation. Pennsylvania had a regulatory framework built around more than a century's experience with conventional oil and gas extraction. Though bad actors existed, most natural gas producers did not operate with careless disregard for the environment, instituting practices to protect surface water and groundwater. But neither the state nor industry was fully prepared for the new management challenges posed by the rapid diffusion of fracking.

As awareness of the impacts grew, regulators strengthened policies intended to safeguard freshwater and human health. To address rising salinity, the state banned shipments of Marcellus wastewaters to municipal treatment plants unless the waste was pretreated to more restrictive standards. Regulations for storing and containing wastewater, drilling fluids, and fracking solutions were updated to lower the likelihood of uncontrolled releases at fracking sites. The state also issued new rules for well construction intended to reduce incidences of methane leakage.

These regulatory improvements have not put Pennsylvania in the clear. In the six years since regulations were strengthened, the state's Department of Environmental Protection has documented more than 100 new cases of water supply contamination caused by oil and gas operations. This figure may underestimate the real extent of the problem, because settlements reached between the industry and homeowners need not be disclosed. To compound these present dangers, new threats to freshwater quality and supply may emerge as infrastructure ages and as industry practices evolve to minimize costs and maximize fossil fuel recovery.

Pennsylvania's experience suggests that the challenge of safeguarding freshwater resources from fracking will persist as long as fossil fuels continue to be pulled from the ground. Meeting this challenge in a sustained way requires management and policy approaches that better leverage data and science in decision-making.

While most of the risks posed to freshwater resources by fracking-related activities have been identified, they have defied quantification. The efficacy of policies that aim to prevent contamination have not been thoroughly tested. Management in the midst of this uncertainty should be adaptive—a scientific way of learning while doing. Adaptive management begins by identifying actions

> **More science is essential, but alone it is not enough to guarantee clean drinking water in areas with fracking or determine how and where unconventional oil and gas development should proceed.**

or interventions that might solve a defined problem, followed by monitoring the outcomes of those interventions, and then making adjustments to resolve any inadequacies. For adaptive management to work, industry must engage with managers and scientists from the environmental community. The track record for this type of collaboration is not especially strong, but there are encouraging signs and reasons for hope.

The nature of interactions between the fossil fuel industry and environmental scientists typically ranges from disregardful to hostile. Environmental scientists have focused on the effects of unconventional oil and gas development on water and air quality, with studies that show adverse effects gaining widespread attention and industry scorn. The industry has tried to discredit these studies, inviting criticism that they are more invested in covering up problems than addressing them.

This adversarial relationship hurts industry and environmental scientists alike. Environmental scientists are excluded from access to monitoring sites, operational information, and other industry data that would strengthen their research. Industry also misses out, scuttling the opportunity to partner with environmental scientists on problem-solving and giving up the chance for constructive dialogue. The tendency for each group to remain in its own silo has engendered mistrust, leading to disagreement that can paralyze progress toward better environmental management.

Though rare, cooperative arrangements with industry enabling scientific assessment of fracking impacts have been forged. For example, a consortium of companies has engaged with universities coordinated largely by the Environmental Defense Fund to assess atmospheric methane emissions from oil and gas operations. I lead a team of researchers at Yale University that has leveraged a collaboration with industry to explore the potential groundwater impacts of shale gas development in Pennsylvania. A formal agreement with Southwestern Energy gave Yale researchers the schedules and locations of gas well projects for the company's Marcellus acreage. With this information, our team installed groundwater monitoring wells immediately adjacent to gas wells and measured changes in water quality over two years as several gas wells were drilled, fracked, and brought into production.

The Yale-Southwestern Energy study is a proof of concept, demonstrating that collaborative, scientific analysis of freshwater impacts of fracking-related activities is feasible. It serves as a template that must be replicated with production companies that operate in different regions and that employ a variety of practices and methodologies. Coordination of this science is critical so that outcomes from different studies can be compared, adaptive management can proceed, and knowledge can be exchanged with policymakers. An advisory board, chaired by a delegate from the host state's department of environmental protection and composed of industry members, as well as qualified scientists, could manage the process.

Someone must pay for this science, of course. The Yale-Southwestern Energy study cost just over $500,000—which may seem expensive but is less than one-fourth of the cost incurred to put one Marcellus well into production. Companies may elect to pay for these studies, recognizing that the investment helps build trust within local communities and contributes to science-based regulation that may be less burdensome to them. State taxes on oil and gas extraction could also pay for the science. Consider that just 1 percent of Pennsylvania's 2018 natural gas impact fee would pay for the first year of eight studies like the one led by Yale. In such cases, funding agreements must be structured to maintain the integrity of the scientific process. Our own experience indicates that it is possible to establish agreement on terms that ensure scientific analyses can proceed without industry interference and that place no restrictions on the dissemination of findings.

More science is essential, but alone it is not enough to guarantee clean drinking water in areas with fracking or determine how and where unconventional oil and gas development should proceed. Policymaking institutions must listen and be responsive to new science. Policymakers must also make resources available to ensure that policies are adequately enforced. And we must make a faithful accounting of fracking costs and benefits that reflects our best knowledge.

Although science is only part of the solution, its proper role in the management of unconventional oil and gas development is to lead the way by providing decision-makers with credible information on environmental impacts and innovative approaches for addressing them. When environmental policy builds on careful science, rigorously analyzed data, and solid facts—pursued without fear of upsetting interested parties or overturning prevailing wisdom—innovative solutions often emerge.

Print Citations

CMS: Saiers, J. "Why Scientists Should Shape Environmental Policy." In *The Reference Shelf: National Debate 2021-2022: Water Resources,* edited by Micah L. Issitt, 46-50. Amenia, NY: Grey House Publishing, 2021.

MLA: Saiers, J. "Why Scientists Should Shape Environmental Policy." *The Reference Shelf: National Debate 2021-2022: Water Resources,* edited by Micah L. Issitt, Grey House Publishing, 2021, pp. 46-50.

APA: Saiers, J. (2021). Why scientists should shape environmental policy. In Micah L. Issitt (Ed.), *The reference shelf: National debate 2021-2022: Water resources* (pp. 46-50). Amenia, NY: Grey House Publishing.

2
Waste and the Water Problem

Photo by Alan Cressier, USGS.

Many areas in the United States still use combined sewer systems that collect rainwater runoff, domestic sewage, and industrial wastewater in the same pipe, leading to problems like this if sewers cannot handle runoff volume.

Sewage and Wastewater Treatment

Water has many uses in human culture. Humans must consume water to survive, and it is essential for every human to have access to clean, fresh water. Clean water is needed for food preparation, and families or individuals who lack access to clean water therefore experience an increased risk of food-borne illness, malnutrition, and hunger. Clean water is also essential is for sanitation. Water is used to collect and remove waste and to clean bodies and homes. Without access to water, individuals suffer from higher rates of skin disorders and infections, and are at much higher risk for food-borne illness.

Collecting and removing human waste is one of the most essential processes for any society, and the effective removal of sewage prevents many common diseases that plague societies without adequate sanitation infrastructure. In addition, when a society fails to effectively manage its waste, essential supplies of water and other resources can become contaminated, leading to outbreaks of disease and other public health emergencies. America, like many nations around the world, is in the midst of what some have called a "sewage crisis," with many communities struggling to effectively manage, dispose of, or isolate sewage from essential supplies of water for sanitation and consumption.

What's Wrong with Sewage?

In the ancient world, humanity had no idea that human waste was dangerous. People eliminated waste directly into lakes or rivers or into simple channels that ultimately carried that waste into some form of reservoir. The situation became worse with the creation of the first "street drains," inlets that allowed residents to deposit waste water into some form of central drainage system. Historians now believe that these types of public drains were first invented in the Mesopotamian Empire of Iraq around 4000–2500 BCE. There is evidence to suggest that societies in ancient Greece and in the Indus Valley created the first organized sewer and drain systems, in which a network of sewers were constructed throughout a city, around 3000 BCE. In the ancient Indus Valley civilizations and later in the Roman Empire, the basic principles of hydroengineering were first established, with humans learning how to create systems to supply homes and villages with water and to carry away dirty water.

The societies of Europe grew out of Roman-Grecian influence and so incorporated subterranean sewer systems into cities and towns as the modern European cultures were established. Draining and sewage systems were likewise imported into the new world with the establishment of the first colonies. Though the principles of sewage management were already well known, only larger cities were typically constructed with a preplanned sewage network. From the Medieval Era through the Colonial Era in the United States, most people chose to live close to a source of water, whether a river, spring, or lake. Communities were also often supplied by wells that utilized water from a nearby stream or lake. This same system was used for waste disposal, so lakes, rivers, and springs became more polluted as populations grew and adopted agricultural or industrial practices. Many rivers and streams were deeply polluted by waste from the meat industry, as the offal, blood, and other tissues of butchered animals were deposited in the same bodies of water providing drinking and sanitary water for communities.[1]

Dutch inventor Antoni van Leeuwenhoek was the first person to observe microbes in a sample of water after he created a series of lenses that increased magnification.[2] The tiny microbes that he first observed in the late 1600s were a revelation to the scientific community, but no one at the time understood the significance of this discovery and what it meant for the management of water resources. At the time, few children survived to adulthood and deadly disease outbreaks occurred seasonally, every year, around the world. In the United States, more than half of all children born died before the age of five. High mortality rate in children and adults was caused by diseases transmitted through water, through contact, and through food, but no one at the time was aware of how this worked. Scientists like Louis Pasteur and Robert Koch were the pioneers who discovered the connection between microbes and illness. Beginning in the latter half of the 1800s, scientists discovered that diseased people and other organisms were found to be carrying strange microorganisms in their blood that weren't present in healthy people or other animals. This was the discovery that led to what is known as "germ theory," the idea that disease is caused by infection by microorganisms, later called bacteria. Later still, scientists would discover that nonliving microbes known as "viruses" could also spread disease through contact or through water supplies.[3]

The realization that microbes caused illness was revolutionary. Over the years that followed, scientists discovered links between many common illnesses and bacteria present either within human bodies or in other parts of the environment. In terms of water resources, the discovery of germ theory opened the door to an understanding of water purification and sanitation. Studies quickly found that the water in wells and rivers contained large colonies of microbes. Eventually, it was discovered that human waste carried microbes from one person to another, and that many diseases spread because of waste within municipal water systems. This was a difficult problem to solve, in part because waste water was intermixed in systems that people used to obtain their drinking and household water. In addition, systems for delivering water to houses or communities had not been constructed so as to prevent contamination from wastewater or pollutants. As the 1800s gave way to the modern era, scientists and urban planners struggled to address these problems and to prevent the spread of disease through municipal waste systems.

Infrastructural Shortcomings

In the United States, at the time people were first learning that dirty water caused disease, many residents were living in communities in which sources of drinking water and water for sanitation were already polluted and in which primitive sewage systems deposited waste directly into the local water reservoirs. It was also in the 1800s that the first "running water" systems were developed, delivering water directly into homes. When this occurred, usage of water skyrocketed, and this dramatically increased demand on existing sewer systems. Municipalities had to create new sewer systems or to change their existing (typically quite simple and primitive) sewer systems to accommodate new flow.

In most American cities and towns, combined sewer overflow, or CSO, systems were created. In these systems, all water sources running into and out of a city are combined. The resulting outflow of water thus contains rainwater runoff combined with sewage from homes and buildings.[4] A few American cities, mostly in California, took a different approach, creating separate lines for rainwater and sewage. These newer cities had the benefit of the discovery of the dangers of sewage, and so were able to invest in infrastructure that preserved rainwater runoff and allowed this water to return to rivers, lakes, or other reservoirs. Most cities, by contrast, used a combined system out of a desire to save on the heavy cost of upgrading existing infrastructure to create a divided system. Allowing rainwater runoff to move through the same system also helped to wash sewage and other waste through the sewers. As scientists learned more about sanitation and public safety, it became clear that CSOs are a major source of pollution and pose a serious health risk.

By the mid-1900s, any city that already had a combined system in place faced major obstacles in terms of upgrading the network. One city—Cambridge, Massachusetts—began a program to create a new separated system in the 1930s and, as of 2021, the project has never been finished. The scope and cost of such a project makes it extremely difficult for cities or towns to gain enough support or to marshal the necessary resources. Writing in *The Atlantic*, Alexis Madrigal argues that the political system in America makes such infrastructure upgrades unlikely because elected officials typically focus on short-term projects that can be completed (or at least significantly developed) during a single election cycle. The need for politicians to advertise accomplishments rather than contributing to longer-term goals for their municipality makes it less likely for municipalities to begin projects that will likely take decades to complete.[5]

To keep communities safe from disease and microbial illness, it is necessary to filter out harmful waste from sewage water and to prevent sewage from leaching into groundwater or natural water ways. There are different ways to do this. One is to use "septic tanks," a system used by around 20 percent of Americans. In this system, waste from a household filters into a tank, where the waste separates into solid and liquid layers. The liquid is pumped into the soil, where bacteria and microbes breakdown the remaining waste, returning the remaining water to groundwater systems. Individuals must service and maintain their own septic tanks and this must be done regularly to prevent pollution from entering the drinking water supplies. An alternative to septic tanks is a waste treatment facility where liquid and solid waste is processed in a way to purify the remaining water and to remove harmful waste and bacteria.

Both septic tanks and municipal waste systems can be problematic. When septic tanks are not well managed, waste can leach directly into streams, lakes, rivers, or other water reservoirs. Likewise, municipal water treatment facilities, which use microbes and chemicals to purify and clean the water, are not always managed effectively. Over the decades, the science of water treatment has changed and some of the older ways of processing wastewater are now thought to be harmful to public health. There are other potential problems as well, such as power outages, overflows due to tropical storms and flooding, etc. Over the decades, sewage treatment facilities in many towns and cities have aged and developed problems. Such facilities are not equipped to handle increasing pressure from weather-related fluctuations or increasing population size, which places additional pressure on waste treatment facilities to manage increasingly large amounts of water and waste.

When wastewater from septic tanks and municipal waste systems flows into waterways, a number of problems can occur. First, waste contains harmful bacteria that directly transmit disease. Second, waste water and industrial runoff can lead to spikes in nutrient levels that can cause "HABs" or "harmful algal blooms," which occur when nutrient polluted water sprout large populations of certain kinds of algae (microbial plants). Algal blooms can kill off vast number of fish, destroy natural communities in lakes and oceanic systems, and pollute entire municipal drinking water supplies, leading to water shortages and illness.[6] Cities in which CSOs are still in place are at much higher risk from dangerous sewage overflows as rainwater surges can wash sewage and industrial waste directly out of the system, leading to massive pollution problems. According to the U.S. Environmental Protection Agency (EPA), CSOs are one of the leading sources of dangerous water pollution in America.

Even communities with updated sewage treatment facilities or with separated systems to protect rainwater runoff and to prevent sewage overflows are not safe from sewage pollution. Many of the cities that still have combined systems are located along waterways that deliver water to many other states. According to *Atlantic* writer Mary Anna Evans, "Waste spilled in the Ohio River affects everyone down the Ohio and the Mississippi, and it contributes to the ongoing woes in the Gulf of Mexico. Even if you don't live in the Northeast, along the Ohio, in the Great Lakes region, along the Mississippi River, or on the Gulf Coast, bear in mind that 40 percent of the commercial seafood caught in the United States comes from the Gulf of Mexico. In other words, when Cincinnati's sewer system overflows into the Ohio, it intrudes into the food chain of a lot of people."[7]

The Elements of a Crisis

Some environmental scientists and specialists in water conservation have described America's struggles with an ageing and problematic waste disposal system as a serious and significant public health crisis. While the obvious solution is to replace infrastructure and to create better and safer systems for managing municipal waste, the cost and difficulty in such an effort prevents many cities and municipalities from initiating these kinds of changes. As with many other aspects of America's struggles with water resources, rural communities and underserved communities are more likely to experience the direct results of sewage system malfunctions or mismanagement and are less likely to be able to access the resources needed to prevent these kinds of problems from developing or to be able to engage in meaningful upgrades. What's more, there is a general lack of public awareness and concern about this problem. Few Americans, especially in areas with sewage treatment systems, are concerned about sewage management until and unless some catastrophe occurs that dramatically impacts the city's capability to manage their sewage system. Large-scale crises may generate intense, but transient, public interest in America's water resource management problems, but this interest typically subsides before politicians are pressured into initiating the kind of reform and improvements necessary to prevent sewage overflows and other dangerous pollution issues connected to the municipal collection and processing of waste.

One of the problems with making progress on America's waste problem is that different political factions prefer different approaches. While some political groups favor public solutions and government investment, other political groups want to turn over responsibility to private companies, allowing free market forces to shape municipal waste management practices. Both avenues to reform have advantages and disadvantages and so political proposals often meet with considerable resistance. In the end, waste management is a public safety and public health issue and the problems facing America's sewage systems are likely to intensify in coming years. America's declining sewage infrastructure has therefore becoming a looming crisis for many communities and, though there has been intense debate about how best to solve this problem, states and municipalities that fail to find solutions risk becoming the next to suffer a major humanitarian tragedy as a result.

Works Used

"Combined Sewer Overflows (CSOs)." *EPA*. National Pollutant Discharge Elimination System. Aug 13, 2020. https://www.epa.gov/npdes/combined-sewer-overflows-csos.

De Feo, Giovanni, et al. "The Historical Development of Sewers Worldwide." *Sustainability*. Vol 6. 2014. https://www.researchgate.net/publication/263278132_The_Historical_Development_of_Sewers_Worldwide.

Evans, Mary Anna. "Flushing the Toilet Has Never Been Riskier." *The Atlantic*. Sep 17, 2015. https://www.theatlantic.com/technology/archive/2015/09/americas-sewage-crisis-public-health/405541/.

Fong, Joss, and Dion Lee. "How Antony van Leeuwenhoek Discovered Bacteria in the 1670s." *Vox*. Oct 24, 2016. https://www.vox.com/2016/8/9/12405306/antoni-van-leeuwenhoek.

Gaynes, Robert P. *Germ Theory*. Washington, D.C.: ASM Press, 2011.

Madrigal, Alexis C. "A Short Masterpiece on the History of Sewers." *The Atlantic*. Oct 5, 2010. https://www.theatlantic.com/technology/archive/2010/10/a-short-masterpiece-on-the-history-of-sewers/64076/.

"What Is a Harmful Algal Bloom?" *NOAA*. Apr 27, 2016. https://www.noaa.gov/what-is-harmful-algal-bloom.

Notes

1. De Feo, et al. "The Historical Development of Sewers Worldwide."
2. Fong and Lee, "How Antoni van Leeuwenhoek Discovered Bacteria in the 1670s."
3. Gaynes, *Germ Theory*.
4. "Combined Sewer Overflows (CSOs)," *EPA*.
5. Madrigal, "A Short Masterpiece on the History of Sewers."
6. "What Is a Harmful Algal Bloom?" *NOAA*.
7. Evans, "Flushing the Toilet Has Never Been Riskier."

Toxic Waters

By Daniel C. Vock
Governing, March 2019

For more than 15 years, Catherine Flowers has been spearheading a lonely and frustrating campaign in Alabama's Black Belt to install and improve a simple but crucial piece of infrastructure for the far-flung homes in the area: septic tanks.

Her efforts began in 2002 shortly after officials in the Black Belt's Lowndes County threatened to jail two dozen residents for inadequate sewage treatment, which is a misdemeanor under Alabama law. Somewhere between 40 and 90 percent of the homes in the county had a failing septic system, or none at all. The residents, who were predominantly black and poor, could not afford the thousands of dollars needed to install new underground sewage tanks. Even if they could afford them, there was no guarantee that the tanks would work in the area's dark clay soil. That soil sits on top of layers of chalk and silt that trap water and prevent it from seeping further into the ground, a huge problem for septic tanks that work by dispersing contaminated water through the ground for filtration.

Even brand-new septic systems often fail in the fields of Alabama if they aren't properly designed for the environment there. Systems specially built for the Black Belt's geology can cost more than $6,000, twice as much as a standard septic system. The most elaborate ones go for as much as $30,000, more than the value of some of the homes they are meant to serve. With all the difficulties, many residents don't bother to install septic systems; they simply run a pipe out of their homes to a ditch nearby.

The threat of arrest is only one of the many dangers that residents with failing or no septic systems can face. Untreated sewage pools in people's yards give off a foul stench. Black water backs up into their sinks, drains and bathtubs. The exposure can have dire consequences for residents' health.

Flowers knows that threat firsthand: A few years ago, she was bitten by a mosquito flying over an uncovered pool of sewage in one resident's yard. The next day, she broke out in a rash all over her body that didn't go away for months. The incident led Flowers to ask questions about the health effects Lowndes County residents were facing. She invited researchers from Baylor College of Medicine to look for a possible resurgence of tropical diseases in the area. They found evidence of hookworm, a disease largely eradicated in most developed countries, in more than a third of the residents they sampled.

That finding brought the attention that Flowers had long been trying to attract. Reporters from *The Guardian*, PBS NewsHour, VICE, Al Jazeera, Fox News and the *New York Times* all came to investigate. So did a United Nations official studying extreme poverty in the United States. Far-off politicians, including New Jersey Sen. Cory Booker and newly elected U.S. Rep. Alexandria Ocasio-Cortez of New York, rallied to the cause.

But there was another group of people who started getting in touch with Flowers. To them, the problems associated with septic systems weren't exotic stories in faraway locales; they were all-too-familiar situations right at home. Flowers started hearing from activists and community leaders from California, Kentucky, Texas and Virginia. Leaky septic tanks cause algae blooms that close beaches on New York's Long Island. They threaten dolphins and other aquatic wildlife in Florida. One of the striking things, Flowers says, is how many of the people affected by wastewater problems are poor or belong to historically marginalized groups. Widespread poverty and lack of political capital only make the task of addressing sanitation issues tougher. "I think the problem is bigger than we realize," Flowers says. "It's not just a one-off thing. Rural communities have ignored this issue for a long time. That's important because, even if we solve the problem with Lowndes County, that doesn't solve the problem for the rest of the country."

Indeed, problems associated with septic systems seem to be getting worse, and not just in rural areas. The number of systems is increasing, fed by population growth and urban sprawl. One out of 5 Americans is dependent on them. Developers regularly install septic tanks in suburban communities to avoid the cost of sewer connections. Meanwhile, septic systems installed decades ago are under stress as population swells in previously rural areas. Climate change can cause new problems, as fierce storms flood drain fields, groundwater levels rise in coastal areas and higher temperatures allow tropical diseases to flourish in exposed pools of sewage.

Simply put, septic systems are getting harder to ignore. Officials at both the state and local levels must increasingly wrestle with how to safeguard individuals' health and protect the environment, without saddling poor residents with the hefty costs of repairing or replacing septic systems.

When Joan Rose set out to study the watersheds in her home state of Michigan a few years ago, her goal wasn't necessarily to focus on septic systems. Rose, a Michigan State University professor and one of the world's leading hydrologists, considers herself a "water detective." By studying the microbiology of water, she can tell you a lot about pollution and whether bacteria in the water came from cattle, pigs or humans.

While studying 64 watersheds on Michigan's Lower Peninsula, Rose found a lot of human-based pollution. She tried to pinpoint where it was originating. "But the only relationship we could find," she says, "was with the increasing number of septic tanks."

Rose discovered that even "working" septic tanks weren't filtering out all the pollution they were designed to keep out of lakes, streams and rivers. "We used to think that once [waste] goes into a soil, we don't have a risk," she says. "We realize now that there are many, many contaminants that move through the soil: viruses, nutrients and even bacteria."

Unlike sewers, which whisk dirty water away through pipes to a water treatment center, septic tanks filter the water onsite. They sort the waste into three layers: scum, sludge and wastewater. Bacteria eventually break down the scum at the top of the tank, while sludge falls to the bottom. (Septic tanks have to be pumped out periodically to work properly.) The wastewater, or effluent, sits in between the scum and the sludge. It flows into underground pipes near the tank and is released into the ground in an area called the drain field. Septic systems rely on the natural filtration of the soil to eliminate the worst contaminants in the water. But most are designed to filter out only disease-causing bacteria and viruses. They aren't capable of removing nitrogen or phosphates, which can wreak havoc on aquatic environments by causing algae blooms, fish kills and ocean dead zones, where most marine life cannot survive.

Rose was telling Michigan residents that their septic systems weren't very good at screening out bacteria. Not surprisingly, she started getting questions about how many of Michigan's 1.4 million septic tanks were failing and where. But her study didn't reveal that kind of detail. In general, she believes, between 10 and 20 percent of septic tanks are failing without the owner's knowledge.

Michigan is the only state in the country that does not have a statewide law governing septic tanks, so the task of keeping track of them falls to the counties. That means the rules about how often or even if septic systems have to be inspected vary by county. It also means that it's hard to track all the septic systems that may im-

Septic systems installed decades ago are under stress as population swells in previously rural areas.

pact a river that flows through several counties. Advocates in Michigan have been pushing state lawmakers for at least 15 years to set up a statewide system. "A huge motivator behind legislation," says Deena Bosworth, the director of governmental affairs for the Michigan Association of Counties, "is that we don't know the extent of the problem."

The most recent effort fell apart because the legislation would have affected the dozen or so counties that already require septic system inspections when properties are being sold. It would have prevented them from requiring inspections beyond statewide minimums, a nonstarter for counties and environmental groups. "Statewide standards aren't out of line," Bosworth says. "But if local governments want to be more restrictive, they should be able to."

Unlike in Michigan, political inaction has brought septic system contamination to crisis levels in Long Island. Suffolk County, on the eastern side of the island across the sound from Connecticut, has 1.5 million people and about 365,000 underground sewage tanks. Nearly all the tanks are leaking harmful pollutants—especially nitrogen—that are threatening the area's environment as well as its economy. Algae blooms have closed beaches. Nitrogen pollution has all but killed off the once-famous clamming industry. And pollution may have made the effects of Hurricane Sandy more extreme by eliminating coastal vegetation and wetlands that could have provided a natural barrier to the storm.

The prevalence of septic systems in the area has stymied economic growth, because they can't handle big developments. They need space for their drain fields, which means they are usually used for small buildings next to empty land, hampering the area's ability to build dense projects. Steve Bellone, the county executive since 2012, has been trying to chip away at the long-standing problem, both by building sewers where feasible and by upgrading existing septic tanks to prevent them from leeching so many harmful chemicals into the soil.

In January, voters in two parts of the county approved $360 million in sewer projects, which Bellone says will serve 6,400 parcels in some of the most ecologically sensitive areas. The key to the new construction was state and federal disaster recovery money for rebuilding after Sandy. County officials selected the projects so that they would help mitigate the impact of future disasters by restoring natural storm barriers. "The marshlands, wetlands and seagrass have been devastated by the decline in water quality and pollution over the last four decades," Bellone says. "This is part of the effort to remediate the pollution in the waterways by reducing nitrogen inputs."

Local property owners also assumed some of the costs of building the sewer improvements. In most cases, though, installing sewer systems is prohibitively expensive for either property owners or the county. So officials are encouraging residents to switch to more advanced septic systems, which can help decrease the amount of nitrogen that gets into the ground and, eventually, into local rivers and Long Island Sound. Qualifying residents are being offered $11,000 grants to install the upgraded systems, plus low-interest loans to cover the rest of the cost. About 100 residents have already installed the new systems.

Bellone says county residents have started recognizing the need for such measures. "The problem with septic systems," he says, "is that they're underground. The saying 'out of sight, out of mind' is apt here. When people buy their houses they know how old the boiler is, how old the roof is. They don't know how old their septic system is or how it's working. But we're really starting to see the results of septic systems: closed beaches, red tide, brown tide, fish kills."

In Alabama, Flowers' advocacy has brought a lot of attention to the situation in Lowndes County. The Alabama Department of Public Health is applying for federal grants to install septic systems for 100 residents in unincorporated areas on a first-come, first-served basis. Residents would pay a one-time fee of $500 or $1,000, depending on the type of septic system installed, plus a monthly fee of $20.

Meanwhile, Flowers and others have been looking for new technology that could replace septic systems with an easier, cheaper way to deal with the persistent problem. Flowers has been talking with Kartik Chandran, an environmental engineering professor at Columbia University whose work focuses on how to use human waste and other wastewater to generate energy and produce agricultural fertilizers.

Flowers is also turning up the heat on the state and federal governments. She joined with Earthjustice, an environmental law firm, to file a civil rights complaint against both the Lowndes County Health Department and the Alabama Department of Public Health. The complaint alleges that the government discriminated against the county's black community when it failed to "abate known insanitary conditions, dismissed a credible outbreak of hookworm and failed to maintain sufficient data regarding the lack of wastewater services, despite knowledge of prior discriminatory acts regarding the high rate of insufficient onsite wastewater systems in the county." The complaint is now before the U.S. Department of Health and Human Services, which will determine whether to pursue an investigation of its own.

Anna Sewell, a water project attorney for Earthjustice, says state and county agencies could start to address the group's concerns by informing residents about the evidence of hookworm infection and how to treat it; by helping families apply for state and federal loans to replace their septic systems; and by conducting a comprehensive survey to determine the extent of the sewage problem in Lowndes County. "The bottom line," she says, "is that agencies have to clean up raw sewage on the ground."

Flowers is keeping her eye on the national picture, even as she hopes to deal with the local crisis. If Lowndes County can take care of the problem, she says, people in other communities might be able to learn from them. "It's not just a regional issue. These crises are happening across the U.S.," she says, "but nobody has investigated it."

Print Citations

CMS: Vock, Daniel C. "Toxic Waters." In *The Reference Shelf: National Debate 2021-2022: Water Resources,* edited by Micah L. Issitt, 59-63. Amenia, NY: Grey House Publishing, 2021.

MLA: Vock, Daniel C. "Toxic Waters." *The Reference Shelf: National Debate 2021-2022: Water Resources,* edited by Micah L. Issitt, Grey House Publishing, 2021, pp. 59-63.

APA: Vock, D. C. (2021). Toxic waters. In Micah L. Issitt (Ed.), *The reference shelf: National debate 2021-2022: Water resources* (pp. 59-63). Amenia, NY: Grey House Publishing.

Filthy Water: A Basic Sanitation Problem Persists in Rural America

By Katherine Bagley
Yale Environment, December 10, 2020

Lowndes County, Alabama lies at the heart of the civil rights movement. Situated between Selma and Montgomery, the rural county is home to most of the route that Martin Luther King Jr. and thousands of activists followed on their historic five-day march in 1965. Beyond its civil rights legacy, however, the county—one of the poorest in the United States—is now becoming known for something far less noble: Up to 90 percent of households have failing or inadequate wastewater systems, causing raw sewage to back up into homes, pool on lawns, and spill into nearby streams and rivers.

Environmental justice activist Catherine Coleman Flowers has spent 20 years bringing attention to what she calls "America's dirty secret." Residents in poor, rural U.S. communities like Lowndes County rely on septic systems to dispose of household wastewater. But as Flowers, founder and director of the Center for Rural Enterprise and Environmental Justice, explains in an interview with *Yale Environment 360*, these systems are expensive to install and maintain—the cost of a new septic system can exceed $20,000, more than many low-income households earn in a year. Federal, state, and local governments don't invest in rural wastewater infrastructure, leaving homeowners on their own to deal with the problem and vulnerable to low-cost contractors and faulty equipment. The result is a public health crisis similar to that found in many developing countries. And climate change—with its more intense rainstorms, sea level rise, and heat—is only exacerbating the problem.

"It's not just Lowndes County," says Flowers, the recipient of a 2020 MacArthur "genius grant" and author of the new book *Waste: One Woman's Fight Against America's Dirty Secret*. "This is a problem throughout rural America... Poor communities across the U.S. are pretty much left to their own devices [when it comes to sanitation]."

Yale Environment 360: You've spent 20 years working on what you call "America's dirty secret"—the lack of basic sanitation in many poor, rural communities, and the public health consequences. When did you first become aware of this problem?

Catherine Coleman Flowers: I first became aware of the problem of sanitation, or the lack of it, in 2002. When I was growing up in Lowndes County, we would have problems with our septic system backing into the home. But we all thought it was essentially a plumbing problem, because no one had done the kind of deep dive that was needed in the community to figure out how many people were dealing with the same problem and what were the factors that contributed to it.

In 2002, [urban policy expert] Bob Woodson came to visit Lowndes County to learn about the challenges of economic development in the region. We were asked by one of the county commissioners to take a detour and go and see a family she wanted me to meet. As we turned off the paved main road onto a dirt road where this family lived, you could see the raw sewage running down the road. The family's mobile home sat on an incline, and we were coming from downhill, and we could see it.

The first person we met was the minister of the local church next to the family compound. He was crying. They had stopped them from having services at his church because he didn't have a functioning septic system. And later we met the family, and they had been arrested, the husband and wife, and were scheduled to go back to court because of this failing septic system. We thought that that was an extreme way of trying to address this, instead of trying to find some solution.

e360: In your book, you state that as many as 90 percent of Lowndes households have failing or inadequate wastewater systems. How did it get to this point?

Flowers: It's not just Lowndes County. I think we have to be clear about that. This is a problem throughout rural America, and since the book has been published, I'm finding other places in suburban areas and in some cities where they use septic systems that are having problems very, very similar to the type of failures we're seeing in Lowndes County. Poor communities across the U.S. are pretty much left to their own devices [when it comes to sanitation] or they don't have the support of the state. If they do get these long grants to build or maintain systems, they're not getting the same quality of service or equipment as you would find in more affluent areas. So they tend to get something that may or may not work, may or may not last, and that is what we've seen.

> Poor communities across the U.S. are pretty much left to their own devices (when it comes to sanitation) or they don't have the support of the state.

Lowndes County, Alabama is 715 square miles. That's a large area. It's bordered by six counties. It is not densely populated. There are about six to seven towns in Lowndes County that are incorporated. Most of it is unincorporated. It's a poor county. Because it's a poor county, it doesn't have the tax base to pay the cost to connect or control municipal sanitation systems. Then the other issue is that because people are not that close together, people in rural communities are held responsible for putting in their own wastewater treatment in a lot of cases. So if they can't afford it, then they can't get it.

e360: As you mentioned earlier, not having a functioning septic system, at least in Alabama, is a criminal misdemeanor, and that residents can be fined $500 for a citation or evicted or arrested. This seems like a system that would perpetuate the already striking inequality of this issue.

Flowers: I agree. We have to get away from these punitive measures so we can find some real solutions. Being punitive, as we've seen, has not provided any solutions, because then it puts all the responsibility on a homeowner who is forced to buy something that first of all, they can't afford, or second, that simply is not working. And it doesn't make sense. It's a vicious circle.

e360: In 2017, your work helped to expose the presence of hookworm in residents of Lowndes County—a parasite found in countries without clean water and adequate sanitation, but that scientists had long believed to be eliminated from the U.S. How shocking was that finding to you?

Flowers: Yes, I was shocked, but even more so, I felt it was almost akin to what people would call a smoking gun for why this issue is so important. Until that time, people were still pushing the narrative of blaming the residents as opposed to understanding that this is an issue that we all need to grapple with. There are places around the country that are dealing with the tough impacts of failing sanitation systems or the lack of sanitation. It's not just in the South, not just in Lowndes County.

The [hookworm] finding helped to raise the level of concern and awareness. For example, one of the first people to reach out to me outside of Alabama was Senator Cory Booker, who actually gave me a call and wanted to come and visit and see for himself. And a lot of people have followed since then. It was also shocking to the rest of the world; it was a mirror that was held up to why in the richest country in the world do we allow this level of inequality to exist? And why haven't we tried to find solutions before now?

But I think it's imperative that we do, because ultimately, now that we know that you can actually test wastewater to see the existence of Covid-19, I'm wondering if anyone has tested raw sewage to see whether Covid exists and whether or not there's a level of exposure that exists in untreated sewage that would not normally exist, especially in rural communities. Lowndes County, Alabama, as it relates to Covid per capita, had the highest death rate and highest infection rate in the state. If you look at Navajo Nation, a place where they have no water infrastructure in some places, which means they have no sanitation infrastructure either, they had high death rates, too, and high infection rates. So we really have to examine how the lack of sanitation and water justice is creating more health barriers and creating more vulnerabilities.

e360: How has climate change, specifically rising seas and more intense storms, exacerbated and will continue to exacerbate this issue?

Flowers: Wastewater disposal technology simply was not designed to take climate change into account. In places like Miami-Dade County, for example, they're already having problems with failing septic systems because of sea level rise. We're going to find that in coastal regions around the country. And then of course, septic systems and the way they function are tied to what's coming from the sky—and we're going to have more deluges of rain. That's part and parcel of climate change. Septic systems can only hold so much water. Once they get full, it pushes that sewage back into the house or something has to break somewhere. It's either going to be on the house, inside the house, or out on top of the ground. There's been evidence of septic systems actually contaminating the drinking water of people that have wells. And the water tables are rising. Lowndes County had a high water table in the first place. Now, with climate change, it's getting even higher, and the type of wastewater disposal systems that are being prescribed by the state *still* do not take into account climate change.

And then of course, the extreme heat. You have raw sewage on the ground in heat, and that's a hotbed of toxic contaminants that could create additional problems in terms of disease.

Right now rural communities are the canary in the coal mine, because they're hidden away from view. That's why I think it's so hard for folks to make policy and try to give suggestions on what they think the solution is—they don't have any clue on what a rural community really is. They have not been there and they're trying to judge it through the lens of an urban area.

e360: What is the solution here? What kinds of partnerships or technology are needed to tackle inadequate wastewater infrastructure in rural communities?

Flowers: Number one is we have to implement the principles of environmental justice—listen to people in the community. I wouldn't be talking to you now if it wasn't for the fact we went from house to house and we talked to over 2,000 residents in Lowndes County to find out what the problems were. We need to teach people in the engineering community, especially in colleges and universities and others who want to partner and be collaborators in finding solutions, how to engage with the community. What does that mean? It doesn't mean going in, doing a survey for a day, and saying, "This is how we fix it," without really doing the deep dive that's necessary. I've been there, I've seen that happen, and people were right back where they were before.

Grants and philanthropic support would be a great start—but really this issue needs to be addressed at the government level. A lot of these local governments can't handle it because they don't have the funds to do it; they don't have the tax base. But we have to make sure that this is addressed, as a public health issue, an environmental justice issue, a social justice issue, an income inequality issue–all of these issues intersect at wastewater. The consequences are too great to ignore.

Print Citations

CMS: Bagley, Katherine. "Filthy Water: A Basic Sanitation Problem Persists in Rural America." In *The Reference Shelf: National Debate 2021-2022: Water Resources,* edited by Micah L. Issitt, 64-68. Amenia, NY: Grey House Publishing, 2021.

MLA: Bagley, Katherine. "Filthy Water: A Basic Sanitation Problem Persists in Rural America." *The Reference Shelf: National Debate 2021-2022: Water Resources,* edited by Micah L. Issitt, Grey House Publishing, 2021, pp. 64-68.

APA: Bagley, K. (2021). Filthy water: A basic sanitation problem persists in rural America. In Micah L. Issitt (Ed.), *The reference shelf: National debate 2021-2022: Water resources* (pp. 64-68). Amenia, NY: Grey House Publishing.

Sewage is Still 'America's Dirty Secret'

By Justine Calma
The Verge, November 13, 2020

Doctors couldn't diagnose the rash spreading across Catherine Flowers' legs and body. But the activist thought it had to do with the day she wore a dress during a visit to a family whose yard featured "a hole in the ground full of raw sewage." "I began to wonder if third-world conditions might be bringing third-world diseases to our region," Flowers writes in her new book, *Waste: One Woman's Fight Against America's Dirty Secret*.

She was right. That rash led to research that found that hookworm, a parasite thought to be pretty much dead in the US, was actually alive and well in the rural Alabama county where she grew up. Without working septic systems, residents were getting sick from raw sewage. Flowers has been on a mission to change things for her community ever since. She is now a recent MacArthur Foundation "genius grant" awardee, and she founded the Center for Rural Enterprise and Environmental Justice (CREEJ).

COVID-19 and Climate Change Are Piling on Top of What's Already a Sh***y Situation

With her latest book, available on November 17th, Flowers is expanding that fight to places across the US which lack the basic infrastructure that many city-dwellers take for granted. Two million Americans lack access to indoor plumbing, a 2019 report found, and that has huge implications for their health. *The Verge* spoke with Flowers about what she's seen and how COVID-19 and climate change are piling on top of what's already a sh***y situation.
(This interview has been edited for length and clarity.)

For someone who isn't familiar with the issues that you've brought light in Lowndes County, Alabama and other rural communities, can you paint a picture of what the problem is?

I've seen three different types of problems. One problem is where people don't have the infrastructure at all. They have a toilet in their home, they flush the toilet and the effluent from the toilet, the wastewater goes out through a PVC pipe into a pit or ditch that they dig or just runs out on top of the ground. Those are people that can't afford that infrastructure, because this is in places like Lowndes County where it's so expensive. One of the families that we're working with recently, we found that it was going to cost $20,000 for a wastewater

> **Two million Americans lack access to indoor plumbing, a 2019 report found, and that has huge implications for their health.**

treatment system because when they went down 25 inches, they struck water.

The second problem that I've seen is when people can afford it, but when they buy it, it doesn't work. Whenever there is a lot of rain or extreme weather conditions, the systems break down. And when it breaks down, it pushes the sewage back into the home.

"Whenever There Is a Lot of Rain or Extreme Weather Conditions, the Systems Break Down."

The third problem that I've seen are big systems and very expensive systems that have been put in place—with wastewater treatment plants and lagoon systems—that fail. And when they fail, again, we have raw sewage either coming into the building or it's out on top of the ground. And in some of those instances, we've seen that people are paying wastewater treatment fees and the systems are not working.

Untreated wastewater can carry the virus that causes COVID-19, although researchers still don't know if a person can get sick from being exposed to it. The CDC says, "At this time, the risk of transmission of the virus that causes COVID-19 through properly designed and maintained sewerage systems is thought to be low." But you've seen a lot of sewage systems that are not properly designed or maintained. Do you have any thoughts about the current situation?

It is a concern to me. Most people are not concerned about it because they don't come in contact with waste, but I'm concerned about those people that do. I can tell you that Lowndes County has the highest per capita COVID-19 infection rate [1 in 13] in the state of Alabama, and also has the highest per capita COVID death rate in the state of Alabama [1 in 335]. I pray that there are no more deaths because I know too many people that have died as a result.

COVID isn't the only global disaster that these communities are facing. Can you tell me a little bit about how climate change impacts the wastewater issues faced by rural areas like Lowndes county?

"Climate Change Has an Impact on Everything."

Climate change has an impact on everything. It has an impact on wastewater technologies, too. Most wastewater technologies are not designed to deal with climate change. The water table is actually getting higher. We're getting more rain. So far this year, we've had at least four storms to come ashore. That's going to continue to be a problem. The clay soil that we have that holds water will continue to hold water. That's not going to change either. The technology needs to change.

This is the time for us to lead globally and find technologies that will better address climate change and wastewater. There are partners that are working with us on trying to find new technological solutions because we realized that it's bigger than Lowndes County. Lowndes County is not the only place in this country that has raw sewage on the ground. Alabama is not the only place in this country that has raw sewage on the ground. So, obviously, it's a bigger problem. A fix is not just to put in a few septic tanks in Lowndes County and think that we solved this.

I wrote the book because I wanted people to understand that it's not just Lowndes County. That's why it's *America's* dirty secret. Lowndes' County is not America's dirty secret. The waste water problem in the US is America's dirty secret.

Despite the fact that a lot of people that live in Lowndes County are descendants of people who may have come to this country as slaves, Lowndes County citizens have always fought for justice, the right to participate in the democratic process, and for economic opportunity going back to the sharecroppers union. This fight, in terms of people stepping out front and sharing their personal struggles with wastewater with the world, it's just a continuation of that history of being on the forefront of positive change that can benefit everyone.

How do you really feel about the moniker, "Erin Brockovich of sewage," that I've seen used to describe your work—even though your work stands on its own?

Yes, it does stand on its own, but if I had to be compared with someone, it's great to be compared with Erin Brockovich. I had seen the movie many years ago, and I've always been a fan of hers. We'll meet virtually for the first time—we're appearing on a panel together at the Texas Book Festival, Saturday.

Print Citations

CMS: Calma, Justine. "Sewage Is Still 'America's Dirty Secret.'" In *The Reference Shelf: National Debate 2021-2022: Water Resources,* edited by Micah L. Issitt, 69-71. Amenia, NY: Grey House Publishing, 2021.

MLA: Calma, Justine. "Sewage Is Still 'America's Dirty Secret.'" *The Reference Shelf: National Debate 2021-2022: Water Resources,* edited by Micah L. Issitt, Grey House Publishing, 2021, pp. 69-71.

APA: Calma, J. (2021). Sewage is still "America's dirty secret." In Micah L. Issitt (Ed.), *The reference shelf: National debate 2021-2022: Water resources* (pp. 69-71). Amenia, NY: Grey House Publishing.

Lethal Algae Blooms—An Ecosystem Out of Balance

By Jeremy Hance

The Guardian, January 4, 2020

On 3 August 2014, residents of Toledo, Ohio, woke to the news that overnight their water supply had become toxic. They were advised not only to avoid drinking the water, but also touching it–no showers, no baths, not even hand-washing.

Boiling the water would only increase its toxicity while drinking it could cause "abnormal liver function, diarrhoea, vomiting, nausea, numbness or dizziness", read a statement from the City of Toledo, warning residents to "seek medical attention if you feel you have been exposed".

Toledo sits on the shores of Lake Erie, one of North America's five great lakes. About half a million residents of the city and surrounding area have relied on Lake Erie for water for hundreds of years.

After the news broke on 3 August bottled water quickly vanished in concentric circles around the city. Eventually, a state of emergency was called and the national guard arrived with drinking water.

Toledo's water crisis lasted for nearly three days. But the water wasn't toxic due to an oil spill or high lead levels, as in Flint, Michigan. Toledo's water was tainted by something altogether different: an algae bloom.

Toledo is not alone. According to scientists, algae blooms are becoming more frequent and more toxic worldwide.

A 14-month long algae bloom in Florida, known as the "red tide", only ended earlier this year, after killing more than 100 manatees, 127 dolphins and 589 sea turtles. Hundreds of tonnes of dead fish also washed ashore. In 2018, there were more than 300 reported incidents of toxic or harmful algae blooms around the world. This year about 130 have been listed on an international database, but that number is expected to increase. Recent reports of a new "red tide" emerging in Florida and more dead wildlife have put the tourist and fishing industries on alert, braced for further devastation. The causes of the blooms vary, and in some cases are never known, but in many parts of the world they are being increasingly linked to climate change and industrialised agriculture.

What Is a Harmful Algae Bloom?

Algae includes everything from micro-algae, like microscopic diatoms, to very large algae, such as seaweed and kelp. Algae are not officially a taxonomic group of creatures (they don't fit into general groups like plants, animals or fungi), but the name is generally used to describe marine or freshwater species that depend on photosynthesis.

An algae bloom occurs when a single member of these species–because of certain conditions–suddenly becomes dominant for a time.

Algae are vital to our survival. It's estimated that at least half of the planet's oxygen comes from these unsung creatures, who produce it through photosynthesis before releasing it into the water. Algae, like land plants, also sequester carbon dioxide; scientists have explored their potential to draw carbon dioxide out of the atmosphere. They have been used as fertiliser, food sources (such as seaweed), and could be a promising source of biofuel in a more sustainable world.

However, some algae blooms can also be harmful–even lethal.

Harmful algae bloom (HAB), as scientists have come to describe the phenomenon, often manifest by forming a kind of scum over a body of water that can be green, blue, brown or even red. But others are completely invisible. The problem has become increasingly widespread and the impact can be deadly to marine life.

Off the eastern coast of the US, a dinoflagellate–a type of marine plankton named *Alexandrium catenella*–has the potential to make shellfish lethal. Its appearance routinely shuts down fisheries, crippling local economies. And it's not just in the US: the same species has shut down mussel farms and recreational collecting of shellfish as far away as New Zealand.

Other blooms wipe out marine life. In 2015, a bloom of various dinoflagellates off the coast of South Africa led to low-oxygen conditions, known as eutrophication, killing 200 tonnes of rock lobster. Freshwater blooms, like those in Lake Erie made up of cyanobacteria or blue-green algae, have not only shut down local water sources but have also been blamed for the death of dogs that had been swimming in them.

It's difficult to make generalisations about harmful algae blooms since specific species have different causes and impacts. Scientists have identified about 100 toxic bloom species in the oceans. Dozens of potentially harmful species of cyanobacteria are known to affect bodies of fresh water.

During most of the past century, harmful algae blooms were rarely headline news, inspiring little scientific study beyond ecological curiosity. That has changed. Algae blooms are notoriously difficult to predict, but a global monitoring group known as HAEDAT is tracking them across the world as they occur. Harmful algae blooms, such as the one that hit Toledo's water supply in 2014, are becoming more common and more toxic–and scientists say humans are to blame.

"There's no question that the HAB problem is a major global issue, and it is growing," said Donald Anderson, director of the US National Office for Harmful Algal Blooms and a lab director at the Woods Hole Oceanographic Institute. "We also have more toxins, more toxic species, more areas and resources affected, and higher economic losses."

Hidden Cost of Ohio's Corn and Soya Bean Boom

The toxic bloom that took over Lake Erie in 2014 was formed by a cyanobacteria known as *Microcystis Aeruginosa,* for which farming is at least partly to blame.

"You have people that still to this day will only use bottled water," says Dr Timothy Davis, an expert in plankton ecology at Bowling Green University, five years after the water crisis and even after Toledo spent $132 million (£101 million) on improving its water treatment plant to handle the blue-green algae.

Lake Erie, the shallowest of North America's Great Lakes, has seen such events in the past. During the 1950s and 60s algae blooms were common, most likely, say researchers, due to poor domestic and industrial wastewater treatment.

"At one point, Lake Erie was considered a dead lake," Davis says. But by the early 1970s, the "dead lake" was resurrected, due to new regulations from the Clean Water Act and the Great Lakes Water Quality Agreement that capped phosphorus loads into the lake at 11,000 tonnes. Phosphorus provides nutrients to plants and is commonly found in manure and produced for fertiliser.

Harmful algae blooms (HAB) often manifest by forming a kind of scum over a body of water that can be green, blue, brown or even red.

Then in the late-1990s, blooms began to reappear. A cyanobacteria bloom requires two things: nutrients and heat. In the case of Lake Erie, nearby farms have become increasingly reliant on large inputs of synthetic fertiliser.

"We went from agriculture that was small farms [and a] variety of crops to larger commercial farms that were harvested for essentially two row crops, corn and soya beans," says Davis. Today, corn and soya beans are Ohio's top crops.

Employing more fertiliser to feed a global market, the farms' excess phosphorus and nitrogen, another plant nutrient, washed out during storms and into the river and streams that feed Lake Erie. About 80% of the nutrients running into Lake Erie are from sources around the Maumee River, which in this case means agricultural runoff from the surrounding farmland.

"If you have an agricultural system where the farmer can only survive by polluting Lake Erie, then there's something fundamentally wrong with that system," says Dr Thomas Bridgeman, director of the Lake Erie Center.

Since the 1990s, Lake Erie has seen a bloom every year–and they appear to be lasting longer and getting larger. This year's bloom in Lake Erie was the fifth largest since 2002–when monitoring began in earnest. It was 620 square miles at its largest after growing throughout August, before dissipating in September.

Meanwhile, climate change has heated up our planet substantially. Nearby Lake Superior, the most northerly of the Great Lakes and the world's largest, has had its first documented cyanobacteria blooms over the past decade. Before climate change, the lake simply would have been too cold for a long-lasting bloom.

It's now almost a certainty that blooms will continue to appear every summer, say researchers, unless Ohio changes its agricultural practices and the global community finally tackles the climate crisis.

"We have to look around and say, 'Look, what do we grow here?'" says Bridgeman. "We grow corn and soya beans. Where does the corn go? It goes into our gas tanks. Where do the soya beans go? They go to China, they go to hogs. Is that really what we want to be doing with our watershed?"

Dead Manatees and Sick Sea Lions

Algal blooms are also becoming more common and severe in many parts of our oceans, harming wildlife and posing potentially dangerous health impacts for local communities.

Scientists say the "red tide" that stuck around the Florida coast from 2017 through to this year may now be a semi-normal part of the ecosystem.

These blooms are pumping poison into the air, known as brevetoxin, which may be harmful to humans if inhaled. Anyone breathing it in can suffer from uncontrollable coughing and a sore throat. "It doesn't make for a pleasant day at the beach," says Malcolm McFarland, a researcher into algae blooms with the Harbor Branch Oceanographic Institute in Fort Pierce, Florida.

It may have long-term health implications as well—one study found that brevetoxin attacked the DNA of lungs in rats, but further research is needed to understand the impact on human health.

Scientists are less certain about the causes of these red tide marine blooms, but both nutrient runoff and climate change may play a role. "The red tide seems to initiate and peak in the rainy season when runoff from the land is highest, and nutrient inputs to freshwater and coastal water bodies spike," says McFarland.

Meanwhile, on the other side of the north American continent, a different red tide is attacking a different species: California is seeing more sick sea lions taken in by rescue centres; pups and adults are dying.

Scientists believe they are suffering from eating fish tainted by *Pseudo-nitzschia australis* algae. The highly toxic algae are fatal at high doses, both to sea lions and humans.

Unlike Florida's red tides, those in California appear to be a very recent arrival. Until the turn of the millennium, large-scale toxic blooms were rare off the coast of California. Then something changed.

"From [2000] forward, we had a very significant bloom every single year with ecosystem impacts in California, and that has never stopped. Not only that, it seemed as though things were getting more and more toxic," says Clarissa Anderson, the executive director at Southern California Coastal Ocean Observing System, nothing that in less than 20 years of research, scientists have seen toxin numbers multiply by 200–from 500 to 100,000 nanograms per litre of sea water.

Anderson says the current best working theory is that increasing carbon sequestration by the oceans–due to the huge increase in greenhouse gas emissions since the industrial revolution–is behind the sudden regularity of these deadly blooms and an increase in their toxicity. She says the study of these events and their toxins is so new that there may be incidents of illness from eating affected fish or shellfish that are misdiagnosed because these poisons are not on the radar of many health organisations.

The Baltic's Dead Zones

Europe has had its own experience of deadly algae blooms that now threaten the future of its fisheries. Last year, the Baltic Sea experienced a bloom so large it could have encompassed Manhattan, and it closed beaches from Finland to Poland.

Finland has been systematically sampling its area of the Baltic since 1979, giving us a clearer idea of the spread and growth of the problem, and what's to blame. In that time, blooms have become larger and longer-lasting, creating dead zones and depleting Baltic fisheries.

Like the example in Lake Erie, the Baltic bloom is caused by an influx of nutrients from agriculture and warming waters.

Scientists are regularly tracking nutrient loads from Finland's rivers into the sea. Data from 2014 in the HELCOM Pollution Load Compilation database, the best currently available, found that more than three-quarters of the nutrient load coming into the Archipelago Sea is from agriculture. The number is surprisingly similar to the proportion coming from industrialised agriculture in Ohio.

The Baltic is a brackish water body, thus supporting blooms typical of both fresh and salt water. But, as in Lake Erie, of real concern are cyanobacteria: several species have been known to produce blooms here.

Below the sea's surface there has been a decline in the more nutritious phytoplankton—and food for fish—and an increase in the potentially toxic species in the more southerly parts of the sea since the early 1980s.

Milder winters and increased rainfall pushing more nutrients into the sea, along with higher surface water temperatures—all due to the climate crisis—are also exacerbating factors, say researchers. Blooms usually begin in July and disappear by August or September. But last year a species particularly resistant to cold remained until November.

"The ice was blue-green because of the cyanobacteria under it," says Sirpa Lehtinen, an expert on plankton for the Marine Research Centre with the Finnish Environmental Institute, who adds that scientists are still trying to work out what this all means for the marine ecosystem, and whether fisheries in the Baltic are in serious long-term peril.

Fixing an Ecosystem Out of Balance

So how can we solve a problem like algae? The answer, says Davis, will be part-regional, part-global solutions. For Lake Erie, it will require agricultural changes—including regulations to reduce the nutrient load—and tackling the climate crisis. But solutions elsewhere may be different, for example, blooms in developing countries might require better wastewater treatment.

The 2014 water crisis in Ohio forced the issue politically which hasn't happened in many other places. Governor Mike DeWine recently announced an initiative called H2Ohio, which is expected to include hundreds of millions of dollars for Lake Erie and other Ohio water bodies over the next 10 years. However, scientists say this is not enough.

"It's going to take a lot more money and a lot more political will than what's happening right now," says Bridgeman.

At the Ohio Department of Agriculture,director Dorothy Pelanda said the department was primarily looking at voluntary programmes based on marketing and education for potential solutions such as cover crops and smarter use of fertiliser. In 2014, Ohio passed new regulations on fertiliser use for farms near the lake: such as not spreading before a storm or on frozen fields.

"We know from science that there is not one solution to every farm … It's about education, it's about being sensitive to what works, what doesn't work," she said. She's hoping to provide increased access for farmers to use high-tech, but often expensive, equipment that can give them a better idea of what parts of their land may need fertiliser and how much.

Pelanda said she's also seen interest in diversifying crops beyond corn and soya beans, to grapes, chestnuts and maple sugar. Asked if voluntary programmes will go far enough, Pelanda says: "That's our challenge. We have to get beyond. We're doing these things … but we're not doing enough of these things. We need to really increase the voluntary adoption of these practices."

Others are more sceptical of voluntary approaches. "We have a long history in this country of a farmer does what he wants on his land. You can choose to take advantage of a programme or something, but you can also choose not to," says Bridgeman, who believes local and federal governments can no longer afford to ignore the climate emergency.

"We need to do something about climate change and we're either going to be paying for it by reducing greenhouse gases or we're going to be paying for it by additional treatment of water," says Bridgeman, adding that most of the blooms around the world have a human element to them.

One thing is certain. Algae blooms aren't going away but are yet another sign—like ocean acidification, vanishing Arctic sea ice, and mass extinction of the Anthropocene—"of an ecosystem that is out of balance," says McFarland.

Print Citations

CMS: Hance, Jeremy. "Lethal Algae Blooms—An Ecosystem Out of Balance." In *The Reference Shelf: National Debate 2021-2022: Water Resources,* edited by Micah L. Issitt, 72-77. Amenia, NY: Grey House Publishing, 2021.

MLA: Hance, Jeremy. "Lethal Algae Blooms—An Ecosystem Out of Balance." *The Reference Shelf: National Debate 2021-2022: Water Resources,* edited by Micah L. Issitt, Grey House Publishing, 2021, pp. 72-77.

APA: Hance, J. (2021). Lethal algae blooms—An ecosystem out of balance. In Micah L. Issitt (Ed.), *The reference shelf: National debate 2021-2022: Water resources* (pp. 72-77). Amenia, NY: Grey House Publishing.

The Science of Harmful Algal Blooms

U.S. Geological Survey, October 24, 2016

Cyanobacterial harmful algal blooms (cyanoHABs) are increasingly a global concern. CyanoHABs can threaten human and aquatic ecosystem health; they can cause major economic damage.

The toxins produced by some species of cyanobacteria (called cyanotoxins) cause acute and chronic illnesses in humans. Harmful algal blooms can adversely affect aquatic ecosystem health, both directly through the presence of these toxins and indirectly through the low dissolved oxygen concentrations and changes in aquatic food webs caused by an overabundance of cyanobacteria. Economic damages related to cyanoHABs include the loss of recreational revenue, decreased property values, and increased drinking-water treatment costs.

Nationwide, toxic cyanobacterial harmful algal blooms have been implicated in human and animal illness and death in at least 43 states. In August 2016, at least 19 states had public health advisories because of cyanoHABs (USEPA, 2016).

Toxic cyanobacterial harmful algal blooms (cyanoHABs) have been implicated in human and animal illness and death in at least 43 states in the United States (Hudnell, 2008; Graham and others, 2009). In August 2016, at least 19 states had public health advisories because of cyanoHABs (U.S. Environmental Protection Agency, 2016).

What Are Cyanobacteria?

Cyanobacteria are naturally occurring microscopic organisms. Although they are true bacteria, they function more like algae in aquatic ecosystems. Thus, they are typically considered to be part of algal communities (this explains why they often are called blue-green algae). Cyanobacterial blooms may appear as discolorations in the water or paint-like scums at the water-surface. Typically, the blooms are blue-green in color, but they also may be yellow, red, or brown.

Cyanobacteria are notorious for producing a variety of compounds that cause water-quality concerns. Cyanobacteria produce taste-and-odor compounds that people are sensitive to at very low concentrations (even parts per trillion) in drinking water. Taste-and-odor compounds may accumulate in fish flesh making it unpalatable, an important concern for the aquaculture industry.

Of greater concern is the production of the toxins that affect human health.

Human ingestion, inhalation, or contact with water containing elevated concentrations of cyanotoxins can cause allergic reactions, dermatitis, gastroenteritis, and seizures.

Recent Science Insights

USGS scientists are leading a diverse range of studies to address cyanoHAB issues in water bodies throughout the United States, using a combination of traditional methods and emerging technologies in collaboration with numerous partners. However, despite advances in scientific understanding of cyanobacteria and associated compounds, many questions remain unanswered about the occurrence, the environmental triggers for toxicity, and the ability to predict the timing and toxicity of cyanoHABs.

Advanced warnings at time scales relevant to cyanoHAB management (hours to days) would allow proactive, rather than reactive, responses to potential events. Sensors that measure cyanobacteria in near real-time show promise for use in early warning systems.

The ability for cyanobacteria to produce cyanotoxins as well as taste-and-odor compounds is caused by genetic distinctions at the subspecies level of the bacteria. By analyzing those distinctions, we can gain a greater understanding of the world of cyanoHABs, an understanding that may lead us to new ways to combat this threat. USGS is developing field and laboratory

> **Nationwide, toxic cyanobacterial harmful algal blooms have been implicated in human and animal illness and deaths in at least 43 states.**

methods to quantify cyanobacterial and associated compounds that include field protocols, field guides, sample preparation techniques, development of assays, and molecular tools.

Nutrient Enrichment: A Key Factor in Occurrences of CyanoHABs

One of the key causes of cyanoHABs is nutrient enrichment. When nutrients from agricultural and urban areas are transported downstream, they can cause cyanoHABs in reservoirs, which can impair drinking-water quality and result in closures of recreational areas.

The USGS, in cooperation with local, state, federal, tribal, and university partners, is pioneering new monitoring, assessment, and modeling approaches to better understand nutrient sources, their transport, and their role in toxic cyanoHABs.

Tracking the Water Quality of the Nation's Streams and Rivers

The USGS monitors nutrient concentrations and flux at key sites nationwide. Annual data are featured at the website, Tracking Water Quality of the Nation's Rivers and Streams.

In addition, the USGS uses advanced optical sensor technology to track nitrate levels in real time at about 135 sites nationwide. These data provide real-time information, improve load calculations, and advance our understanding of processes controlling nutrient variability. The data are publicly available at the website, WaterQuality Watch.

Identifying Nutrient Sources and Hotspots

USGS models of nutrient concentrations and loads in streams provide an important tool for identifying nutrient sources. Estimates derived from these models provide insights into which areas and sources are contributing the largest amounts of nutrients to local streams, lakes, and reservoirs. The models also enable the tracking of nutrients and their sources from local streams to the Nation's estuaries and the Great Lakes. See website, Tracking the Source and Quantity of Nutrients to the Nation's Estuaries.

Print Citations

CMS: "The Science of Harmful Algal Blooms." In *The Reference Shelf: National Debate 2021-2022: Water Resources,* edited by Micah L. Issitt, 78-80. Amenia, NY: Grey House Publishing, 2021.

MLA: "The Science of Harmful Algal Blooms." *The Reference Shelf: National Debate 2021-2022: Water Resources,* edited by Micah L. Issitt, Grey House Publishing, 2021, pp. 78-80.

APA: U.S. Geological Survey. (2021). The science of harmful algal blooms. In Micah L. Issitt (Ed.), *The reference shelf: National debate 2021-2022: Water resources* (pp. 78-80). Amenia, NY: Grey House Publishing.

A Hacker Tried to Poison a Florida City's Water Supply, Officials Say

By Andy Greenberg
Wired, February 8, 2021

Around 8 AM on Friday morning, an employee of a water treatment plant in the 15,000-person city of Oldsmar, Florida, noticed that his mouse cursor was moving strangely on his computer screen, out of his control, as local police would later tell it. Initially, he wasn't concerned; the plant used the remote-access software Team-Viewer to allow staff to share screens and troubleshoot IT issues, and his boss often connected to his computer to monitor the facility's systems.

But a few hours later, police say, the plant operator noticed his mouse moving out of his control again. This time there would be no illusion of benign monitoring from a supervisor or IT person. The cursor began clicking through the water treatment plant's controls. Within seconds, the intruder was attempting to change the water supply's levels of sodium hydroxide, also known as lye or caustic soda, moving the setting from 100 parts per million to 11,100 parts per million. In low concentrations the corrosive chemical regulates the PH level of potable water. At high levels, it severely damages any human tissue it touches.

According to city officials, the operator quickly spotted the intrusion and returned the sodium hydroxide to normal levels. Even if he hadn't, the poisoned water would have taken 24 to 36 hours to reach the city's population, and automated PH testing safeguards would have triggered an alarm and caught the change before anyone was harmed, they say.

But if the events described by local officials are confirmed—they have yet to be corroborated firsthand by external security auditors—they may well represent a rare publicly reported cyberintrusion aimed at actively sabotaging the systems that control a US city's critical infrastructure. "This is dangerous stuff," said Bob Gualtieri, the sheriff of Pinellas County, Florida, of which Oldsmar is a part, in a press conference Monday afternoon. "This is somebody that is trying, it appears on the surface, to do something bad."

In a follow-up call with WIRED, Gualtieri said that the hacker appears to have compromised the water treatment plant's TeamViewer software to gain remote access to the target computer, and that network logs confirm the operator's mouse takeover story. But the sheriff had little else to share about how the hacker accessed TeamViewer or gained initial access to the plant's IT network. He also provided no details as to how the intruder broke into the so-called operational technology network that controls physical equipment in industrial control systems and is typically segregated from the internet-connected IT network.

The intruder was attempting to change the water supply's levels of sodium hydroxide, also known as lye or caustic soda.

Gualtieri said the city's own forensic investigators, as well as the FBI and Secret Service, are seeking those answers. "That's the million-dollar question, and it's a point of concern, because we don't know where the hole is and how sophisticated these people are," Gualtieri said. "Did this come from down the street or outside the country? No idea."

Security professionals have long advised not only segregating IT and OT networks for maximal security but also limiting or ideally eliminating all connections from operational technology systems to the internet. But Gualtieri conceded that the plant's OT systems were externally accessible, and that all evidence points to the attacker accessing them from the internet. "There is merit to the point that critical infrastructure components shouldn't be connected," Gualtieri said. "If you're connected, you're vulnerable."

Gualtieri said that the water treatment facility had uninstalled TeamViewer since the attack, but he couldn't otherwise comment on what other security measures the plant was taking to remove the intruder's access or prevent another breach. He added that officials have warned all government organizations in the wider Tampa Bay area to review their security protocols and make updates to protect themselves. "We want to make sure that everyone realizes these kinds of bad actors are out there. It's happening," Oldmar mayor Eric Seidel said in a press conference. "So really take a hard look at what you have in place."

As unprecedented as Oldmar's public announcement of a cybersabotage attempt on its water systems may be, the attack it describes is hardly unique, says Lesley Carhart, a principal threat analyst at industrial control system security firm Dragos. She says she's seen incidents firsthand in which even unsophisticated hackers access software applications that offer control of physical equipment—such as the TeamViewer remote access tool reportedly used in Oldmar or the human-machine interfaces (HMIs) that directly control equipment—and start messing with them. Thousands of such systems are discoverable over the internet with search tools like Shodan, she points out. It's often only the complexity and safeguards in industrial control systems that prevent hacker meddling from having serious consequences.

"Do I think that on a regular basis people are logging in to HMI systems and hitting buttons? Absolutely," says Carhart. "Do those things have a measurable impact on the real world? Very rarely."

Carhart points to a comparable incident—albeit one carried out by an insider rather than an external attacker—when a disgruntled IT consultant for a sewage treatment plant in the Australian shire of Maroochy used his remote access to dump millions of gallons of raw sewage into local parks and rivers. On the other end of the sophistication spectrum, the Russian hacker group known as Sandworm in December 2015 hijacked a remote-access software similar to the TeamViewer program used in Oldmar to open circuit breakers in Ukrainian electric utilities, turning off the power to a quarter-million civilians. And there's an even more direct precedent: In 2016, Verizon Security Solutions reported that hackers broke into an unidentified water utility and changed the chemical levels.

Water treatment and sewage plants, Carhart says, are often some of the most digitally vulnerable critical infrastructure targets in the United States, made more so by the budget cuts and remote work scenarios imposed by the Covid-19 pandemic. She says she has dealt with entire cities whose municipal water treatment plant has only a single IT person.

«They›re doing whatever they have to keep water flowing and sewage treated. If they don›t have the resources to do that and do cybersecurity, what are they going to do?» she asks.

"They're going to keep the process running, keep society running. That's what they have to do."

Print Citations

CMS: Greenberg, Andy. "A Hacker Tried to Poison a Florida City's Water Supply, Officials Say." In *The Reference Shelf: National Debate 2021-2022: Water Resources,* edited by Micah L. Issitt, 81-83. Amenia, NY: Grey House Publishing, 2021.

MLA: Greenberg, Andy. "A Hacker Tried to Poison a Florida City's Water Supply, Officials Say." *The Reference Shelf: National Debate 2021-2022: Water Resources,* edited by Micah L. Issitt, Grey House Publishing, 2021, pp. 81-83.

APA: Greenberg, A. (2021). A hacker tried to poison a Florida city's water supply, officials say. In Micah L. Issitt (Ed.), *The reference shelf: National debate 2021-2022: Water resources* (pp. 81-83). Amenia, NY: Grey House Publishing.

3
Protecting Natural Water Bodies

Industrial waste and raw sewage passes from Mexicali (Mexico) into Calexico, California, in the New River.

Protecting Rivers, Lakes, and Watersheds

The water resources available to residents of any state also include the natural reservoirs of water that exist in the state, whether or not any of those natural water sources are used directly to supply drinking water to any of the communities. America's streams, rivers, lakes, and springs provide water to millions of Americans, but are also essential for the health of America's broader ecosystems. These, in turn, provide the resources that Americans depend on, both directly in terms of food but also in regulating the environment and creating the conditions necessary to maintain healthy agricultural territories and to moderate climate.

Industrial waste and municipal sewage pose a serious threat to the health of natural waterways and reservoirs, and this, in turn, threatens the lives and welfare of all Americans. Rivers and streams carry water across many states and ultimately feed into oceanic spillways, and thus pollution entering rivers or streams can affect lives distant from the pollution source. Water pollution problems in cities and towns also contributes to the decline of oceanic health and this ultimately poses a threat to people living across the United States and in many other countries. For many years, scientists and experts in environmental remediation have been trying to spread awareness about the crisis that America is facing with regard to preserving natural water systems. In a very real sense, at the current level of decline, many American rivers, lakes, and other reservoirs are very much under threat. Failure to make progress with regard to water conservation could pose a threat to the continuation of human life.

Watersheds and Waterways

While most Americans are at least basically familiar with lakes, streams, rivers, and ponds, fewer Americans might understand how special areas called "watersheds" function in the circulation of water through an environment. A watershed is an area of land that channels rainfall and snowmelt into streams, creeks, and rivers, and that eventually leads water all the way to "outflow points," where the water deposited in the terrestrial environment reenters the ocean. Watersheds, also known as "drainage basins" may stretch over thousands of square miles, while others may be significantly smaller. The Mississippi River watershed is the nation's largest, draining 1.15 million square miles of land into the rivers and encompassing territory within 31 states and two Canadian provinces.[1]

Pollution, whether coming from municipal sewage systems, agricultural processes, or rural waste systems, floods into the nation's watersheds where some of the water soaks into the soil, while the remaining water rejoins natural waterways en route to the ocean. Water coming through the watersheds is essential to human life. This water grows crops and provides drinking and household water for residents of the nation's cities and towns. When water enters watersheds, the water is filtered through the soil, where plants absorb excess nutrients and use the water and nutrients to fuel growth. Cities and towns use municipal sewage systems or septic systems to prevent pollution from washing into the watersheds and so from pollution natural waterways. When these systems fail, or when waste management systems are overwhelmed by flooding or heavy rains, pollutants flood into watersheds and from there into rivers, streams, lakes, and the ocean. This pollution then threatens the health of aquatic ecosystems and all living creatures that depend on aquatic resources.[2]

Sewage system malfunctions are but one of the many sources of pollution that threaten the health of the nation's watersheds and waterways. For instance, gardening, both commercial and residential, has the potential to introduce pollutants to watersheds. The U.S. Environmental Protection Agency (EPA) has estimated that commercial corn production and residential agriculture distribute pollutants and harmful chemicals across most of the American landscape and into the outflows that lead to the oceans. The issue of watershed and waterway preservation first gained widespread public attention in the 1960s; since then environmentalist organizations have been encouraging American companies and individual citizens to adopt changes that can help to preserve remaining water and to reduce the introduction of pollutants. These changes include utilizing organic gardening techniques, reducing or eliminating pesticides and agricultural chemicals, and installing "low-flow" toilets and waste-reducing utilities in homes and businesses to limit water waste. Other environmental techniques can also be used to reduce the impact of pollution, such as planting and maintaining "rain gardens" and other biological barriers that will remove pollutants from drainage water as it moves through an environment.

Each year, research studies add new information to the collective knowledge of pollution and its impact on the environment. For instance, a 2017 study of Iowa corn agriculture found that mass agriculture was a major contributor to watershed pollution and that farmers, especially those managing large-scale agricultural programs, had not embraced methods to reduce runoff or fertilizer pollution.[3] Numerous studies over the decades have demonstrated the environmental hazards of large-scale agriculture, which pollutes both air and water, but critics argue that states and the federal government have not imposed sufficient restrictions and regulations to control this problem. According to the National Resources Defense Council, agricultural pollution is one of the primary global threats to air and water quality. Sources include waste runoff into natural water systems, fertilizer pollution, and methane pollution, which contributes to climate change.[4]

While some regions face problems involving polluted water, in other parts of America the growing problem is a lack of water. Human-mediated climate change is changing the environment of the earth and, in arid areas where water resources are limited, this has led to increasing drought and issues involving water supply. In part of California, Arizona, Nevada, and many other states, drought has become increasingly common and naturally occurring drought cycles are changing, with periods of drought becoming more intense and longer lasting. This strains water resources in areas where limited rainfall and runoff leads to limited water reserves. A Harvard University study published in 2019 indicated that widespread "water scarcity" issues and water shortages will become increasingly common in the United States in coming decades.[5]

Climate change is increasing the frequency of climate fluctuations and, despite resistance from political factions aligned with corporate interests, decades of evidence proves that human activity, in the form of air pollution, water pollution, agriculture, and fossil fuel harvesting, is the primary agent of climate change. As the climate continues to change, climatic disturbances involving tropical storms, flooding, and drought will all become more common and more severe. On one hand, this will mean that more and more Americans (and people around the world) will have difficulty accessing clean water, but it will also mean that pollution from residential and commercial sources will become more of a problem. Flooding and tropical storms, which cause overflows in sewage management systems and wash terrestrial pollution into waterways, will therefore intensify existing concerns over watershed and waterway pollution and preservation. Efforts to address this problem are complicated by disagreements over the allocation of tax revenues and by the high cost of environmental remediation and protection. Though there is considerable debate over how to accomplish the goal of protecting water resources, it is clear that the threats facing America's water resources are growing in number and intensifying and that some strategy for mitigating these threats is necessary.[6]

Federal and State Regulations

The early 1970s was the culmination of an environmentalist movement that began in the late 1940s. American environmentalism goes back much further than the early twentieth century, and there were environmentalist movements in the United States stretching back even to the Colonial era as colonists first realized how their efforts to build agricultural settlements was pollution rivers and driving needed animal resources from the nation's growing towns and settlements. The very first environmental laws passed in the nations came about in the colonies, where laws limited hunting and logging activities to ensure access to resources in later years. In the 1800s, industrial manufacturing and development spread rapidly across the United States and, as this occurred, pollution levels skyrocketed. In cities with large industrial processing industries, air pollution became such a severe problem that mass respiratory illness was common. Meanwhile, the nation's first large-scale corporations operated in a completely unregulated environment. Waste from manufacturing was pumped into the nation's watersheds and, sometimes, directly into rivers, streams, or lakes.

One of the most famous examples of industrial era pollution is the Cuyahoga River, which runs past the city of Cleveland. For many years, the city's steel industry pumped millions of gallons of toxic waste into the river. By the late 1800s, residents of Cleveland and other communities bordering the Cuyahoga River complained of floating debris and oil, foul smelling water, and a dramatic loss in biodiversity. In 1868, in what was the first of several times, the Cuyahoga River actually caught fire, with flames wicking over the deposits of oil and chemicals floating on the top of the water. The burning of the river was a local controversy in the 1800s, but captured little in the way of national attention. However, the river caught fire at least six more times. One of the final fires, in 1969, drew widespread media attention and became a turning point for water preservation legislation. From this controversy, the City of Cleveland and the state of Ohio adopted new policies and regulations and invested in a large-scale effort to protect and preserve the river.[7]

State governments enacted regulations on water pollution long before there were any commensurate federal regulations in place. However, not all states were equally aggressive when it came to reducing air and water pollution and this is a national problem because pollutants emanating from any region ultimately impact those living in many other regions. Air pollution, for instance, does not remain in the area where pollutants are released, but travels through air currents to other states. Water pollution likewise travels through rivers, streams, and creeks across state and regional borders, ultimately impacting the ocean. While state and municipal governments put effort into controlling local pollution rates, even states with aggressive pollution control regulations faced the threat of pollution from unregulated states. For this reason, the preservation of resources is an issue that must be managed at the national level as well as at the state and municipal level.

The nation's first federal law on water pollution was the Rivers and Harbors Act of 1824. This limited piece of legislation was the first time that the federal government tried to assert control over state management of waterways. This was controversial at the time, and there was significant resistance from factions of Americans dedicated to preserving state autonomy, but the courts ruled that the government had the power to enforce federal regulations on water resources in furtherance of commercial trade or national security. The Rivers and Harbors Act was primarily instituted to facilitate the passage of commercial goods through waterways, but it was also important for the preservation of natural waterways because it was the first time that the federal government prohibited states from damming or diverting rivers with widespread national interest. These principles, and the legal precedent established through the act, facilitated the passage of the nation's first law directly targeting water pollution, the Federal Water Pollution Control Act of 1948.

The 1948 act was well-intentioned, arising directly from public concern over the increasingly evident pollution in the nation's rivers and other waterways, but the act was insufficient for a number of reasons. For one, politicians allied with corporate interests ensured that enforcement measures were limited and thus there were few consequences for individuals or companies that violated the laws. In addition, the law did not directly prohibit commercial interests from discharging pollution into waterways or watersheds but simply required states to engage in remediation measures to ensure public safety. The act also fell short in that it did not consider the health of aquatic ecosystems and wildlife and focused entirely on human use and welfare. Last, the 1948 act only considered "point source" pollution, which is pollution that directly impacts a specific waterway. A great deal of the pollution introduced to America's watersheds and waterways does not fall into this category and is instead categorized as "nonpoint source" pollution, which means that the initial source of pollution may be somewhat distant from a specific waterway. Farm runoff, fertilizers and insecticides, and residential pollution typically falls into the nonpoint source category and the 1948 water act did nothing to reduce or address these sources of pollution.[8]

The most significant water pollution legislation in American history is the Clean Water Act (CWA), a 1972 law that greatly expanded on the 1948 act. The CWA fully banned point-source pollution, meaning that it prohibited any company from discharging pollution directly into a watershed or waterway. The law further empowered the newly created EPA to implement pollution regulations, including changing or amending rules for industrial pollution and domestic sewage management. The CWA also provided federal funding for sewage control and funded research and conservation efforts. This was the first federal water preservation law to take the conservation of aquatic ecosystems into consideration and this, alone, made the law far more effective because it encouraged state authorities to utilize biodiversity and ecosystem quality as a measure of pollution control and management efforts. The 1972 law has been updated on a number of occasions. In the 1980s, federal revenues were expanded for treatment plant programs and in the 1990s additional provisions were added specifically to address pollution in the Great Lakes region.[9]

An Evolving Goal

The vast majority of Americans were supportive of the Clean Water Act and other environmental legislative initiatives of the 1970s and, though polling on the issue is rarely undertaken, there is considerable indicating that a majority of Americans continue to support maintaining and even strengthening federal and state regulations on water and air pollution. A 2016 Kaiser Family Foundation poll, for instance, found that contaminated drinking water ranked as one of the most widespread concerns for citizens. Polls have also found that majorities across political parties, age ranges, and ideological factions are supportive of efforts to improve water quality and are willing to pay to improve or enhance existing efforts. A 2017 poll from the Water Foundation found that 88 percent of Americans across all categories "strongly" support ensuring safe drinking water and a full 77 percent strongly support protecting forests and aquatic ecosystems.[10]

Corporations are the greatest impediment to enforcing and strengthening the CWA and other legislative efforts to protect water resources. Environmental regulations represent an increased cost to many companies, and this cost reduces profit for shareholders, owners, and upper-level managers. Companies therefore expend resources to purchase support from politicians and to discourage public support for legislation involving stronger environmental regulations on things like pollution and water safety. For many states, the cost of remediation is now prohibitively high and this coupled with corporate resistance prevents many states and municipalities from taking steps to improve water management systems. The modern debate over the protection of natural water reservoirs therefore often hinges on municipal and state economies and depends on the degree to which residents and managers of a municipality emphasize economic profit or long-term societal health and stability.

Works Used

"Climate Change and Water—Warmer Oceans, Flooding and Droughts." *EEA*. European Environment Agency. Nov 23, 2020. https://www.eea.europa.eu/signals/signals-2018-content-list/articles/climate-change-and-water-2014.

"Future Widespread Water Shortage Likely in U.S." *SITN*. Science in the News. Mar 20, 2019. https://sitn.hms.harvard.edu/flash/2019/widespread-water-shortage-likely-in-u-s-caused-by-population-growth-and-climate-change/.

"History of the Clean Water Act." *EPA*. https://www.epa.gov/laws-regulations/history-clean-water-act.

"Implementation of the Federal Water Pollution Control Act (Regulation and Monitoring of Toxic and Hazardous Chemicals)." Hearings before the Subcommittee on Oversights and Review of the Committee on Public Works and Transportation U.S. House of Representatives. *U.S. Government Printing Office*, 1980, p. 1904.

Lindwall, Courtney. "Industrial Agricultural Pollution 101." *NRDC*. Jul 31, 2019. https://www.nrdc.org/stories/industrial-agricultural-pollution-101.

Rotman, Michael. "Cuyahoga River Fire." *Cleveland Historical*. 2021. Oct 5, 2019. https://clevelandhistorical.org/items/show/63.

Royte, Elizabeth. "The Simple River-Cleaning Tactics That Big Farms Ignore." *National Geographic*. Dec 7, 2017. https://www.nationalgeographic.com/science/article/iowa-agriculture-runoff-water-pollution-environment.

"Water Public Opinion Polls and Data." *Water Polls*. 2021. https://waterpolls.org/.

"Watersheds, Flooding, and Pollution." *NOAA*. National Oceanic and Atmospheric Administration. 2021. https://www.noaa.gov/education/resource-collections/freshwater/watersheds-flooding-and-pollution.

"What Is a watershed?" *NOAA*. National Oceanic and Atmospheric Administration. Feb 26, 2021. https://oceanservice.noaa.gov/facts/watershed.html.

Notes

1. "What Is a Watershed," *NOAA*.
2. "Watersheds, Flooding, and Pollution," *NOAA*.
3. Royte, "The Simple River-Cleaning Tactics That Big Farms Ignore."
4. Lindwall, "Industrial Agricultural Pollution 101."
5. "Future Widespread Water Shortage Likely in U.S.," *SITN*.
6. "Climate Change and Water—Warmer Oceans, Flooding and Droughts," *EEA*.
7. Rotman, "Cuyahoga River Fire."
8. "Implementation of the Federal Water Pollution Control Act (Regulation and Monitoring of Toxic and Hazardous Chemicals)," *U.S. Government Printing Office*, p. 1904.

9. "History of the Clean Water Act," *EPA*.
10. "Water Public Opinion Polls and Data," *Water Polls.org*.

Healthy Watersheds Protection: Basic Information and Answers to Frequent Questions

U.S. Environmental Protection Agency, March 5, 2018

What Is a Watershed?

A watershed—the land area that drains to one stream, lake or river—affects the water quality in the water body that it surrounds. Like water bodies (e.g., lakes, rivers, and streams), individual watersheds share similarities but also differ in many ways. Every inch of the United States is part of a watershed—in other words, all land drains into a lake, river, stream or other water body and directly affects its quality. Because we all live on the land, we all live in a watershed—thus watershed condition is important to everyone.

Watersheds exist at different geographic scales, too. The Mississippi River has a huge watershed that covers all or parts of 33 states. You might live in that watershed, but at the same time you live in a watershed of a smaller, local stream or river that flows eventually into the Mississippi. EPA's healthy watersheds activities mainly focus on these smaller watersheds.

What Is a Healthy Watershed?

A healthy watershed is one in which natural land cover supports:

- dynamic hydrologic and geomorphologic processes within their natural range of variation,
- habitat of sufficient size and connectivity to support native aquatic and riparian species, and
- physical and chemical water quality conditions able to support healthy biological communities.

Natural vegetative cover in the landscape, including the riparian zone, helps maintain the natural *flow regime** and fluctuations in water levels in lakes and wetlands. This, in turn, helps maintain natural geomorphic processes, such as sediment storage and deposition, that form the basis of aquatic habitats. Connectivity of aquatic and riparian habitats in the longitudinal, lateral, vertical, and temporal dimensions helps ensure the flow of chemical and physical materials and movement of biota among habitats.

A healthy watershed has the structure and function in place to support healthy aquatic ecosystems. Key components of a healthy watershed include:

- intact and functioning headwater streams, floodplains, riparian corridors, biotic refugia, instream habitat, and biotic communities;

- natural vegetation in the landscape; and

- hydrology, sediment transport, fluvial geomorphology, and disturbance regimes expected for its location.

*A stream's *flow regime* refers to its characteristic pattern of flow magnitude, timing, frequency, duration, and rate of change. The flow regime plays a central role in shaping aquatic ecosystems and the health of biological communities. Alteration of natural flow regimes (e.g., more frequent floods) can reduce the quantity and quality of aquatic habitat, degrade aquatic life, and result in the loss of ecosystem services.

Are Healthy Watersheds Very Common?

Unfortunately, not. Healthy watersheds are uncommon, particularly in the eastern U.S. as well as in most other parts of the nation that are urbanized, farmed, or mined. Large tracts of protected wildlands, mostly in the western U.S., are where most healthy watersheds can be found. However, some healthy watersheds exist in many regions of the country where water pollution has been prevented or well controlled, and where communities maintain the benefits of their clean waterways.

How Might Healthy Watersheds Affect Me?

You may potentially benefit from healthy watersheds in numerous ways, generally unseen and unrecognized by the average citizen:

- Healthy watersheds are necessary for virtually any high quality outdoor recreation sites involving the use of lakes, rivers, or streams. Great fishing opportunities are usually due to healthy watersheds that surround the waters that people love to fish.

- Your drinking water, if it comes from a surface water source, might be substantially less expensive to treat, if a healthy watershed around the water source filters pollution for free.

- Your property values may be higher, if you are fortunate enough to reside near healthy rather than impaired waters.

You and your community's quality of life may be better in these and other ways due to healthy watersheds; now, imagine how unhealthy watersheds might affect you as well.

Why Do Watersheds Need to Be Protected?

Healthy watersheds not only affect water quality in a good way, but also provide greater benefits to the communities of people and wildlife that live there.

A watershed—the land area that drains to a stream, lake or river—affects the water quality in the water body that it surrounds. Healthy watersheds not only help protect water quality, but also provide greater benefits than degraded watersheds to the people and wildlife that live there. We all live in a watershed, and watershed condition is important to everyone and everything that uses and needs water.

Healthy watersheds provide critical services, such as clean drinking water, productive fisheries, and outdoor recreation, that support our economies, environment and quality of life. The health of clean waters is heavily influenced by the condition of their surrounding watersheds, mainly because pollutants can wash off from the land to the water and cause substantial harm.

Streams, lakes, rivers and other waters are interconnected with the landscape and all its activities through their watersheds. They are influenced by naturally varying lake levels, water movement to and from groundwater, and amount of stream flow. Other factors, such as forest fires, stormwater runoff patterns, and the location and amount of pollution sources, also influence the health of our waters.

> **Healthy watersheds are necessary for virtually any high quality outdoor recreation sites involving the use of lakes, rivers, or streams.**

These dynamics between the land and the water largely determine the health of our waterways and the types of aquatic life found in a particular area. Effective protection of aquatic ecosystems recognizes their connectivity with each other and with their surrounding watersheds. Unfortunately, human activities have greatly altered many waters and their watersheds. For example:

- Over the last 50 years, coastal and freshwater wetlands have declined; surface water and groundwater withdrawals have increased by 46%; and non-native fish have established themselves in many watersheds (Heinz Center, 2008).

- A national water quality survey of the nation's rivers and streams showed that 55% of the nation's flowing waters are in poor biological condition and 23% are in fair biological condition (U.S. EPA, 2013). Compared to a 2006 survey (U.S. EPA, 2006), which only assessed wadeable streams, 7% fewer stream miles were in good condition.

- Nearly 40% of fish in North American freshwater streams, rivers and lakes are found to be vulnerable, threatened or endangered; nearly twice as many as were included on the imperiled list from a similar survey conducted in 1989 (Jelks et al., 2008)

- Rainbow trout habitat loss from warmer water temperatures associated with climate change already has been observed in the southern Appalachians (Flebbe et al., 2006).

Why Is EPA Concerned with Healthy Watersheds?

One of EPA's most important jobs is to work with states and others to achieve the Clean Water Act's primary goal—restore and maintain the integrity of the nation's waters. Despite this law's many pollution control successes, tens of thousands of streams, rivers and lakes have been reported as still impaired. The great majority of these involve pollution sources in their watersheds—the land area that surrounds and drains into these waters. Knowing the conditions in watersheds is crucial for restoring areas with degraded water quality, as well as protecting healthy waters from emerging problems before expensive damages occur.

Achieving the Clean Water Act's main goal depends on having good information about watersheds—their environmental conditions, possible pollution sources, and factors that may influence restoration and protection of water quality. EPA is investing in developing scientifically sound and consistent data sources, and making this information public and easily accessible to the wide variety of our partners working toward clean and healthy waters.

What Is Being Done to Protect Healthy Watersheds?

A very wide range of activities could be called healthy watersheds protection. These may include regulatory and non-regulatory approaches. EPA's healthy watersheds protection activities are nonregulatory. Approaches used at state and local level could be either. The private sector is also actively involved in many forms of protection.

After decades of focusing almost exclusively on restoring impaired waters, EPA created the Healthy Watersheds Program (HWP) to bring more emphasis to proactively protecting high quality waters, following the Clean Water Act (CWA)'s objective "...to restore and maintain the chemical, physical, and biological integrity of the Nation's waters." The HWP takes a non-regulatory, collaborative approach to maintaining clean waters by supporting EPA and its partners in their efforts to identify, assess and protect watershed health through Clean Water Act programs. This approach is essential for addressing future threats such as:

- emerging water quality problems,
- loss and fragmentation of aquatic habitat,
- altered water flow and availability,
- invasive species, and
- climate change.

How Is a Healthy Watershed Identified?

There are literally hundreds of watershed characteristics (such as environmental traits, sources of degradation, and community factors) that may influence environmental health and quality of life, for better or worse. Identifying and comparing these characteristics is known as watershed assessment. This process is the main way to compare watershed condition across large areas such as states, and find the healthy watersheds among the rest.

What Is Evaluated in a Healthy Watersheds Assessment?

EPA's process for assessing healthy watersheds looks at small scale watersheds—either catchments (which average about one square mile in area) or HUC12 watersheds (which average about 35 square miles in area). The factors for describing and comparing watersheds, called *indicators*, are selected specifically for the area of the country being studied. Although custom selections of indicators are made to suit the study area, all assessments develop a comparative index of watershed health and index of watershed vulnerability. These complementary indices help states and other users find out where the healthiest watersheds are, and also what their level of vulnerability might be.

How Much Healthy Watersheds Assessment Has Been Done in the U.S.?

Several states have developed statewide assessments of their healthy watersheds on their own over the past decade. EPA has partnered with states and watershed groups in several additional locales to generate more statewide watershed assessments. However, in many states, there are still no completed studies to identify the healthy watersheds or their vulnerabilities. EPA is currently working to provide these states with preliminary healthy watersheds assessments.

Print Citations

CMS: "Healthy Watersheds Protection: Basic Information and Answers to Frequent Questions." In *The Reference Shelf: National Debate 2021-2022: Water Resources,* edited by Micah L. Issitt, 95-99. Amenia, NY: Grey House Publishing, 2021.

MLA: "Healthy Watersheds Protection: Basic Information and Answers to Frequent Questions." *The Reference Shelf: National Debate 2021-2022: Water Resources,* edited by Micah L. Issitt, Grey House Publishing, 2021, pp. 95-99.

APA: U.S. Environmental Protection Agency. (2021). Healthy watersheds protection: Basic information and answers to frequent questions. In Micah L. Issitt (Ed.), *The reference shelf: National debate 2021-2022: Water resources* (pp. 95-99). Amenia, NY: Grey House Publishing.

Debunking the Trump Administration's New Water Rule

By Ryan Richards

Center for American Progress, March 27, 2019

In February, the U.S. Environmental Protection Agency (EPA) released its revised "Waters of the United States" (WOTUS) rule. The proposed rule dramatically restricts what falls under the purview of the Clean Water Act, the environmental law that has led to the cleanup of thousands of rivers and lakes in the United States. The U.S. Geological Survey has estimated that the rule would remove federal protections for 18 percent of stream and river miles and 51 percent of wetlands in the United States, putting protections at their lowest levels since the Reagan administration and leaving millions of Americans vulnerable to polluted water.

Despite EPA Administrator Andrew Wheeler's claim that the changes were made to simplify what waterways are covered by the Clean Water Act, a close reading of the rule suggests that the changes add little clarity. In fact, experts have pointed out that the definitions used in the new rule are so general—and stray so far from sound science—that consultants may be required to determine whether a water body falls under federal jurisdiction. This would place further stress on farmers and landowners who are making good-faith efforts to follow the law.

While Wheeler recently claimed that "access to clean drinking water worldwide is 'the biggest environmental threat'," the rule appears to be yet another gift from Trump's EPA to polluters, especially the coal and hard-rock mining industries that have already benefited from myriad Trump administration policies. The proposed rule's shift away from science will seriously undermine water quality improvements that have been achieved since the Clean Water Act became law. Not only will the rule's narrowed definitions overwhelm states with new regulatory responsibilities, but the rule will also kneecap the booming restoration economy. This has been key to drawing billions of dollars in private investment to support environmental restoration and protection.

What Counts as WOTUS?

Passed in 1972, the Clean Water Act gives the EPA and the Army Corps of Engineers the responsibility to regulate water pollution. The agencies have written several rules since 1972 to define the bodies of water they must oversee, with new rules

being promulgated in re-
sponse to court decisions.
The most recent case, *Ra-*
panos v. United States, was
decided in 2006; the decision was 4-1-4 and defined

Instead of empowering states, the proposed rule appears to be an end run to gut environmental protections at all levels of government.

federal jurisdiction as ap-
plying to traditionally navigable waters as well as other waters with a "significant
nexus" to navigable waters. The latter refers to those water bodies that affect the
chemical, physical, or biological health of navigable waters.

In 2015, the EPA concluded a four-year scientific review of the nation's rivers
and wetlands to determine what counted as a "significant nexus" under the *Rapa-*
nos decision. It also released a rule that applied this definition to water bodies. However, industry opposed the rule, and over the subsequent years, litigation limited its
implementation to 26 states.

Instead of fighting for the rulemaking and ensuring strong protections against
water pollution, the Trump administration has continued its track record of supporting industry interests at the expense of the American public. The proposed new
WOTUS rule eliminates the categories introduced in the 2015 rule, limiting federal protections to broad categories of "traditional navigable waters"—seas, lakes,
permanent or intermittent rivers, and wetlands that either feed into or out of these
water bodies. The proposed rule also explicitly excludes ephemeral streams, which
flow during and shortly after precipitation events, and wetlands without surface
connections to traditional navigable waters. The proposed rule also leaves open the
option of removing intermittent rivers and streams before its finalization.

The New Rule Benefits Industry at the Expense of Public Health

A close reading of the proposed rule shows that it includes a big exemption that
benefits mining companies. Specifically, it explicitly excludes "water-filled depressions created in upland incidental to mining or construction activity." While the
2015 rule excluded dry land depressions created by mining or construction activity,
it clarified that ephemeral and intermittent streams could still be considered waters
of the United States, even if they were dry part of the year.

Ephemeral and intermittent streams are a critical part of hydrology in much of
the country, where seasonal rainfall means that many streams and rivers do not flow
year round. One example of this is an arroyo in the American Southwest, a stream
that flows only during and after rains, not permanently, because the region receives
so little precipitation. Including these seasonal streams under the WOTUS rule is
essential, as mining activities in these areas have a major effect on the quality of
water downstream.

Yet mining groups have been quietly advocating for a new WOTUS rule.
While farm groups opposing WOTUS have received most of the media attention, lobbying records indicate that since 2017, the National Mining Association alone has spent $3.5 million on lobbying activities related to the new WOTUS

rule. Several coal and hard-rock mining companies also list millions of dollars in WOTUS advocacy in their lobbying reports. Given the unequivocal link between mining and water contamination, these groups have a clear incentive to advocate for the narrowest definition of "waters of the United States."

Trump's 2019 "Economic Report of the President" confirms that the proposed WOTUS rule is intended as a handout to the mining industry, calling it one of "the most economically significant deregulatory actions for energy" currently underway. This aligns with the Trump administration's stated priorities to support coal and extractive industries; it also follows ongoing efforts to weaken environmental and public health standards to benefit these interests by weakening EPA rules on mercury pollution and supporting the successful nullification of the Department of the Interior's Stream Protection Rule under the Congressional Review Act.

The New Rule Leaves States Holding the Bag

Instead of empowering states, the proposed rule appears to be an end run to gut environmental protections at all levels of government.

By removing federal oversight of clean water in many areas, the proposed rule punts a significant amount of responsibility to individual states, many of which are under-resourced and legally unprepared to take on permitting and enforcement. In fact, fewer than half of states have their own permitting programs for protecting wetlands, with many of the remaining states relying on federal standards or joint programs with the Army Corps of Engineers for monitoring and enforcement. Even where these programs exist, it is not guaranteed that states will have the staff capacity to ensure that similar levels of protection are maintained. A 2015 survey by the Association of State Wetland Managers finds that only 10 states have more than 20 staff members devoted to wetlands-related regulatory or monitoring work.

States' lack of staff and funding to regulate water quality, combined with the Trump administration walking away from its responsibilities, means that it simply won't get done—and that communities will be left vulnerable to water pollution. The Trump administration's redefinition of WOTUS is part of a broader effort to eliminate large portions of the EPA's historical responsibilities, ostensibly handing them off to state and local agencies. However, the administration's talking points run counter to the decadeslong history of federal-state cooperation that has improved water quality across the country.

The New Rule Hamstrings Private Investment in Conservation Innovation

The rollback of federal protections also threatens to undercut some of the most successful examples of using market-based tools to improve environmental quality. Mitigation—the restoration or improvement of habitats to compensate for the impacts of development—was pioneered under the Clean Water Act to address the effects of infrastructure on wetlands and streams.

The mitigation banking system has boomed in the past decade. It grants private businesses credits for investing in restoration; businesses can then sell these credits to developers who need to compensate for the impacts of development. More effective than requiring developers to oversee on-site restoration projects, the mitigation banking industry now dominates the emerging restoration economy—a sector that employs 126,000 people and generates $9.5 billion annually. More than 1,800 banks are approved to sell credits for wetland and stream restoration, and the practice has cut permitting times in half for development projects.

Because the proposed rule cuts 50 percent of wetlands and nearly 20 percent of stream and river miles from consideration under the Clean Water Act, the mitigation banking industry would face severe uncertainty if the rule were to be finalized. As discussed above, states are unlikely to fill the gap in protections that the proposed rule creates, so the change would effectively eliminate a large portion of the demand for the mitigation credits that fuel the industry. Turning off the tap for private investment in conservation is bad for business. Mitigation banks often invest in conservation easements and restoration projects years before any credits are approved for sale, so the proposed new rule would negate significant investments in bodies of water that are no longer regulated.

Conclusion

Despite the administration's claims, the proposed Waters of the United States rule would not simplify the regulatory process or provide any clarity for farmers. Instead, it appears to be a giveaway to the mining industry that would hamstring efforts to effectively protect the nation's waters from pollution and would place an undue burden on states. The new rule would also stifle the booming restoration economy and limit safeguards for some of the most toxic forms of development. Congress should press the EPA and the U.S. Army Corps of Engineers to ensure that the rule reflects the best science—and it should hold the administration accountable for this blatant attempt to give handouts to favor big polluters at the expense of public health.

Print Citations

CMS: Richards, Ryan. "Debunking the Trump Administration's New Water Rule." In *The Reference Shelf: National Debate 2021-2022: Water Resources,* edited by Micah L. Issitt, 100-103. Amenia, NY: Grey House Publishing, 2021.

MLA: Richards, Ryan. "Debunking the Trump Administration's New Water Rule." *The Reference Shelf: National Debate 2021-2022: Water Resources,* edited by Micah L. Issitt, Grey House Publishing, 2021, pp. 100-103.

APA: Richards, R. (2021). Debunking the Trump administration's new water rule. In Micah L. Issitt (Ed.), *The reference shelf: National debate 2021-2022: Water resources* (pp. 100-103). Amenia, NY: Grey House Publishing.

Three-Eyed Fish and Two-Headed Turtles? The Stench of this River Spanning U.S.- Mexico Border Is Legendary

By Brittny Mejia
LA Times, May 2, 2018

Reporting from Calexico, Calif.—The river is so foul that rumors swirl about two-headed turtles and three-eyed fish. If you fall in, locals joke, you might sprout a third arm.

So go the stories about the New River, whose putrid green water runs like a primordial stew from Mexico's sprawling city of Mexicali through California's Imperial Valley.

The river, with skull-and-crossbone signs warning about the danger it poses, reminds Calexico resident Carlos Fernandez of a scene in *The Simpsons Movie* where Homer Simpson disposes of pig feces by dumping them into a lake.

"That's the river," the 34-year-old said. "I'm surprised there's no glass biodome over us yet."

For decades, government agencies have grappled over what to do about the New River. And while it is cleaner than it once was, it is still such a cesspool of pollution that Imperial Valley residents believe it will never be restored.

Last year, the California Environmental Protection Agency announced an agreement to move forward on a project that will improve water quality in the New River, once designated the most polluted in America.

"It's a historic problem," said Jose Angel, the executive officer with the California Regional Water Quality Control Board Region 7. "No one would like that running through their neighborhood, so why should it run through Calexico?"

There's a 30-foot gap in the border fence separating Mexicali and its American neighbor, Calexico, allowing the river to flow through, and some crossing the border illegally know that the waist-high water is so disgusting that Border Patrol agents won't get in to try to catch them. This year, workers are constructing a 30-foot-tall bollard-style barrier, which could eliminate the gap and cut off access to those trying to cross illegally.

David Kim, a Border Patrol assistant chief patrol agent for the El Centro sector, had to see a doctor after he fell into the river in 2001 while following a group of migrants.

The doctor asked him if the water had gotten in his eyes or mouth and then took a blood sample. A couple of weeks later Kim came back to get blood drawn again to make sure he was OK.

"We don't tell agents they have to get in the water at all, because we know how dirty it is," Kim said.

Fouled with trash and waste, the river flows for 16 miles through Mexicali and then for about 60 miles through the Imperial Valley before emptying into the Salton Sea.

Health guidelines state that fecal coliform bacteria levels in water designated for recreation, estimated using a process called the Most Probable Number (MPN) method, should not exceed a value of 400 MPN per 100 milliliters. In the New River, the fecal coliforms are in the range of 5,000 to 12,000 MPN per 100 milliliters—and that's when the flow from Mexicali isn't at its worst.

The situation has gotten significantly better in the last decade. But the New River has defied a complete makeover.

"Even though we managed to get rid of the raw sewage from Mexicali through implementation of national projects ... the river doesn't meet our standards," Angel said. "It does pose a public health threat to anyone who comes in contact with that water."

The New River was created in 1905 when the flooding Colorado River jumped its banks south of the border and flowed north until it filled what was then known as the Salton Sink and is now the Salton Sea. Because much of the Imperial Valley is below sea level, the New River flows north.

As Mexicali grew as a manufacturing and population center, so did the problems of the river, which has no substantial tributaries, making runoff and sewage outfall its only main sources of water.

About 15 years ago, parts of the river that flowed through Mexicali's metropolitan area were enclosed. The only reminders of the river's existence in the area close to the border is the street's name, Bulevar Río Nuevo, and the above-ground grates from which the stink emanates on broiling days.

Enrique Vallejo has lived in a home along the river in Mexicali since he was 12. Now 51, he can still recall the green tinge to the water and the mosquitoes that swarmed over the waterway in years past. When it would rain, the river would overflow, sending filthy water streaming into his house.

To Vallejo, the river "was a dump."

"We were so grateful when it was covered. It was a huge change," he said.

Across the border, officials are also hoping for a change, after Calexico, Imperial County and the Imperial Irrigation District signed a memorandum of understanding last October regarding maintenance and operation of a New River improvement project.

The project, which has been in the works since 2016, includes installment of a trash screen just downstream from the Mexico border, piping polluted water away from Calexico to wetlands and aeration structures for remediation, as well as replacing polluted water with treated wastewater from the city's treatment plant.

Two years ago, the state Legislature · appropriated $1.4 million to fund the planning, design and environmental review of the project. With the memorandum of understanding in place, the planning and design contract was put out for bid at the end of 2017 and awarded in March. Design and planning is expected to be completed in October.

Fouled with trash and waste, the river flows for 16 miles through Mexicali and then for about 60 miles through the Imperial Valley before emptying into the Salton Sea.

"This agreement marks an important milestone in our efforts to improve the health of the New River," California Secretary for Environmental Protection Matthew Rodriquez said last year.

Martha Fernandez has lived in her home on Calexico Street for 16 years, but first heard about the river when she moved to Calexico in 1980. For a while, she would walk along its banks.

Then, eight years ago, a yellow sign went up across from her house with a warning in Spanish and English between two skull-and-crossbone symbols:

"Contaminated soil and New River water
Keep Out!!"

After the sign appeared, her walks stopped.

Along Calexico's streets near the river, some residents expressed doubt that there would be follow-through on cleaning up the river.

From the backyard of his house on Emilia Drive, Joe Valencia has a view of the New River. Valencia, who has lived in the Imperial Valley for 40 years, knows by now that you don't fish in it.

"I haven't seen anything change in the years I'm growing up," the 47-year-old said. "I have my kids coming up and I don't think they'll even see any change either."

On a recent morning, a Border Patrol agent sat in his green-and-white car, eyes trained on the gap in the fence above the New River. In Mexicali, workers were focused on constructing the new port of entry, while the agent was focused on catching migrants attempting to cross illegally.

Foamy water flowed from the Mexico side and out along the river's banks, which are littered with water bottles, clothing, shoes and butane lighters.

Fish jumped out from the brown water and pigeons and sparrows circled above it, occasionally dropping down to take a drink from the water, where old tires had settled at the bottom. A light breeze made the smell slightly more bearable.

"I've heard of DNA mutations happening to the animals, three-eyed fish and I don't know what else," a trainee at a recent Border Patrol citizen's academy said as he looked into the water, prompting peals of laughter from agents.

"I wouldn't be shocked," Agent Juan Gonzalez responded. "If someone told me they found a three-eyed catfish in there I'd be like, yeah."

"Or a bird that could play guitar," Agent Joel Merino added. "Probably."

The day Agent David Kim fell into the water, he had stepped down onto what he thought was a solid embankment. It turned out to be a crust over the water. He sank down to his knees in water that had the consistency of oil.

"The smell that came up, it smelled like an outhouse," Kim recalled. "Immediately, just that smell started making my stomach turn. I was stuck in my boots, I couldn't move, because it was just so thick around my legs."

Kim lay on his stomach and crawled out. A couple of weeks after he gave his second blood sample, the doctor called to tell him his blood was all clear and that he had not contracted any infectious diseases.

"It has improved a lot," Kim said of the river water. "But when people say it's not as bad as it used to be, it's still really bad."

Agents often spot migrants in the river and warn them that they are in polluted water. In life or death situations—such as when a migrant is drowning—agents have entered the water for rescues.

Kim said he thinks most migrants don't know how dangerous the polluted water is. But he thinks smugglers do—and try to use it to their advantage.

"They know that as long as you stay in this water you're pretty safe—relatively speaking. You're safe from us, from being arrested," Kim said. "But as far as being safe health-wise ... there's no way to know how many people have contracted something from the water that have been in there."

Print Citations

CMS: Mejia, Brittny. "Three-Eyed Fish and Two-Headed Turtles? The Stench of This River Spanning U.S.–Mexico Border Is Legendary." In *The Reference Shelf: National Debate 2021-2022: Water Resources,* edited by Micah L. Issitt, 104-107. Amenia, NY: Grey House Publishing, 2021.

MLA: Mejia, Brittny. "Three-Eyed Fish and Two-Headed Turtles? The Stench of This River Spanning U.S.–Mexico Border Is Legendary." *The Reference Shelf: National Debate 2021-2022: Water Resources,* edited by Micah L. Issitt, Grey House Publishing, 2021, pp. 104-107.

APA: Mejia, B. (2021). Three-eyed fish and two-headed turtles? The stench of this river spanning U.S.–Mexico border is legendary. In Micah L. Issitt (Ed.), *The reference shelf: National debate 2021-2022: Water resources* (pp. 104-107). Amenia, NY: Grey House Publishing.

US States Face Water Crisis as Global Heating Increases Strain on Supplies

By Emily Holden

The Guardian, August 6, 2019

A handful of US states—including New Mexico and California—are facing significant strains on their water supplies that will only intensify with global heating, according to new rankings.

New Mexico tops the list and is the only state with "extremely high" pressures on its water availability. The state's score is on par with the United Arab Emirates in the Middle East and Eritrea in Africa, the World Resources Institute (WRI) found.

California ranks second, followed by Arizona, Colorado and Nebraska.

"We're stretching our water supply pretty much as far as it can go … and even further," said Leah Schleifer, a spokeswoman for WRI's water program.

Experts with WRI said the data shows a global water crisis.

"The picture is alarming in many places around the globe, but it's very important to note that water stress is not destiny," said Betsy Otto, WRI's global water director. "What we can't afford to do any longer is pretend that the situation will resolve itself."

The global research organization compared the water available in aqueducts to the amount withdrawn for homes, industries, irrigation and livestock.

Around the world, stress on water supplies can exacerbate conflict and migration, threaten food supplies and pose risks for water-dependent industries, including mining and manufacturing, WRI notes.

The US overall is not among the world's most at-risk countries, although Mexico ranks No 24. A 2010 study predicted that climate-driven changes in crop yields in Mexico would lead to more emigration to the United States. And the global climate crisis is increasingly being recognized as a major factor in the exodus from Central America to the US.

Worldwide, at the top of the list are Qatar, Israel, Lebanon, the Palestinian Territories and Iran. A total of 17 countries are facing "extremely high" risks and another 27 are facing "high" risks.

Scientists have also linked the violence and civil war in Syria to a drought driven by rising temperatures and massive water withdrawals. In the African Sahel, a semi-arid region that stretches coast to coast across northern Africa below the Sahara, they have documented similar water stresses as millions have migrated out of the countryside.

WRI's experts explained that water stress is different from drought. But places where people are using water at a faster rate than it is replaced could see serious problems if they hit a drought—or a prolonged period without enough rain.

Around the world, stress on water supplies can exacerbate conflict and migration, threaten food supplies and pose risks for water-dependent industries, including mining and manufacturing.

"With respect to climate change we know that in many places what we're going to be seeing is more erratic, more unpredictable hydrology, precipitation. Either too much or too little, often in the same places," Otto said.

The mid-latitudes around the globe are likely to receive less rainfall as temperatures rise. And they will be using more water, as crops draw up more water during dry periods and people use water-dependent electricity to run air conditioners, Otto said.

A recent analysis of 12m wells in the US found that as groundwater supplies are depleted, people and industry are digging deeper. Researchers called the trend an "unsustainable stopgap" that is only available to those who can afford it and where hydrologic conditions allow.

The last widespread drought in the US was in 2012, when more than 80% of the country experienced abnormal dryness or worse, and two-thirds of the country experienced drought, said Brad Rippey, a meteorologist for the agriculture department.

California saw an extended drought with conditions beginning in 2011 and not subsiding across the state until the last couple of years.

The state is expected to see huge population growth at the same time temperatures could be 5F warmer, sea levels keep rising and water from melting snowpack declines, said Joaquin Esquivel, chairman of the California water resources control board.

In the 2010s, drought hit the US islands of Puerto Rico and the Virgin Islands. In 2016 it swept through the north-east. And in 2017 made its way through the northern plains.

Today, south-east Alaska's rainforest is feeling the most intense drought in the country.

World Bank research has emphasized that "while the consequences of drought are often invisible, they are significant and cause 'misery in slow motion.'"

Print Citations

CMS: Holden, Emily. "US States Face Water Crisis as Global Heating Increases Strain on Supplies." In *The Reference Shelf: National Debate 2021-2022: Water Resources,* edited by Micah L. Issitt, 108-110. Amenia, NY: Grey House Publishing, 2021.

MLA: Holden, Emily. "US States Face Water Crisis as Global Heating Increases Strain on Supplies." *The Reference Shelf: National Debate 2021-2022: Water Resources,* edited by Micah L. Issitt, Grey House Publishing, 2021, pp. 108-110.

APA: Holden, E. (2021). US states face water crisis as global heating increases strain on supplies. In Micah L. Issitt (Ed.), *The reference shelf: National debate 2021-2022: Water resources* (pp. 108-110). Amenia, NY: Grey House Publishing.

Countries, Home to One-Quarter of the World's Population, Face Extremely High Water Stress

By Rutger Willem Hofste, Paul Reig, and Leah Schleifer
World Resources Institute, August 6, 2019

Once-unthinkable water crises are becoming commonplace.

Reservoirs in Chennai, India's sixth-largest city, are nearly dry right now. Last year, residents of Cape Town, South Africa narrowly avoided their own "Day Zero" water shut-off. And the year before that, Rome rationed water to conserve scarce resources.

The reasons for these crises go far deeper than drought: Through new hydrological models, WRI found that water withdrawals globally have more than doubled since the 1960s due to growing demand—and they show no signs of slowing down.

New data from WRI's Aqueduct tools reveal that 17 countries—home to one-quarter of the world's population—face "extremely high" levels of baseline water stress, where irrigated agriculture, industries and municipalities withdraw more than 80% of their available supply on average every year. Forty-four countries, home to one-third of the world, face "high" levels of stress, where on average more than 40% of available supply is withdrawn every year. (Check your country's water stress level in the full rankings at the end of this post.) Such a narrow gap between supply and demand leaves countries vulnerable to fluctuations like droughts or increased water withdrawals, which is why we're seeing more and more communities facing their own "Day Zeros" and other crises.

Water Stress Creates Ripple Effects Throughout Societies and Economies

Water stress poses serious threats to human lives, livelihoods and business stability. It's poised to worsen unless countries act: Population growth, socioeconomic development and urbanization are increasing water demands, while climate change can make precipitation and demand more variable.

We're already witnessing some of these impacts play out around the world. . . .

Middle East and North Africa (MENA) Is the Most Water-Stressed Region on Earth

Twelve out of the 17 most water-stressed countries are in the Middle East and North Africa (MENA). The region is hot and dry, so water supply is low to begin with, but growing demands have pushed countries further into extreme stress. Climate change is set to complicate matters further: The World Bank found that this region has the greatest expected economic losses from climate-related water scarcity, estimated at 6-14% of GDP by 2050.

Yet there are untapped opportunities to boost water security in MENA. About 82% of the region's wastewater is not reused; harnessing this resource would generate a new source of clean water. Leaders in treatment and reuse are already emerging: Oman, ranked #16 on our list of water-stressed countries, treats 100% of its collected wastewater and reuses 78% of it.

> **Forty-four countries, home to one-third of the world, face "high" levels of stress, where on average more than 40% of available supply is withdrawn every year.**

About 84% of all wastewater collected in Gulf Cooperation Council countries (Bahrain, Kuwait, Oman, Qatar, Saudi Arabia and the United Arab Emirates) is treated to safe levels, but only 44% goes on to be reused.

India's Water Stress Goes Beyond the Surface

India's water challenges extend beyond current events in Chennai. Last year, the National Institution for Transforming India (NITI Aayog), a government research agency, declared that the country is "suffering from the worst water crisis in its history, and millions of lives and livelihoods are under threat." Aqueduct's findings put this crisis in context: India ranks 13th for overall water stress and has more than three times the population of the other 17 extremely highly stressed countries combined.

The new Aqueduct data includes both surface and groundwater stress for the first time. In addition to rivers, lakes and streams, India's groundwater resources are severely overdrawn, largely to provide water for irrigation. Groundwater tables in some northern aquifers declined at a rate of more than 8 centimeters per year from 1990-2014.

India is starting to take critical steps to mitigate water stress, including setting up the Jal Shakti Ministry to prioritize all water issues—including supply, drinking water and sanitation—under one national government umbrella. Other solutions the country could pursue include more efficient irrigation; conserving and restoring lakes, floodplains, and groundwater recharge areas; and collecting and storing rainwater.

Pockets of Extreme Water Stress Exist Even in Countries with Low Overall Water Stress

While it's helpful for policymakers to understand and take action on water stress at the national level, water is an inherently local issue. That's why in addition to ranking countries' water stress, Aqueduct includes data at the sub-national and sub-watershed levels.

It's clear that even in countries with low overall water stress, communities may still be experiencing extremely stressed conditions. For example, South Africa and the United States rank #48 and #71 on WRI's list, respectively, yet the Western Cape (the state home to Cape Town) and New Mexico experience extremely high stress levels. The populations in these two states rival those of entire nations on the list of most water-stressed countries.

Water Stress Is Not Your Destiny

Water stress is just one dimension of water security. Like any challenge, its outlook depends on management. Even countries with relatively high water stress have effectively secured their water supplies through proper management.

Saudi Arabia, ranked #8 for water stress, prices water to incentivize conservation. Its new Qatrah ("droplet" in Arabic) program sets water conservation targets and aims to reduce water usage 43% within the next decade. Namibia, one of the most arid countries in the world, has been turning sewage water into drinking water for the past 50 years. And Australia nearly halved domestic water use to avert its own Day Zero moment during the Millennium Drought. The country's water-trading scheme, the largest in the world, allows for smart allocation of water among users in the face of variable supplies.

Why Rank Water Stress in Countries and States?

Water does not follow boundaries set by humans—rivers run across countries, and a flood may only affect a few city blocks. For this reason, most water-related information is collected at a watershed or sub-watershed scale. Yet the policy decisions required to reverse water stress—like setting withdrawal caps, encouraging wastewater treatment and establishing pricing schemes—primarily take place at an administrative scale, such as at a country, state or provincial level.

Data broken down by watershed is more useful to a scientist than a member of parliament. This presents a challenge for decision-makers keen to inform policy with the best available data on water risks. To aid with this process, WRI produces national and sub-national estimates of water stress, drought and flood risks that can help decision-makers better understand exposure to water challenges.

3 Ways to Reduce Water Stress

In any geography, water stress can be reduced by measures ranging from common sense to cutting-edge. There are countless solutions, but here are three of the most straightforward:

1. Increase agricultural efficiency: The world needs to make every drop of water go further in its food systems. Farmers can use seeds that require less water and improve their irrigation techniques by using precision watering rather than flooding their fields. Financiers can provide capital for water productivity investments, while engineers can develop technologies that improve efficiency in agriculture. And consumers can reduce food loss and waste, which uses one-quarter of all agricultural water.

2. Invest in grey and green infrastructure: Aqueduct's new data shows that water stress can vary tremendously over the year. WRI and the World Bank's research shows that built infrastructure (like pipes and treatment plants) and green infrastructure (like wetlands and healthy watersheds) can work in tandem to tackle issues of both water supply and water quality.

3. Treat, reuse and recycle: We need to stop thinking of wastewater as waste. Treating and reusing it creates a "new" water source. There are also useful resources in wastewater that can be harvested to help lower water treatment costs. For example, plants in Xiangyang, China and Washington, D.C. reuse or sell the energy- and nutrient-rich byproducts captured during wastewater treatment.

The data is clear: There are undeniably worrying trends in water. But by taking action now and investing in better management, we can solve water issues for the good of people, economies and the planet.

Print Citations

CMS: Hofste, Rutger Willem, Paul Reig, and Leah Schleifer. "Countries, Home to One-Quarter of the World's Population, Face Extremely High Water Stress." In *The Reference Shelf: National Debate 2021-2022: Water Resources,* edited by Micah L. Issitt, 111-114. Amenia, NY: Grey House Publishing, 2021.

MLA: Hofste, Rutger Willem, Paul Reig, and Leah Schleifer. "Countries, Home to One-Quarter of the World's Population, Face Extremely High Water Stress." *The Reference Shelf: National Debate 2021-2022: Water Resources,* edited by Micah L. Issitt, Grey House Publishing, 2021, pp. 111-114.

APA: Hofste, R. W., Reig, P., & Schleifer, L. (2021). Countries, home to one-quarter of the world's population, face extremely high water stress. In Micah L. Issitt (Ed.), *The reference shelf: National debate 2021-2022: Water resources* (pp. 111-114). Amenia, NY: Grey House Publishing.

4
Finding Solutions

By U.S. Geological Survey, Office of Water Quality.

A river polluted by sediment.

Solutions and Strategies

America's water crisis has many dimensions. From industrial pollution to climate change and the increasing frequency of natural disasters, citizens and organizations focused on environmental protection and remediation face a growing list of challenges. But there are many people working on innovative solutions. Solutions to the nation's water crises sometimes involve governmental investment and, at other times, call on community and local efforts or on technological innovation.

Governmental and Private Innovation

It is virtually impossible to protect the nation's water resources utilizing only local solutions because the nation's waterways and watersheds are all connected. Pollution in any region has the potential to impact the entire nation as pollutants move through watersheds and waterways, and eventually into the ocean. Combating water pollution has long been a battle between those concerned about water quality and public health and those who seek to avoid or curtail environmental regulations because of excessive costs. Prior to the 1972 Clean Water Act (CWA), politicians and lobbyists in many states derailed efforts to establish stronger water conservation standards. In a number of states, corporations continued to dump pollutants directly into rivers, lakes, or into the ocean, posing a serious threat to animal and plant life across the nation. The 1972 amendments of the CWA provided a national framework for water conservation, and this meant stronger controls on corporate activities that might impact water systems.

Since the CWA was passed, with widespread bi-partisan and public support, hundreds of streams, lakes, rivers, and watersheds have been improved with cleanup and anti-pollution efforts. A study published in the *Proceedings of the National Academy of Sciences* indicated that water quality had improved across the United States since the establishment of the CWA. However, the research team also noted that the cost of environmental protection and remediation remained high compared to achievement, providing one of the primary counterpoints used to argue against the CWA by corporate lobbyists and allied politicians.[1]

Some activists have been pushing for updates to the CWA or for other amendments to strengthen regulations on water preservation, while others are lobbying the central government to amend regulations so as to reduce the burden on businesses. The Donald Trump administration deemphasized environmental protection and weakened both the Clean Water and Clean Air Acts. President Joe Biden's administration reversed many of these changes, but it remains to be seen whether the Biden administration will introduce any innovation into federal efforts to preserve water resources.

Opponents of regulation argue that free market forces can best combat pollution and water quality issues. This philosophy says that consumers can put pressure on corporations by supporting corporations whose practices reflect their interests. The corporations can then reinvest profits to reduce the environmental impact of their activities or to support other forms of environmental improvement. A number of corporations have committed to certain environmental goals, such as the Coca-Cola Company, which supports a watershed restoration program that replenishes an equivalent amount of water each year to what the corporation uses in producing its products. A number of corporations with connections to California, a state coping with both pollution and water shortages, joined together to form a foundation that supports legislation on sustainability in water management.[2]

While corporate involvement in sustainability and preservation programs may be seen as a welcome addition to the broader goal of preserving water resources, corporations involved in these efforts have limited commitment because activities undertaken by many of those same corporations directly contribute to water safety and quality issues. Coca-Cola, for instance, packages its produces in plastic, which contributes to plastic pollution in rivers and streams, and therefore contributes to the growing problem of "microplastics," tiny fragments of plastic that have been found throughout earth's ecosystems and that greatly damage aquatic life and also threaten human health. Thus, while the corporate approach can provide significant benefits, corporations have a conflict of interest in protecting their profit, rather than to working toward common welfare, and thus many feel that corporate involvement in water preservation cannot supplant the need for oversight and regulation in the public interest.[3]

Economically, while the cost of maintaining and preserving water is considerable, studies indicate that, with sufficient investment, it is possible to guarantee water quality for all Americans while also preserving watersheds and waterways to ensure that clean water remains available. Meanwhile, the cost of poor water quality is also significant. The World Bank estimates that disease outbreaks, loss of productivity, and other problems associated with pollution and water quality issues costs billions in lost revenues around the world. Further, states facing limitations on the availability of water, or safe drinking water, are less able to expand and grow, because access to water is a prime component in economic growth.

One of the biggest challenges in combating water pollution and protecting water quality is updating municipal infrastructure for water management. Not only is this an essential aspect of preserving resources, but is also one of the most contentious. While polls indicate widespread support for efforts to improve or protect water resources in the general sense, residents of communities may be less sanguine when it comes to direct tax expenditures and less supportive when it comes to support long-term municipal projects that might strain local resources and/or inconvenience their lives. It can therefore be difficult for municipalities to build support for local initiatives in specific. As of 2021, it is unclear how America will cope with the pressing need for infrastructural repair, but experts in the field have warned that the nation's deteriorating infrastructure is among the nation's most pressing problems and that Americans in many communities will face an increasing threat of sewage and pollution problems in the future if some method cannot be found to engage in significant and widespread reform of the nation's sewage and water management systems.

Technology and Opportunity

When it comes to preserving water sources, beyond the debates over regulation and private investment, there is the possibility that new technological innovations may be useful in preserving remaining waterways and preventing pollution. While there are many technological innovations in development or being used to combat water resource issues, not all of these solutions are equally advantageous. There are, for instance, a number of companies currently working on methods to "desalinate" ocean water, which would then make more of the world's oceanic water resources available for uses that require freshwater. Desalination is utilized in parts of Africa and in the Middle East and can provide a solution in regions where water scarcity is a perennial problem. There are companies currently working on large=scale desalination programs that would be better able to provide large quantities of drinking or irrigation water for communities facing water shortages, but ultimately this is a set of solutions designed to combat desertification and water scarcity, but that may otherwise be counterproductive. Research indicates that desalination is costly, wasteful, and produces toxic byproducts that will ultimately contribute to water safety issues in many of the communities in which this process is being implemented.[4]

There are other solutions that have fewer complications and that, if implemented, could greatly transform efforts to preserve water without creating new problems. For instance, irrigation systems utilized in many farms and commercial agricultural companies are inefficient. Newer methods of irrigating and providing water for crop growth could reduce the use of freshwater for agriculture by as much as 25 percent. This could result in massive improvements to water preservation efforts as nearly 40 percent of all freshwater used in the United States is used for agriculture. Another potential solution in areas where water shortages are the key problem might be to "recycle" wastewater to meet certain needs. In California, a number of cities have been introducing a process to introduce a certain percentage of recycled wastewater into supplies used for agriculture, irrigation, dust control, and cooling industrial facilities.[5]

While some states are using recycled water for nonpotable uses, there are processes that can be used to clean and process wastewater that will make that water safe for consumption. Probably the biggest impediment to such an effort is that citizens may be unwilling to trust the quality of water than had once been polluted with excrement and other waste. Writing in *Nature*, Ceclia Tortajada and Pierre van Rensburg argue that "There is no room for squeamishness in the face of the world's growing water shortage." The authors demonstrate that sensationalized media coverage validates incorrect ideas about the use of recycled water that discourages consumption, even as the recycling of water is the best current solution to water shortages in many parts of the world.[6]

It is possible, also, that wastewater may find other industrial and commercial uses as well. There have been efforts to utilize wastewater to manufacture biogas, thus reducing the amount of freshwater consumed for this purpose and creating a new industrial use for wastewater that could increase profits within the industry. Even more innovative solutions are also on the horizon, such as system developed by Ohio University Professor Russ Gerardine, who has pioneered a method for removing hydrogen from ammonia and urea present in urine and then was able to use this extracted hydrogen to power a small fuel cell. In areas where large amounts of urine are collected, such as in sports stadiums, airports, or facilities housing large populations of workers, extracted hydrogen could be used to provide a portion of the electrical energy consumed by that building or facility. While an innovation like this does not necessary result in saving water, such solutions provide a way to recycle waste and so provide extra economic benefit to the processes already needed to collect and process liquid waste.[7]

One of the benefits to federal investment in water quality is that it provides revenues for startup and individuals interested in water conservation or protection. Back in 2009, research firm McKinsey published a quarterly report arguing that there were significant business opportunities in the realm of water purification, preservation, and in developing new technology to meet water resource goals. McKinsey researchers noted that there were likely to be developing business opportunities in water treatment and in the distribution of treated water. Efficiency research and improvement was another arena in which McKinsey's researchers saw expanding opportunities moving forward. Further, green and sustainable agriculture and equipment to facilitate sustainable agriculture was another arena in which growth led to new opportunities for profit.[8] Likewise, a more recent (2015) article from *Tech Crunch* looked at how a new group of "water startups" in California capitalized over the state's dwindling water supplies by offering water delivery, preservation, and processing. *Tech Crunch* reporters noted that the water industry itself is worth more than $600 billion in annual revenues, and that concern about water scarcity and quality is increasing, thus providing more interest in water management and pollution solutions for companies.[9]

Community Engagement

Access to water isn't only about sourcing and distributing an essential and valuable resource, it's also a matter of improving and sustaining communities and cultures. Humanity has long chosen to establish communities near waterways and watersheds, both for convenience and pleasure. While water is necessary for life and hygiene, both natural sources of water and supplied water also provide many recreational and emotional benefits for communities. From fishing to canoeing to swimming pools, water is a significant feature in many people's lives that provides pleasure as well as serving as an irreplaceable resource. The effort to protect and preserve water can also anchor a community and can bring people together to work on shared goals.

There are many examples from countries around the world of members of local communities working together to clean rivers and streams and engaging in other projects to provide or distribute water or to otherwise help to preserve local resources. Further, such efforts do not need to be entirely community funded. The U.S. Environmental Protection Agency (EPA), through the CWA provides small grants and limited assistance for community efforts to improve water quality. A local community program in the Greater Boston area, for instance, succeeded thanks to a small grant from the EPA that was used to purchase monitoring equipment and eventually grew to include a variety of local and national partners who have donated in the effort to restore the city's "Big River," which has been devastated by pollution over past decades.[10] With sufficient effort, small-scale community projects can attract powerful partners and federal investment, which can transform a local effort into something transformative.

Works Used

"The Business Opportunity in Water Conservation." *McKinsey Quarterly*. Dec 1, 2009. https://www.mckinsey.com/business-functions/sustainability/our-insights/the-business-opportunity-in-water-conservation.

"How Technology Is Providing Solutions for Clean Water." *Ohio University*. Mar 2, 2021. Retrieved from https://onlinemasters.ohio.edu/blog/how-technology-is-providing-solutions-for-clean-water/.

James, Kirsten. "Report: How the Biggest Companies Score on Water Sustainability." *Water Deeply*. The New Humanitarian. Mar 22, 2018. Retrieved from https://deeply.thenewhumanitarian.org/water/community/2018/03/22/report-how-the-biggest-companies-score-on-water-sustainability,

Manke, Kara. "Clean Water Act Dramatically Cut Pollution in U.S. Waterways." *Berkeley News*. Oct 8, 2018. https://news.berkeley.edu/2018/10/08/clean-water-act-dramatically-cut-pollution-in-u-s-waterways/.

Pechet, Tamin. "Turning Water Problems into Business Opportunities." *Tech Crunch*. Jun 22, 2015. https://techcrunch.com/2015/06/22/turning-water-problems-into-business-opportunities/.

Simon, Matt. "Desalination Is Booming: But What About All That Toxic Brine?" *Wired*. Jan 14, 2019. https://www.wired.com/story/desalination-is-booming-but-what-about-all-that-toxic-brine/.

Tortajada, Cecilia, and Pierre van Rensburg. "Drink More Recycled Wastewater." *Nature*. Dec 31, 2019. https://www.nature.com/articles/d41586-019-03913-6.

"Water." *World Bank*. Understanding Poverty. Mar 01, 2021. https://www.worldbank.org/en/topic/water/overview.

"Water Recycling." *CASA*. California Association of Sanitation Agencies. 2021. https://casaweb.org/renewable-resources/water-recycling/.

"What Communities Are Doing." *EPA*. Urban Waters. Aug 11, 2020. https://www.epa.gov/urbanwaters/what-communities-are-doing.

Notes

1. Manke, "Clean Water Act Dramatically Cut Pollution in U.S. Waterways."
2. James, "Report: How the Biggest Companies Score on Water Sustainability."
3. "Water," *World Bank*.
4. Simon, "Desalination Is Booming: But What About All That Toxic Brine?"
5. "Water Recycling," *CASA*.
6. Torgajada and van Rensburg, "Drink More Recycled Wastewater."
7. "How Technology Is Providing Solutions for Clean Water," *Ohio University*.
8. "The Business Opportunity in Water Conservation," *McKinsey Quarterly*.
9. Pechet, "Turning Water Problems into Business Opportunities."
10. "What Communities Are Doing," *EPA*.

Our Cities' Water Systems Are Becoming Obsolete: What Will Replace Them?

By Brad Plumer
Vox, December 19, 2014

Most of us in the United States don't give much thought to our drinking water. When we turn on our faucets, clean drinking water comes out. When we flush our toilets, the waste goes away. Simple, right?

But as David Sedlak explains in his fascinating book, *Water 4.0: The Past, Present, and Future of the World's Most Vital Resource*, nothing about water has ever been simple. The urban water systems we rely on so heavily were developed in response to three major crises stretching back centuries—from water shortages in the Roman Empire to cholera outbreaks in the Industrial Revolution to polluted lakes in the United States in the 1970s.

And now, Sedlak writes, we're about to face a fourth major water crisis—"as continued population growth and climate change stretch the ability of urban water systems to meet our needs."

During past crises, engineers came up with ingenious technical fixes. The Romans perfected systems for bringing freshwater from faraway sources to crowded cities. In the 19th and 20th centuries, Europe and the United States developed water-treatment methods—sand filtration and chlorination—to clean up drinking water so that it didn't make people sick. And, in the 1970s, the US enacted the Clean Water Act to fund waste-treatment plants, so that we were no longer choking our lakes, rivers, and streams with raw sewage.

Those fixes worked well. But now cities are facing a fresh round of problems—in need of further, drastic fixes. Many of the pipes and sewage-treatment plants we've built will soon reach the end of their lifespans and require big, costly upgrades. In the Northeast, cities have grown so large that sewage systems are struggling to rein in overflow during big storms. And in the Southwest, cities like Phoenix and Las Vegas are grappling with a lack of water—a problem that will become more dire if global warming makes drought more common.

I talked to Sedlak in October about his book and how our water systems will have to change in the future. There's no one single technology that will fix all of our water woes, he says. Some cities will simply have to plunk down billions to update their aging pipes and plants—although many will try to postpone fixes for as long as possible. "Historically, we've always been reluctant to spend money on water systems

> **"Historically, we've always been reluctant to spend money on water systems until a real crisis comes along."**

until a real crisis comes along," Sedlak says. "And we're starting to enter one of those periods."

Meanwhile, better conservation can help water-stressed cities—but only up to a point. Many cities in the Southwest may have to look to new technologies, such as water recycling, desalination, or even radically decentralized water systems. Some of these technologies have drawbacks (desalination uses an enormous amount of energy, for one), but they could become more common in the years ahead.

Sedlak is the co-director of the Berkeley Water Center, and the director of the Institute for Environmental and Science and Engineering at the University of California, Berkeley. A lightly edited transcript of our interview is below.

How Water Systems Evolved: From the Romans to the 1970s

To understand why our current water systems are entering a new crisis era, it's worth going back and understanding how we got here. "I like to describe the history of urban water systems as a series of three big revolutions," Sedlak says. "Water systems tend to remain static for long periods of time, and it's only when the system is under stress that people decide to allocate the resources necessary to bring about a change."

Water 1.0—bringing drinking water to cities. "The first of these water revolutions, I credit to the Romans and call it 'Water 1.0,'" he begins. "Rome was a very large city, anywhere from 500,000 to 1 million people at its height, and it was impossible to provide everyone there drinking water from the Tiber River and local groundwater sources alone. So the Romans brought in water from the nearby countryside—the system that included those famous Roman aqueducts. And because the Romans were so wealthy and had such sophisticated engineering, they were able to provide their citizens something like 100 gallons per person per day—which is comparable to what we provide in modern cities."

"That system of bringing in imported water via a gravity-fed system, distributing it around the city, and then ultimately disposing of it through an underground sewer network, really laid the ground for the next 1,900 years of urban water."

Water 2.0—water treatment. "Water 1.0 was a great idea, and made it possible for people to have large quantities of inexpensive water come into their homes. But it then led to a new problem in the modern age. Steam engines and water wheels allowed us to pressurize water and deliver it to the home, which led to inventions like the toilet and shower. We were using so much water that it had to go somewhere."

"Before, human waste could go into night-soil buckets and it would get taken to the countryside [for use as fertilizer]. But now we were putting human waste into water and putting it in the sewer, and if you lived downstream from a city that was doing this, this was contaminating your drinking water supply. So in the 19th century and early 20th century, it was commonplace to have waterborne disease outbreaks like cholera and typhoid fever."

"Many cities dealt with this problem by bringing in water from places that weren't contaminated. But there was one city that couldn't do this—Lawrence, Massachusetts, which was downstream from the textile manufacturing city of Lowell. Wastewater from Lowell was contaminating the Merrimack, but Lawrence had no other alternative. So [in the 1880s] they turned to engineers at MIT, who came up with the simple idea of filtering water through sand as a way of removing typhoid fever bacteria. That was later coupled with chlorination of water and basically solved the problem of waterborne disease outbreaks."

"I call that Water 2.0, because it really was a revolution. That technology extended the lifespan of the average American by something like 15 years. The National Academy of Engineering ranked drinking-water treatment right up there with electricity and air travel as the biggest innovations of the 20th century."

Water 3.0—paying for sewage treatment. "But there was still a problem. We were still putting more sewage into our rivers and lakes. And even though we could still pull out clean drinking water from those polluted sources, that sewage was causing ecological damage. Between the 1920s and the 1970s, our rivers and lakes and estuaries really got degraded—there were discussions of the Great Lakes dying, the waterfronts of big cities reeked from sewage going directly into the river. You had fish kills, algae blooms."

"Now, we actually had the technology to treat sewage—this was perfected between the 1920s and 1940s. But cities didn't want to pay for them. It wasn't until the late 1960s and early 1970s that the public got concerned about environmental problems and Congress passed the Clean Water Act, which created a federal system for underwriting the cost of sewage-treatment plants. For a 20-year period, starting in 1972, the federal government paid up to 75 percent of the cost of building sewage treatment plants. And we largely made these polluted rivers and lakes, once again fishable, swimmable, and in many cases drinkable. That was water 3.0."

Now Our Urban Water Systems Are Starting to Break Down

So what are the biggest problems facing water systems today? "I would categorize the stresses on our modern water infrastructure into three groups," says Sedlak.

(1) Our water infrastructure needs costly upgrades: "First, when we built all this water infrastructure, we didn't think hard enough about creating a system to fund its upkeep, maintenance, and replacement. We had a federal grant system to build these treatment plants, but needed to set aside money to rebuild them."

"So now we're entering a period where many of the water pipes and treatment plants built throughout the 20th century are falling apart and need to be replaced at almost the exact same time. This puts a tremendous financial strain on our water utilities, and they're really limited on how much they can raise our water rates, because no one likes their water bill going up."

(2) Many sewer systems are becoming overloaded: "The second strain I see on our urban water systems is particularly relevant in places with a lot of rain and

snow—the Northeast and the Midwest and even the Pacific Northwest. Many of these cities built what are known as 'combined sewer systems,' where all of the storm runoff gets routed through the sewage treatment plant."

"But as cities have grown and we haven't kept up with increasing the size of pipe network, there's a tremendous need to upgrade our systems to handle that large volume of water that comes in every time it rains. Cities like Indianapolis and Philadelphia and Seattle are struggling to spend hundreds of millions of dollars or billions to upgrade their systems to prevent raw sewage from leaking out of the treatment plants during large storms."

(3) Water scarcity in drought-prone areas: "The third stress on urban water systems is more relevant in places where we don't have enough water. That would be the West and Southwest and increasingly the Southeast of the United States."

"In these areas we see tremendous population growth. Ten of the country's 20 largest metropolitan areas are located in the South or West in areas where there's just not enough water supply. And our conservation efforts are starting to reach their limits. We're also realizing that some of these regions are most prone to climate change. So we see drought in California, drought in Texas, until recently the drought in the Colorado River basin, and that has sparked real concerns about providing cities in this region with enough water in the future."

Climate change will make this all harder. "The most recent global climate models suggest that the wet places will get wetter and the dry places will get drier. And that's exactly the wrong thing for the water infrastructure that we have. Cities in the North and Northeast that are struggling with combined sewer overflows can expect more big storms and stress on their systems. And cities in the South and Southwest can expect longer drought periods and higher water demand as temperature gets higher."

Cities Are Already Struggling to Deal with These Crises

"The situation that many utilities find themselves in could be described as 'muddle on in the best way possible,'" Sedlak says.

"So, for example, in the case of cities that struggle to dispose of all the storm water that overwhelm their sewage treatment plants, many cities are building gigantic pipe networks to intercept rainwater and hold it underground temporarily so it doesn't overwhelm the treatment plants when it rains. In those cities you see increases in people's water bills. But it's difficult to do this—people tend to notice anytime their water bill goes up faster than inflation."

Meanwhile, in the Southwest, many cities have been pushing for conservation measures to save water—but even those have limits. "When you look at where water goes in the western United States," Sedlak says, "almost half of the water that comes to our cities that are grappling with water-supply problems goes outdoors to lawns. So the logical thing is to try to discourage people who live in arid climates from having green lawns—or at least encourage more appropriate landscaping."

But this is easier said than done. "Simply raising someone's water rates is hard because there are poor people in the community who struggle to pay their water bills. So you can try to come up with system that penalizes people for high water use. But it takes more than a $50 or $100 month water bill to get someone with a lush green lawn to change their behavior."

"The other strategy available to utilities is more of a carrot approach—that is, to provide people with incentives for replacing their lawns with desert-friendly plants. But that requires a fair amount of effort and community outreach to do."

Possible Fixes: Water Recycling, Desalination, Decentralization

In his book, Sedlak makes clear that we still don't know exactly how cities will deal with all of the water crises they're now facing—from overflows in the Northeast to drought in the Southwest. But he explores a number of nascent technologies that might play a much bigger role:

Water recycling: "We now have the ability to recycle water within cities," Sedlak says. "And that idea of taking our wastewater and using it again in a centralized fashion is really revolutionary. It extends our water supply with a source of water that is largely resistant to drought."

"The first generation of water reuse focused on taking wastewater effluent for industrial purposes—like water for cooling towers or oil refineries or using the water for landscape irrigation and agriculture. Those approaches are well established. But the forefront of water reuse is today is treating that water to a point where it can be introduced back into the drinking water supply."

This isn't *quite* as novel as it sounds. "When we look at southern California, there are a number of cities that have engaged in this practice for decades," Sedlak says. "They take the wastewater effluent, they subject it to reverse osmosis, then treat it with another oxidation process. And that water is so clean that it's hard to distinguish it from a distilled water that you would buy at the store. They then put it back in the aquifer."

"The real direction this is going is a practice called direct potable reuse—where people take wastewater and treat it and put it *directly* into a drinking water treatment plant. And that's already starting to happen. We have a couple of projects in Texas starting to deliver water this way, in Odessa and Midland. There's one in a town called Big Spring."

Desalination: Many people still think of desalinating sewater as something that's too costly to work. Not so, explains Sedlak. "Seawater desalination has undergone tremendous technological advances just in the past decade. When Australia struggled with their millennial drought or when Israel and Spain have grappled with their water supply needs, seawater desalination was a major part of solution."

Unfortunately, this solution also comes with drawbacks. "There are lots of concerns over energy consumption and greenhouse-gas emissions and the possible damage that desalination plants can cause to the aquatic environment. I think the ecological damage from desalination has largely been addressed through projects in Australia. But it's really this concern about energy consumption that is slowing down desalination's movement in the western United States."

"Still, there's a big desalination plant, a 50-million-gallon a day plant being built in Carlsbad, just north of San Diego and there's a large seawater desalination operating in Tampa. So there are examples, and the jury's out on whether it will become more widespread."

Decentralization: Many cities currently have centralized water systems—all the water comes from one big water treatment plant, and all the waste goes to one big sewage-treatment plant. But as water becomes scarce in areas and older systems come under strain, more places may decide to decentralize their systems.

"In North America, remember, most people live in suburbs," Sedlak says. "So we have the potential to build our water infrastructure in a distributed fashion. We might build a small wastewater treatment plant for a small neighborhood, and use that water for local landscape irrigation—or even recycle it for drinking water—instead of sending that water all the way back to a centralized treatment plant many miles away and then pumping it back to the community. That would give us tremendous potential for saving energy and avoiding the need to maintain and operate a large underground networks of pipes.

So What's Standing in the Way of "Water 4.0"?

"The first obstacle is that people don't want to spend the money until there's a crisis," Sedlak says. "It's only once crises occur, people to start investing money very quickly. We see that with respect to flood control infrastructure in New Orleans and New York City. People had issued warnings that those cities were susceptible to major hurricanes, but we had to wait for those hurricanes to hit."

"Similarly when you look at the questions of drought, or combined sewer overflows or decaying pipes—prior to an emergency, the public's hesitant to make the investment. So the challenge for water engineers is to try to have the right technologies available, so that when society decides it's time for a change, these are the shovel-ready projects that we build. Because if we don't do the demonstration-scale projects and learn about the pros and cons of different approaches, we'll just continue to build more of the same."

I asked Sedlak whether climate change might be more difficult to plan future water systems—since we don't know for sure how future rainfall patterns will change. "I think there's a fair amount of uncertainty in terms of no longer being able to use the historic record to predict rainfall patterns in the future," he says.

"But I also don't think the increased uncertainty should push us to try to make our water systems more robust than they are now. So that if the worst comes to pass, we'll be ready for it. Unlike our cellphones or computers that we replace every four or five years, investments in water infrastructure take decades to plan and are intended to last 40 or 50 or 100 years. So when we make those investments it's important to get it right."

Print Citations

CMS: Plumer, Brad. "Our Cities' Water Systems Are Becoming Obsolete: What Will Replace Them?" In *The Reference Shelf: National Debate 2021-2022: Water Resources,* edited by Micah L. Issitt, 123-129. Amenia, NY: Grey House Publishing, 2021.

MLA: Plumer, Brad. "Our Cities' Water Systems Are Becoming Obsolete: What Will Replace Them?" *The Reference Shelf: National Debate 2021-2022: Water Resources,* edited by Micah L. Issitt, Grey House Publishing, 2021, pp. 123-129.

APA: Plumer, B. (2021). Our cities' water systems are becoming obsolete: What will replace them? In Micah L. Issitt (Ed.), *The reference shelf: National debate 2021-2022: Water resources* (pp. 123-129). Amenia, NY: Grey House Publishing.

It Could Only Cost 1% of GDP to Solve Global Water Crises

By Colin Strong and Samantha Kuzma
World Resources Institute, January 21, 2020

Statistics on global water challenges are daunting: 3 billion people don't have basic handwashing facilities. A quarter of the world's population live in countries facing extremely high water stress. There are more than 500 dead zones—areas of the ocean without enough oxygen for most marine life to survive—from untreated wastewater.

The solutions to the world's water crises, though, cost far less than you might think. New WRI research found that securing water for our societies by 2030 could cost just over 1% of global GDP—about 29 cents per person, per day from 2015-2030.

And the economic benefits outweigh the costs. Every dollar invested in water access and sanitation yields an average $6.80 in returns. The World Bank found that failing to implement better water management policies could result in regional GDP losses from 2-10% by 2050.

What Is Sustainable Water Management?

Sustainable water management is the desired end-state for achieving water security. It consists of six strategies that can ensure access to water and sanitation for all by 2030, including:

- Delivering safely managed drinking water to all populations without access.

- Delivering safely managed sanitation and hygiene services to all populations without access.

- Treating all industrial wastewater to tertiary treatment levels.

- Reducing nutrient loading to acceptable concentrations within water bodies.

- Addressing water scarcity by bringing water withdrawals in line with water demand while accounting for environmental flow rates.

- Adopting water management, regulations and legislation to accompany the above sets of solutions.

While conserving water-related ecosystems is not explicitly addressed in this framework, many of the strategies incorporate aspects of ecosystem protection, such as preserving environmental flows while tackling water scarcity and reducing dead zones by eliminating water pollution.

Sustainable Water Management Can Achieve Water Security for All

The paper analyzed what it could take to achieve a combination of six strategies that, taken together, can provide water security. We've named this desired end-state "sustainable water management." . . . Our definition of sustainable water management matches generally to UN Sustainable Development Goal number six (SDG 6), which calls for "access to water and sanitation for all" by 2030. We calculated the investments needed to tackle each of the six strategies in a given country.

We found that 75 countries can achieve sustainable water management at 2% or less of their annual GDP; 70 countries can get there with 2-8% of GDP; and 17 countries will require more than 8% of their GDP to solve their water problems.

Every country faces different types of water challenges and will need to prioritize different tasks to achieve sustainable water management, such as treating wastewater, delivering clean drinking water, adopting stronger water management policies and investing in vital infrastructure. The relative cost share of each of these tactics varies considerably by country.

In 75 Countries—Including the US and South Africa—Achieving Sustainable Water Management Costs Less than 2% of GDP

For 75 countries representing half the global population, achieving sustainable water management is well within reach, requiring less than 2% of GDP.

In the United States, for example, the estimated cost to deliver sustainable water management is only 0.78% of GDP. The largest investment gap is solving water scarcity, which makes up 67% of the country's costs to achieving "water for all." (Note: this does not include the cost of replacing existing infrastructure, such as pipes, that may have reached the end of its effective life.)

These costs are nothing compared to the damages the country will incur should water scarcity continue. In California, for example, water scarcity and drought fueled the forest fires that caused $24 billion in damages in 2018 and will negatively affect the quality of drinking water for years to come. A forthcoming study by the U.S. Forest Service found that nearly half of river basins that supply water to the United States may not be able to satisfy demands, which could constrain municipal needs, agricultural production and industrial growth.

South Africa's water crisis came under global scrutiny when Cape Town, the nation's second-largest city, narrowly avoided a "Day Zero" water shut-off in 2018. Yet even in the face of severe risks, it could cost less than 2% of South Africa's GDP in 2030 to tackle its water issues. More than half of the costs are associated with providing drinking water and sanitation, while addressing scarcity comprises about 20% of the total cost.

17 Countries Need the Most Help in Solving Water Problems

Seventeen countries, representing 10% of the global population, need more than 8% of their annual GDP to deliver sustainable water management. This is due to both very limited water management and infrastructure and relatively poor economies. These countries will need assistance from development banks and other financing and development organizations if they are to fully solve their water challenges.

Achieving sustainable water management in Mali, for example, could require more than 8% of the country's 2030 GDP. Like many countries in sub-Saharan Africa—including Eritrea, Zimbabwe and Sierra Leone—delivering access to drinking water and sanitation services is the top cost category for Mali, accounting for 58% of total costs. Drinking water and sanitation costs are close-

---

Sustainable water management is the desired end-state for achieving water security.

---

ly connected—countries where clean and accessible drinking water is scarce tend to also have gaps in access to sanitation, and vice versa. Countries with high drinking water and sanitation costs also tend to require much larger percentages of GDP to deliver sustainable water management.

Countries, states and governments around the world should pay attention to, and invest in, water security outside their own boundaries. Water crises cascade beyond national borders: Droughts and water stress can contribute to violent conflict, migration and regional instability. In Mali, violence is already erupting between farmers and pastoralists over increasingly scarce water and land resources. Water shortages can hurt agriculture, raising the prices of staple crops around the world. This can cause poor nutrition, hurt the global economy and further contribute to conflict. For example, droughts in 2010 in Russia, Ukraine, China and Argentina caused spikes in wheat prices, which experts say was one of many driving forces of the Arab Spring.

Achieving Sustainable Water Management in Every Country

We estimated costs using global data, so they should not be taken as precise costs or specific policy recommendations. Effective management of water resources requires a deeper dive into local conditions, taking into consideration national water challenges, localized data and the political landscape. The numbers above should be used as a jumping-off point for further research and an initial screen for the countries that need investment the most.

At a broad level, though, the solutions to water-related challenges are already understood. Reducing our collective thirst through demand-management solutions like efficient irrigation often reduces water scarcity, while maintaining productivity and business viability. Nature-based infrastructure, which harnesses ecosystems like forests and wetlands in tandem with traditional infrastructure like pipes and pumps, has major benefits for both water quantity and quality.

The solutions to the world's water crises are readily available; what's missing is the money (from public and private sectors) and political will needed to implement them. It's time that water solutions be seen not as a burden, but as an opportunity. Resolving the world's shared water challenges improves the lives and livelihoods for billions, benefits the ecosystems around us, and can yield significant returns on investment.

Print Citations

CMS: Strong, Colin, and Samantha Kuzma. "It Could Only Cost 1% of GDP to Solve Global Water Crises." In *The Reference Shelf: National Debate 2021-2022: Water Resources,* edited by Micah L. Issitt, 130-133. Amenia, NY: Grey House Publishing, 2021.

MLA: Strong, Colin, and Samantha Kuzma. "It Could Only Cost 1% of GDP to Solve Global Water Crises." *The Reference Shelf: National Debate 2021-2022: Water Resources,* edited by Micah L. Issitt, Grey House Publishing, 2021, pp. 130-133.

APA: Strong, C., & Kuzma, S. (2021). It could only cost 1% of GDP to solve global water crises. In Micah L. Issitt (Ed.), *The reference shelf: National debate 2021-2022: Water resources* (pp. 130-133). Amenia, NY: Grey House Publishing.

How Monitoring Local Water Supplies Can Build Community

By John M. Carroll

The Conversation, October 17, 2018

Water insecurity is a touchstone for 2018. Our planet isn't running out of water, but various kinds of mismanagement have led to local water crises across the planet, directly threatening millions of people.

Ensuring water quality requires regular testing, protecting source water, monitoring and repairing distribution systems, treatment plants and other infrastructure, and developing the ability to recycle water and desalinate salt water. These activities require many types of specialists. But they can also benefit from the direct participation of engaged citizens, who themselves can also benefit from getting involved with this work.

Most of my career has focused on information sciences and technology. Over the past 40 years, I have investigated cases in which people creatively mastered information and technology that was poorly designed relative to their needs, or applied technology to problems it was not originally designed for, such as strengthening local heritage, community governance or collaborative learning. I have learned that making technology effective often requires the creative engagement of everyone who is affected by it.

Contemporary reports on failing water systems tend to overlook the critical roles that citizens can play in addressing environmental challenges at the local level. Water systems are human-technology interactions. Engaged and informed volunteers who are committed to protecting water quality are as critical to a successful water system as pumps and filters.

Taking Responsibility for Water Systems

In the course of a research project on citizen-initiated health collaborations, I learned that people in my own community in central Pennsylvania were deeply involved in monitoring local water quality. Many Americans probably think of this as a job for state or local government agencies. But it also can be a community engagement activity, much like working at a food bank, driving for Meals on Wheels or building homes with Habitat for Humanity.

This does not mean the work is any less about environmental protection. Rather, it incorporates environmental protection

Water systems are human-technology interactions.

into the core of hyperlocal community work – the actions people take locally to strengthen their communities.

Roughly 100,000 people live in the Spring Creek watershed in central Pennsylvania. Spring Creek is a well-known trout fishery, but the region faces ongoing water quality challenges, including agricultural runoff, stormwater silt and invasive species. It also has legacy pollution sources, including abandoned clay and coal mines and a chemical plant that was a Superfund site in the 1980s. Future challenges include a threat of runoff from Marcellus Shale gas drilling.

Several dozen local groups–including nonprofits, municipal entities and regional water and sewer authorities–carry out a wide variety of water quality testing programs. Each group gathers and organizes its own data sets, but they also coordinate through overlapping memberships, arrangements to share equipment, space, funding and data, and initiatives involving multiple townships and boroughs, which the groups sometimes create themselves.

Spring Creek is a stream in the West Branch of the Susquehanna River watershed. Within this 146-square-mile watershed, there are at least seven springs that each produce more than 1 million gallons per day of clean, cold water. Spring Creek Watershed Atlas, CC BY-ND

Citizen Water Monitoring Connects Communities

Although these groups have only a few hundred members in total, they are involved in many activities. They advise municipalities and the public on watershed issues, such as development proposals. They also coordinate planning among towns, conduct outreach programs at public schools, observe and collect samples at field sites, and interact with testing laboratories and government agencies.

Some groups have developed data sets and analyses that are curated and published online or available by request. They also have produced a community watershed atlas, which explains what the watershed is, how it works and how it serves the people who live in it.

Several groups that mainly collect data consist almost entirely of older adults. For example, members of the Pennsylvania Senior Environmental Corps work in teams of four to six, regularly visiting sites throughout the watershed to measure about 40 data points per site, including water chemistry, stream flow characteristics and counts of macro invertebrates.

Members of Trout Unlimited focus specifically on indicators of healthy fish populations, such as identifying trout spawning nests. This involves regular physical work and social interaction, so the groups coproduce better community and personal health as they protect local water resources.

Trout Unlimited volunteers work to identify high-quality trout streams in Pennsylvania and target them for protection.

There are 350 local nonprofit water quality groups in Pennsylvania alone. These volunteer groups could be seen as a transitional workaround whose work will eventually be replaced by remote sensor networks. But that is a narrow view of what they do for local communities and for people. Automation will not engage citizens in learning about water resources, or provide meaningful and rigorous tasks that motivate them to be active outdoors.

Leveraging Citizen Water Activism More Effectively

These water monitoring initiatives are sustainable and valuable. They are a hyperlocal variety of citizen science—citizens organizing and carrying out water monitoring activities in their own communities.

Their work produces more than data. It strengthens trust and social capital throughout the community, and makes people more aware of local water challenges. It cultivates critical environmental knowledge and skills, and gives volunteers meaningful work.

But it could be even more beneficial. My Penn State colleagues and I are working with citizens in central Pennsylvania to design and develop a community water quality data platform, which would integrate and amplify local groups' and government agencies' diverse data sets, making it easier to visualize and analyze water quality data.

Clean water groups could use this tool to explore scenarios, such as enhancing riparian buffers—planted zones near stream banks—to mitigate impacts from springtime agricultural runoff or summertime thermal pollution episodes. Using data this way could make watershed events and patterns more accessible to residents, and more effective as opportunities for learning and engagement.

This platform could make it easier for citizens to become knowledgeable about water resources, and more generally, about data visualization and analysis and data-driven thinking. We do not think fixing failing water systems should be up to citizens, but we believe it is better for everyone if citizens are informed and engaged about their water supplies. It would be nice to assume that responsible authorities will ensure our water is clean and safe, but examples like the drinking water crisis in Flint, Michigan, show that this is not always true.

In Spring Creek, and probably many other locations, promising local networks like this are hidden in plain sight. Once they are identified, communities can leverage them. And others can work to foster them where they do not yet exist.

Print Citations

CMS: Carroll, John M. "How Monitoring Local Water Supplies Can Build Community." In *The Reference Shelf: National Debate 2021-2022: Water Resources,* edited by Micah L. Issitt, 134-137. Amenia, NY: Grey House Publishing, 2021.

MLA: Carroll, John M. "How Monitoring Local Water Supplies Can Build Community." *The Reference Shelf: National Debate 2021-2022: Water Resources,* edited by Micah L. Issitt, Grey House Publishing, 2021, pp. 134-137.

APA: Carroll, J. M. (2021). How monitoring local water supplies can build community. In Micah L. Issitt (Ed.), *The reference shelf: National debate 2021-2022: Water resources* (pp. 134-137). Amenia, NY: Grey House Publishing.

Could These Five Innovations Help Solve the Global Water Crisis?

By Rosie Spinks
The Guardian, **February 13, 2017**

The global water crisis has many causes, requiring many different solutions. As 1.2 billion people live in areas of water scarcity, these solutions must span policy, technology, and behaviour change to make a real difference.

A number of technological innovations address the crisis in novel ways. We asked two water experts–Vincent Casey, senior water and sanitation adviser at WaterAid, and Hannah Safford, an energy and environmental policy analyst–to assess some of the most creative approaches.

In partnership with nonprofit Water is Life, researchers at Carnegie Mellon University developed this education and filtration tool. Each page of the book provides basic water and sanitation advice, such as the importance of keeping contaminants like rubbish and faeces away from water, often unknown in developing countries. Perhaps more novel is that the advice is printed on "scientific coffee filter" paper that can be used to purify drinking water and reduce 99.9% of bacteria. Each book has enough filtration sheets to provide its reader with clean water for four years. It's being distributed in Ghana, Kenya, Haiti, Ethiopia, India and Tanzania, and a Farsi version of the book is in development.

Casey: Many different filter products will purify water and remove pathogens, but it needs to have a demand from users. It also needs to be affordable [in the local context] or come with some credit mechanism. Filters play a crucial role in making the water safe, but if you're not blocking other routes of transmission (e.g., flies on food, handwashing after toilet use) you will still have problems. In other words, any filter has to be part of a combined solution.

WaterSeer

It looks like a well, but instead of withdrawing groundwater, the WaterSeer uses the surrounding environment to extract water from the atmosphere. It is planted six feet below the surface, where its lower chamber is surrounded by cool earth. Above ground, wind spins a turbine which spins fan blades inside the device. These blades send the air into an internal condensation chamber where, as the warm air cools, the vapour condenses on the sides of the chamber. Water then flows down to the lower chamber and can be extracted with a simple pump and hose. In ideal conditions, it can collect 37 litres of water a day. Developed by VICI labs in the US, the project is being tested by the National Peace Corps Association and will be piloted later this year.

Casey: If we take sub-Saharan Africa as an example, groundwater tends to be available in most places we work–about 20m below the surface. So it's a management or infrastructure problem that prevents people accessing water, not a lack of it. It's not really about fixing the problem with technology; it's about fixing the system. With this example, I would imagine there could be problem with vandalism, as the device seems quite fragile. However, that's not to say that technology is not part of the solution–it has a role, but it's makes up 20% of the whole picture, along with policy and management.

Graphene Filters

Desalination, converting saltwater into freshwater, has historically been too expensive and energy-intensive to serve as a widespread solution for improving access. However, Lockheed Martin has developed and patented a Perforene graphene filter which it claims would reduce the energy cost of conventional reverse osmosis desalination by 20%, while withstanding higher pressure and temperatures. The perforated, hyper-permeable filter is one atom thick and is said to improve the flow of water compared to conventional methods by 500%. While the technology would be hugely beneficial to the oil and gas sector, which reportedly produces 18bn gallons of wastewater each year, the company is also researching other applications for the technology, including in food and energy generation.

> Emphasis should be place on smart water management, reducing water losses, and increasing the uptake of water-efficient technolgies practices.

Safford: Desalination should only be used as a last resort. Emphasis should be placed on smart water management, reducing water losses, and increasing the uptake of water-efficient technologies practices. But in regions where there is truly not enough freshwater to meet demand, a cheaper and less energy-intensive desalination method is certainly a good thing.

Fog Catchers

Vast mesh nets capture moisture from fog, which drips into collection trays after condensation. The largest of these projects is on the slopes of Mount Boutmezguida, a microclimate in Morocco where 6,300 litres of water can be harvested per day. The water is clean, free and instant, which is perhaps why Dar Si Hmad–the nonprofit responsible for the project–as awarded the UN's 2016 Momentum for

Change award. First developed in South America, fog catching systems also exist in Chile, Peru, Ghana, Eritrea, South Africa and California.

Safford: Fog catching could provide a sustainable supply of drinking water for small communities in water-scarce regions, but it is unlikely to generate enough water to significantly increase water supplies. The Mount Boutmezguida project only generates enough water to serve about 160 people per day–a project of a similar size in a developed country would serve a smaller number of people [due to higher consumption habits].

Solar Crop

In hot and dry climates, many farmers pump groundwater to irrigate crops, and there has been a growth in the use of solar-powered pumps. A problem arises when farmers view solar energy as free, as it can cause overirrigation. A part-technological, part policy and management solution by CGIAR's research programme on water, land and ecosystems, and in partnership with the International Water Management Institute (IWMI), incentivises farmers using solar pumps to sell excess power back to the grid. The guaranteed buy-back scheme produces a "triple win"; farmers gain income, the state gains electricity reserves, and the water source is conserved by curbing usage–all while reducing carbon emissions. The scheme is being piloted in Gujarat, and IWMI estimates that solarising India's 20m irrigation wells could reduce carbon emissions by 4-5% per year.

Casey: A good initiative addressing a serious problem through changes to policy and management, not just focusing on a technical solution. In addition, selling electricity back to the grid could generate revenue to conduct maintenance on these pumps–a good sign for the sustainability of the arrangement.

Print Citations

CMS: Spinks, Rosie. "Could These Five Innovations Help Solve the Global Water Crisis?" In *The Reference Shelf: National Debate 2021-2022: Water Resources,* edited by Micah L. Issitt, 138-140. Amenia, NY: Grey House Publishing, 2021.

MLA: Spinks, Rosie. "Could These Five Innovations Help Solve the Global Water Crisis?" *The Reference Shelf: National Debate 2021-2022: Water Resources,* edited by Micah L. Issitt, Grey House Publishing, 2021, pp. 138-140.

APA: Spinks, R. (2021). Could these five innovations help solve the global water crisis? In Micah L. Issitt (Ed.), *The reference shelf: National debate 2021-2022: Water resources* (pp. 138-140). Amenia, NY: Grey House Publishing.

Seagrass a Powerful Ally in the Fight Against Climate Change Says Seychelles-Based Expert

By Matthew Morgan

The PEW Charitable Trusts, **March 1, 2021**

For the last five decades, conservation biologist Jeanne A. Mortimer has traveled the world, researching marine turtles and their habitats—particularly seagrass. In 1981, her passion for sea turtles drew her to migrate to Seychelles, an island nation in the Indian Ocean off the coast of East Africa, where seagrass ecosystems are very important to sea turtle populations and fisheries. Mortimer now coordinates research and conservation projects for seagrass and educates people about its importance as a critical marine habitat—and its value as a nature-based solution in the fight against climate change.

This interview with Mortimer—which took place on one of her favorite occasions, World Seagrass Day—has been edited for clarity and length.

Q: What brought you to Seychelles?

A: I first arrived here 40 years ago to study sea turtle populations. I had just completed my Ph.D. at the University of Florida, where my doctoral research focused on nesting turtles at Ascension Island in the south Atlantic Ocean—and the Government of Seychelles wanted to better understand the status of turtles in their waters. At the time there was both local and international concern that turtles were being overexploited, and the country was keen to move forward with science-based management recommendations.

Q: And that led to your interest in studying seagrass?

A: Green turtles are voracious herbivores in those parts of the world where they feed on seagrass meadows. In fact, during my master's research, I had studied the ecology of green turtles foraging in seagrass meadows along the eastern coast of Nicaragua. At that time, in the mid-1970s, we didn't know whether green turtles were more interested in the seagrass itself or in eating the other organisms found on the seagrass blades. It turns out that the green turtles were in fact focused on eating the young fresh shoots of seagrass, while hawksbill turtles in Seychelles feed on the invertebrate animals and plants growing amongst the seagrasses.

Q: March is seagrass awareness month. So what do you want people to know about seagrass?

A: People need to realize that seagrass has biological, chemical, and physical importance on a grand scale. Seagrass comprises expansive and highly productive ecosystems that provide food and habitat to thousands of animal and plant species, many of which have commercial importance to humans or are endangered. Seagrass meadows physically protect our coastlines from erosion: During heavy storms, seagrass root mats hold tightly to the seafloor, keeping the plants in place. Meanwhile their leaves baffle wave action and currents, causing sediment to settle quickly so it's not transported to locations where it doesn't belong—such as on top of living coral reefs. And through photosynthesis, seagrass removes carbon dioxide (CO_2) from the water and replaces it with oxygen that fish, coral, and other marine animals need to breathe.

Q: So seagrass plays a role in carbon sequestration?

A: Yes, seagrass research has come a long way since the 1970s, and we now know that seagrass efficiently sequesters carbon by storing it in the underlying soil—trapping it there for long periods of time. In fact, scientists estimate that around 10% of the total organic carbon sequestered in the ocean is buried in seagrass beds.

Q: Why is this carbon burial important? And how does it work?

A: We know that the burning of fossil fuels through human activity has increased CO_2 levels in the atmosphere, which promotes climate change. But seagrasses can lock away some of this carbon: As the seagrass sheds leaves or dies, the dead plant material gets trapped in the low-oxygen sediments on the ocean floor, where the carbon is stored for very long periods of time safely away from the atmosphere. So, seagrass meadows are a natural carbon sink—making them important nature-based solutions to climate change.

Q: How are seagrasses faring worldwide?

A: The loss of seagrass ecosystems is accelerating, and some researchers estimate that we've lost 30% of the world's seagrass since scientists first started monitoring seagrass coverage back in 1879. That makes it urgent that we protect seagrass ecosystems.

Q: What about in Seychelles?

A: The human population of Seychelles is right around 100,000, and almost all of them live in the inner islands—where large expanses of seagrass have been lost to coastal reclamation projects, and more such projects are being considered. Mechanical damage caused by boat propellers and trampling, as well as by pollution from sewage outflow and agricultural runoff, pose further threats.

In contrast, most seagrass meadows in the

> **The loss of seagrass ecosystems is accelerating, and some researchers estimate that we've lost 30% of the world's seagrass since scientists first started monitoring seagrass coverage back in 1879.**

outer islands of the archipelago remain in a relatively healthy state. Unfortunately, that doesn't compensate for the damaged seagrass in the inner islands because the species composition of both plants and animals in seagrass meadows in the inner islands differs greatly from that in the outer islands. At least one seagrass species in the inner islands, *Enhalus acoroides*, is on the verge of extinction due to habitat destruction.

Q: Can you say more about current seagrass research?

A: Research underway in Seychelles includes identifying what seagrass species occur, in what density, and over how great an area. During 2021, a seagrass mapping and carbon assessment project will begin in which Seychelles stakeholders, including Island Conservation Society, a local conservation nongovernmental organization; University of Seychelles; and Seychelles Conservation and Climate Adaptation Trust, an independent trust, will—in partnership with Oxford University—map our seagrass ecosystems using a combination of ground truthing and satellite imagery and estimate the carbon stored in these ecosystems. This project will provide the data the Government of Seychelles needs to support seagrass protections in its Nationally Determined Contributions and thereby include nature-based solutions as part of its commitment toward the Paris Climate Agreement.

Q: One final question: Is it true that in Seychelles you're known as "Madame Turtle"?

A: Seychellois people like nicknames, and beginning in 1981 people started referring to me as "Madanm Torti"—which means "Madame Turtle" in Seychellois Creole. Over the years I became familiar to people during televised public awareness campaigns about turtle conservation, so by now many Seychellois who don't know my real name recognize me as "Madanm Torti." I answer to either name.

Print Citations

CMS: Morgan, Matthew. "Seagrass a Powerful Ally in the Fight Against Climate Change Says Seychelles-Based Expert." In *The Reference Shelf: National Debate 2021-2022: Water Resources,* edited by Micah L. Issitt, 141-144. Amenia, NY: Grey House Publishing, 2021.

MLA: Morgan, Matthew. "Seagrass a Powerful Ally in the Fight Against Climate Change Says Seychelles-Based Expert." *The Reference Shelf: National Debate 2021-2022: Water Resources,* edited by Micah L. Issitt, Grey House Publishing, 2021, pp. 141-144.

APA: Morgan, M. (2021). Seagrass a powerful ally in the fight against climate change says Seychelles-based expert. In Micah L. Issitt (Ed.), *The reference shelf: National debate 2021-2022: Water resources* (pp. 141-144). Amenia, NY: Grey House Publishing.

In New Mexico, Pecos River Sustains Communities, Traditions, and Wildlife

By Nicole Cordan

The PEW Charitable Trusts, July 22, 2020

The Pecos River in northern New Mexico is the lifeblood of a vibrant riverine eco-system, supporting numerous wildlife species while providing clean drinking wa-ter to surrounding communities and locally renowned trout fishing and whitewater boating. Originating in the Pecos Wilderness of the Sangre de Cristo Mountains, the Pecos River is in the southernmost section of the Rocky Mountains. It flows through broad valleys, conifer forests, deep canyons, and desert tablelands and is home to rainbow, Rio Grande cutthroat, and brown trout. With a watershed extend-ing over 400 square miles, the Pecos is a cold-water oasis in a desert-like environ-ment.

A local coalition of tribal leaders, business owners, water users, anglers, and con-servationists has been working to preserve the rivers and streams in this productive and valuable watershed for current and future generations. On April 20, that work took a big step forward when the New Mexico Acequia Association, San Miguel County, the Town of Pecos, the Upper Pecos Watershed Association, and Molino de la Isla Organics LLC, a large local farm, submitted a petition asking the state government to designate 14.1 miles of the Pecos River and 56.2 miles of its tribu-taries in the Upper Pecos Watershed as Outstanding National Resource Waters (ONRWs) under the federal Clean Water Act.

By taking that action the state would help local farms, including many run by families, that rely on access to clean water from these rivers for crop irrigation, among other uses. The designation would also help sustain consumer spending that's part of the $2.3 billion annual outdoor recreation economy in the state.

The ONRW provisions in the Clean Water Act allow states to permanently pro-tect their highest quality, most valued surface waters, such as rivers, streams, lakes, or wetlands. ONRW designation means that no new or increased pollution is al-lowed on a waterway, although current uses may continue—including traditional activities such as grazing and acequia operations.

As people say, *agua es vida*, and the waters and aquatic life of New Mexico's Upper Pecos Watershed have supported the Pecos Pueblo people for generations and remain culturally significant to them today. Farmers, ranchers, and anglers also depend on the watershed for their livelihoods and way of life. Thanks in part to

> The ONRW provisions in the Clean Water Act allow states to permanently protect their highest quality, most valued surface waters, such as rivers, streams, lakes, or wetlands.

a long history of respect for and stewardship of the environment among those who live in the area, most of the waters of the Upper Pecos remain clean and healthy, and eligible for ONRW designation.

ONRW designation would help protect the Pecos watershed from numerous threats, including erosion and runoff from new road construction and extractive activities that could degrade these pristine waters. And, as droughts and monsoons in the region worsen—due, experts say, to climate change—safeguarding clean, free-flowing water is even more important.

In the coming months, the public will have an opportunity to submit comments on the ONRW petition to New Mexico's Water Quality Control Commission. The commission will weigh the contributions of the river to downstream water users, outdoor enthusiasts, tribal interests, and traditional uses against future activities that would exploit the watershed. The *Pew Charitable Trusts* joins the petitioners in urging the commission to safeguard this natural asset to help current and future generations of New Mexicans and visitors thrive.

Print Citations

CMS: Cordan, Nicole. "In New Mexico, Pecos River Sustains Communities, Traditions, and Wildlife." In *The Reference Shelf: National Debate 2021-2022: Water Resources,* edited by Micah L. Issitt, 145-146. Amenia, NY: Grey House Publishing, 2021.

MLA: Cordan, Nicole. "In New Mexico, Pecos River Sustains Communities, Traditions, and Wildlife." *The Reference Shelf: National Debate 2021-2022: Water Resources,* edited by Micah L. Issitt, Grey House Publishing, 2021, pp. 145-146.

APA: Cordan, N. (2021). In New Mexico, Pecos River sustains communities, traditions, and wildlife. In Micah L. Issitt (Ed.), *The reference shelf: National debate 2021-2022: Water resources* (pp. 145-146). Amenia, NY: Grey House Publishing.

5
Policy Issues

By Lynn Betts, USDA Natural Resources Conservation Service, via Wikimedia.

Topsoil runoff from mass agriculture is one of the issues states and the federal government must address.

State and Federal Water Policy

The debate over how to manage the nation's water resources often devolves into a contest between political factions. On one side of the table are those who prioritize economic growth, especially of corporations that place large demands on water resources or whose operations produce pollution and degrade water supplies. On the other side of the debate are those who prioritize public health and environmental stability. The American people do not fall cleanly into either side of this debate. In public opinion polls, Americans tend to favor protecting the environment, water resources, and public health in the general sense, but may oppose more specific policies put forward to address these problems. For instance, voters might feel they are committed to environmentalism, but might oppose a municipal bill because it requires an increase in taxes, or may oppose a federal bill because they have also been led to believe that governmental "interference" in industry is detrimental to their well-being.

Environmentalism and Partisan Politics

Interestingly, the American environmental movement was once very much connected to American conservatism. In the early twentieth century, it was conservative politicians (like Teddy Roosevelt) who were most active in preserving America's natural resources and in combating corporate destruction of the environment. This was because, at the time, conservative Americans felt that preserving America's rivers, lakes, streams, oceans, and the broader forests, prairies, and ecosystems of the country was an important part of conserving America's culture and traditions. Further, the preservation of natural resources is essential to any American whose lives or livelihoods depends on them. Farmers cannot thrive without fresh, clean water. Fishermen cannot thrive without rich populations of fish and other sea creatures. For anyone whose profession or whose recreational life is enriched or dependent on nature, environmental conservation is an essential goal.

The strong links between American conservatism and environmental protections remained in place until well into the latter half of the twentieth century. In the 1970s, when the Clean Air Act (CAA) passed through Congress, there was widespread bipartisan support. Though there were intense debates and negotiations, only one Representative voted against the CAA. The Clean Water Act (CWA) was a bit more contentious, but still received passionate support and endorsement by Republicans of the era. In 1974, it was Republican Senator James Buckley, and four other Republicans, who endorsed a bill to strengthen the Clean Air Act with an absolute prohibition on dumping in national parks and federal lands.[1]

It wasn't until the Reagan Administration that the conservative movement in America began moving away from environmentalism. Reagan's legacy on the environment is mixed. His presidency came at a time when the Republican Party was divided between the older generation, who had embraced environmentalism as part of conservatism, and a new generation more closely linked to corporate interests. Reagan did not aggressively push deregulation, but he had no personal interest in environmental protection and did not make it a priority.[2] In 1981, Reagan famously said that trees produce more pollution than automobiles, demonstrating the direction in which American conservatism was heading. Reagan had simply misunderstood data on the issue which shows that trees and forests emit volatile compounds into the air, such as the hydrocarbon known as isoprene. However, these gases are harmless until they interact with nitrogen oxides, which are released from the burning of coal and other fossil fuels.[3] Reagan's mistaken belief that trees produce "pollution," is not simply the result of Reagan's own failure to understand the science on the issue. His administration was being advised by representatives with ties to the automotive and fossil fuel industries who were paid to discourage regulation. These individuals purposefully misled Americans and allied politicians by producing misleading reports to deemphasize the impact of fossil fuel pollution.

Reagan, the most popular Republican president in twentieth-century American politics, was the first president whose views on the environment were shaped primarily by lobbying from the fossil fuel industry, rather than by the desire to preserve resources for future generations. Reagan's successor and vice president, George H.W. Bush, adopted a moderate approach to environmental protections, and in some ways marked a return to the Republicanism of the past, where conservation and conservatism were more closely allied. By the time the next Republican administration came to power, under Bush's son, George W. Bush, things had changed. The younger Bush reduced environmental regulation, refused to embrace the overwhelming scientific consensus on climate change, and abandoned decades of legislation on protecting natural ecosystems and wildlife. This change occurred because the younger Bush, like Reagan, was personally and professionally indebted to the fossil fuel industry. As a result, the policies his administration put forward were designed to protect and enhance oil industry profits, and not to protect resources or prevent pollution. Across the country older Republican politicians with ties to conservation efforts were replaced by politicians with closer links to the fossil fuel industry and other industries linked to pollution and this pushed the Republican Party, and American Conservatism, away from environmental stewardship.[4]

As the Republican Party moved away from environmentalism, Democratic Party politicians increasingly adopted environmentalist policies. However, Democratic Party commitment to environmental and resource protection was and remains largely moderate in character. The Democratic Party politician with the strongest personal and professional commitment to the environment, former Vice President Al Gore, failed to win the 2000 election and so it is unknown how the nation's environmental legacy might be different if Gore's stewardship had been put into place. Since the 2000s, the Green Party, a progressive political movement that focuses heavily on environmental protection, has been the primary environmentalist political movement in the United States. The Green Party has been visible in pursuing federal office, including the presidency, but the party has not succeeded to gain much in the way of traction at the state level. For this reason, the Green Party is not an effective force in American politics and can, at best, be considered a protest movement that reduces the strength of the moderate progressive political movement without accomplishing anything meaningful in terms of legislation.

In the 2010s and 2020s, environmental policies have been difficult to achieve. The Republican Party and the Democratic Party have often been at a deadlock in terms of passing new legislation and many of the policy changes that have come about since the 2000s have been accomplished through Executive Order or through U.S. Environmental Protection Agency (EPA) policy changes without new legislation being adopted at the congressional level. States have, in many ways, taken the lead in passing new environmental regulations but such actions have limited efficacy when it comes to air and water quality, because the nation's air and water resources are, to a great extent, shared resources. While states can therefore take action to update their infrastructure, to preserve remaining water reserves, or to implement new "green technology" that reduces pollution, unless all states adopt similar measures, pollution and degradation will continue and will ultimately impact all Americans.

Green Energy and the Business Angle

The right-wing shift away from environmental and resource protection occurred, in part, because the American conservative movement became more intimately linked to the fossil fuel industry. George W. Bush was actually the founder of Arbusto Energy, an oil and gas exploration company he founded in 1977, and his family's personal fortunes depended on the profits derived from this industry.[5] It is perhaps unsurprising, therefore, that he favored policies that benefitted the fossil fuel industry at the expense of public welfare or environmental conservation.

Donald Trump, like Bush, had invested heavily in fossil fuels on a personal level and his campaign for the presidency, and subsequent fundraising efforts, depended heavily on this industry. In addition, Trump, a New York City socialite who took over his father's real estate business, had little personal interest in environmentalism or utilizing the nation's natural resources for recreation. Over the course of his controversial single-term presidency, Trump greatly reduced protections on clean water and air and engaged in efforts to "deregulate" industries involved in environmental activities. What this means, in basic terms, is that the Trump Administration made it possible for corporations to earn more profit, by decreasing the level of corporate responsibility for preserving or conserving natural resources.[6]

Fossil fuel corporations view environmental regulation and climate change mediating policies as a threat, because these regulations reduce their potential for profit. Consider, for instance, the debate over whether or not automobile manufacturers had to install "catalytic converters" in the 1960s and 1970s. This technology was proven to greatly reduce automotive air pollution, but automotive companies fought against legislation to require catalytic converters, because being forced to do so cost money and reduced profit.[7] This is essentially what is still happening in America.

To combat climate change and to protect air and water quality, it is necessary for America to move away from fossil fuels and towards renewable and sustainable forms of energy. Industries that contribute to climate change, such as the fossil fuel industry, the automotive industry, large-scale agriculture, and industrial manufacturing, object to making the changes needed to achieve this goal, because doing so would reduce their potential for profit. The question facing Americans therefore is whether it is more important to protect these industries from a reduction in profit, or whether it is preferable to combat climate change and to preserve remaining natural resources.

Debates about environmentalism, protecting natural resources, and similar topics are often portrayed as a simplified ideological choice. Many Americans believe that protecting the environment or natural resources necessarily puts a strain on the economy, but this is not necessarily the case. There are many studies, a growing body of international research suggesting that pollution costs more than can be countered by the benefit of unregulated commerce and that there are more opportunities in sustainable development than in continuing to invest in unsustainable resource exploitation.

One study, a 2015 report published in the *Lancet Commission on Pollution and Health*, found that 16 percent of all premature deaths around the world are caused by pollution of water and air. In total, the world's nations spend 16 percent of revenues, or $4.6 trillion, to fight the ill effects of pollution in their environment. Further, the commission's economic analysis indicated that $1 that Americans invest in clean air, results in $30 dollars in return, in the form of enhanced public health and other benefits.[8] Numerous reports have also shown that green energy and sustainable development are the fastest growing segments of the U.S. economy. Since 2000, the solar and wind energy industries have grown dramatically, while employment and profits from the fossil fuel industry, the automotive industry, and other industries linked to environmentally-destructive practices, have declined.

However, the potential economic benefits of environmental development do not mean that there aren't ways that environmental regulation might be improved to benefit businesses forced to adjust to new regulations or to protect workers in those industries whose lives might be disturbed by regulation. While there is an absolutist movement against any environmental regulations, there are other moderate critics who argue that environmental policies can be improved so as to prevent overly burdening businesses while still accomplishing goals with regard to protecting national resources. This more nuanced dimension of the policy debate is often obscured by the more aggressively absolutist actors in this broader debate.

In the 2020s, the primary debate over environmentalism revolves around the Green New Deal (GND), a series of proposals supported by progressive politicians seeking to dramatically increase investment in green and sustainable energy and technology, while taking equally aggressive steps to control pollution and to protect remaining resources. Currently, American politicians, ideologues, and industry experts have been debating this issue through the media, both social and traditional. The GND has been designed as an effort to balance economic stability and growth against the existential threat of climate change and other environmental problems, but there is little agreement about whether or not adopting policies in this vein would be beneficial for America.

Predictably, there are some politicians and industry representatives who have portrayed the GND as a fundamental threat to American prosperity. There is little evidence to support this broader dismissal, but there are individual aspects of GND policy proposals that have come under scrutiny and that might be subject to more specific and focused debate. At present, there are few conservative politicians who support the GND, and few progressive politicians who do not support it, but the American people are divided on the issue. There is widespread, bipartisan support for the goals of the overall program, but less agreement over how to fund and implement legislation that could allow the nation to achieve those goals.[9] The public discussion of the issue has been heavily influenced by misinformation and propaganda seeking to portray the GND as anti-American, "socialist," or "bad for business." While there may be numerous legitimate criticisms that could be applied to the GND, none of these more generalized and nebulous characterizations is substantive. As of 2021, the future of American water resources is uncertain, in part, because of the heavily politicized debate. It remains to be seen if politicians and scientists can provide enough clarity to shift public opinion either away from or towards adopting more aggressive policies in the future.

Water Resources and National Security

There is another dimension to protecting America's water resources in that a nation's water supplies and the safety and security of those resources is one dimension of a nation's broader national security situation. While the connections between national security and water security may not be immediately apparent to many, there are many ways in which the state of a nation's water resources can affect the nation's security apparatus.

For one thing, water shortages and pollution can drive migration, create food shortages, and can, in many other ways, destabilize societies. This can lead to refugee crises and many other kinds of humanitarian emergencies and these, in turn, can create national security hazards even for nations distant to where these crises emerge. For several decades, security experts have warned that climate change is creating regional conflicts, especially in areas where water scarcity has been a chief concern. The ongoing civil war in the Sudan is one of a number of military conflicts that are directly related to climate change and the loss of water reserves. Not only has the Sudanese civil war create a refugee crisis that has impacted neighboring nations and much of Europe, but the conflict also makes it difficult for foreign nations operating within sub-Saharan Africa. This includes many European nations that have been active in the region both to protect access and combating the destabilization caused by the rise of antigovernment radical regimes. There are substantive links between the intensification of climate change, the loss of access to water resources, and the rise in sub-Saharan radicalism. Many of the individuals who have joined radical groups in the region are responding not only to the influence of radical issue entrepreneurs, but also to a loss of livelihood and stability that is linked to increasing drought cycles and the broader impact of climate change.[10] Because the major pollution-producing nations of the world, such as the United States, China, and India, have not effectively worked to address climate change, it is likely that climate-related military conflict will also intensify in the future.

It is also possible, as water shortages become more common, that many nations around the world could experience increased internal conflict. More than one-third of the United States is at risk for severe water scarcity issues in the future and, as this occurs, internal conflict between the states could intensify. It is likely that water scarcity will put increasing pressure on certain communities and may fuel the expansion of domestic terrorism and radicalism in the United States as it has in other parts of the world. Further, as fossil fuel companies attempt to continue normal operations despite the impact of their businesses on the broader environment, conflict between American environmental activists and corporations is likely to intensify. This might result in radical or militant citizen action against these corporations and could intensify other kinds of conflict as well.

Another way in which water resources impact national security involves the capability to supply and sustain national security agencies and military organizations. In the United States, studies have found that a number of military bases and training facilities are under threat for water shortages.[11] In 2020, a national screening program found that the water supplies at 678 military installations showed toxic levels of fluorinated chemicals known as per- and polyfluoroalkyl substances (PFAS). These toxic chemicals came from groundwater that the installations were using for drinking water, but the situation is complicated by the use of aqueous film-forming foam (AFFF), a fire-fighting chemical used in military bases that contains toxic levels of PFAS that can leach into water supplies. The military bases also produce massive amounts of pollutants and waste that can overflow strained sewage systems, further contributing to water quality issues.[12] Any threat to the health, welfare, or effective function of U.S. military bases is, quite obviously, a direct threat to America's national security preparedness and functionality and thus water shortages and water pollution are direct threats to U.S. national security on the domestic level, while these same factors are a threat to international stability and so create the potential for conflict on the global stage.

Finally, as climate change intensifies the threat of water shortages around the world, existing supplies of fresh water will become an increasingly valuable resource in nearly every country around the world. It is possible, as this situation progresses, that water resources may become an increasingly attractive military target or a target for radicals hoping to destabilizing governmental regimes. Over the longer term, water resources are a cornerstone of national security and the stability of every nation depends on maintaining access to water. As the nation moves towards through the current water crisis, then, it will become increasingly essential for Americans to consider not only their own immediate welfare, but how their nation's actions on climate change and other water preservation measures, may leave their country exposed and vulnerable in the changing world.

Works Used

Cohen, Steve. "The Human and Financial Cost of Pollution." *State of the Planet.* Columbia University. Oct 23, 2017. https://blogs.ei.columbia.edu/2017/10/23/the-human-and-financial-cost-of-pollution/.

Dickstein, Corey. "GAO: 102 Military Bases Face Water Shortage Risk; Pentagon Must Track Issue Better." *Stars and Stripes.* Dec 3, 2019. https://www.stripes.com/news/us/gao-102-military-bases-face-water-shortage-risk-pentagon-must-track-issue-better-1.609642.

Goldenberg, Suzanne. "The Worst of Times: Bush's Environmental Legacy Examined." *The Guardian.* Jan 16, 2009. https://www.theguardian.com/politics/2009/jan/16/greenpolitics-georgebush.

Grandoni, Dino, and Scott Clement. "Americans Like Green New Deal's Goals, but They Reject Paying Trillions to Reach Them." *Washington Post.* Nov 27 2019. https://www.washingtonpost.com/climate-environment/2019/11/27/americans-like-green-new-deals-goals-they-reject-paying-trillions-reach-them/.

Hampton, Liz. "Factbox: U.S. Oil and Gas Regulatory Rollbacks under Trump." *Reuters.* Aug 29, 2019. https://www.reuters.com/article/us-usa-climate-regulations-factbox/factbox-u-s-oil-and-gas-regulatory-rollbacks-under-trump-idUSKCN1VJ2BP.

Hayes, Jared and Scott Faber. "UPDATED MAP: Suspected and Confirmed PFAS Pollution at U.S. Military Bases." *EWG.* Apr 2, 2020. https://www.ewg.org/news-and-analysis/2020/04/updated-map-suspected-and-confirmed-pfas-pollution-us-military-bases.

"How Technology Is Providing Solutions for Clean Water." *Ohio University.* Mar 2, 2021. https://onlinemasters.ohio.edu/blog/how-technology-is-providing-solutions-for-clean-water/.

Jackson, Brooks. "Bush as Businessman." *CNN.* May 13, 1999. https://www.cnn.com/ALLPOLITICS/stories/1999/05/13/president.2000/jackson.bush/.

"'Killer' Trees? Not Exactly." *Earth Observatory.* Sep 30, 2013. https://earthobservatory.nasa.gov/images/84021/killer-trees-not-exactly.

Shabecoff, Philip. "Reagan and Environment: To Many, a Stalemate." *New York Times.* Jan 2, 1989. https://www.nytimes.com/1989/01/02/us/reagan-and-environment-to-many-a-stalemate.html.

Tamvada, Jagannadha Pawan, and Mili Shrivastava. "Going Green Dramatically Benefits Businesses—It Should Be Central to Their Coronavirus Recovery Strategy." *The Conversation.* Aug 17, 2020. https://theconversation.com/going-green-dramatically-benefits-businesses-it-should-be-central-to-their-coronavirus-recovery-strategy-143855.

Verhoeven, Harry. "Climate Change, Conflict and Development in Sudan: Global Neo-Malthusian Narratives and Local Power Struggles." *Development and Change.* Vol 42, No 3, 2011.

Weisskopf, Michael. "Auto-Pollution Debate Has Ring of the Past." *Washington Post.* Mar 26, 1990. https://www.washingtonpost.com/archive/politics/1990/03/26/

auto-pollution-debate-has-ring-of-the-past/d1650ba3-2896-44fa-ac1b-4e28aca78674/.

Notes

1. Fuller, "Environmental Policy Is Partisan: It Wasn't Always."
2. Shabecoff, "Reagan and Environment: To Many, a Stalemate."
3. "'Killer' Trees? Not Exactly," *Earth Observatory*.
4. Goldenberg, "The Worst of Times: Bush's Environmental Legacy Examined."
5. Jackson, "Bush as Businessman."
6. Hampton, "Factbox: U.S. Oil and Gas Regulatory Rollbacks under Trump."
7. Weisskopf, "Auto-Pollution Debate Has Ring of the Past."
8. Cohen, "The Human and Financial Cost of Pollution."
9. Grandoni and Clement, "Americans Like Green New Deal's Goals but They Reject Paying Trillions to Reach Them."
10. Verhoeven, "Climate Change, Conflict and Development in Sudan: Global Neo-Malthusian Narratives and Local Power Struggles."
11. Dickstein, "GAO: 102 Military Bases Face Water Shortage Risk; Pentagon Must Track Issue Better."
12. Hayes and Faber, "UPDATED MAP: Suspected and Confirmed PFAS Pollution at U.S. Military Bases."

Trump's Environmental Policies Rule Only Part of America

By Alex Guillen, Beatrice Jin, and Eric Wolff
Politico, September 19, 2018

The stark political divide between conservative and liberal states mirrors a growing chasm on environmental policy and pollution across the country as the Trump administration dials down federal regulations and blue states step in to pursue their own rules.

The split has been decades in the making, with states that voted for President Donald Trump growing increasingly angry about the expanding role of the federal government and blue states pressing for tighter regulations to deal with greenhouse gases and other pollutants that threaten air and water. But Trump's dramatic deregulatory agenda has prompted many states to accelerate their own efforts to curb pollution.

The result: In an increasing number of practical ways, industries such as electric power, automaking, farming and refrigeration must simultaneously operate both in Trump's America and in a much more liberal country. Besides worsening an already-ugly division between Republican- and Democratic-led states, the trend also threatens to burden many of the same businesses that Trump says he's trying to help.

"I'm not surprised about this trend," said Dallas Burtraw, a senior fellow at the think tank Resources for the Future. "The way the red-blue divide is occurring increasingly seems like the policies at the state level are aligning with the politics."

2016 Election Results

POLITICO compared how states have split on key environmental issues—climate change, vehicle efficiency, pollution from coolants and clean water—with the 2016 presidential election results, and the correlation is striking.

The red-blue divide is not always perfectly neat—Republican-dominated states like Texas and Iowa are national leaders in wind power—but the partisan fights in Washington (D.C.) over environmental issues are filtering down to the states, which are often responding with their own action.

"People still want clean air and clean water, and if they believe the federal government isn't doing its part to deliver and to enforce environmental requirements, then they'll look to their states," said Carol Browner, the Clinton-era Environmental Protection Agency administrator and climate adviser to President Barack Obama.

"Carbon Intensity" Predicted the 2016 Vote

On a key metric of climate change, the divide between red states and blue states is noteworthy: Of the 28 most-carbon-intensive states, all but one went for Trump in 2016. At the other end of the spectrum, the 14 least-carbon-intensive states voted for Hillary Clinton. A state's carbon intensity—the amount of CO_2 emissions divided by gross domestic product—depends on factors such as how it produces its electricity, vehicle miles driven, prevalence of energy-intensive activities such as manufacturing, and the ratio of rural to urban populations.

States can influence their emissions by adopting policies such as clean energy standards or incentives for public transit or electric vehicles. But the divide is likely to widen after the Trump administration rolled back many climate change policies, including walking away from the U.S. promises under the Paris climate agreement. After that announcement, 16 states—mostly those won by Clinton—created the U.S. Climate Alliance to try to meet the targets under the Paris pact.

Clinton States Fight Weak Trump Auto Rule

The Trump administration is hitting the brakes on auto emissions rules created under Obama, but more than a dozen states plan to align with California's stricter standards instead. Federal law gives California unique power to enact rules more stringent than the federal government's, and other states can choose to follow Sacramento's lead instead of the federal standards. Thirteen states and Washington, D.C., are set to follow California's rules, and together they represent more than a third of the nation's auto market.

> **Trump's dramatic deregulatory agenda has prompted many states to accelerate their own efforts to curb pollution.**

The Trump administration says it will revoke California's authority to set its own rules, a move that would set off a court fight that many experts say might favor the Golden State. Should California prevail in the legal battle, the U.S. auto market could face two separate sets of emissions rules that vary depending on the state.

Most experts agree that that would be a disaster for automakers, who are pressing the Trump administration to pull back on its proposal and maintain one national standard. But until one side swerves, California and the Trump administration are speeding toward a head-on collision.

Clinton States Go It Alone on Potent Greenhouse Gas

The Trump EPA suspended an Obama rule that would have phased out hydrofluorocarbons used in refrigerators and air conditioners even though there is little opposition to eliminating the powerful greenhouse gas.

U.S. manufacturers support a shift away from HFCs, and they had hoped a phase-out would open up markets to newer replacement chemicals they have developed that don't contribute to climate change. Now they hope that blue states can agree on a single regulation that would create momentum for a new national rule, and also ratification of an international treaty that would cut down HFC use worldwide.

The 16-state U.S. Climate Alliance said in June that all its member states would seek ways to cut HFCs and other short-term greenhouse gases. California Gov. Jerry Brown signed legislation last week that would mimic EPA's suspended rule in the Golden State, and New York Gov. Andrew Cuomo promised to do the same by regulation.

Trump States Want More Water Control

Judging exactly what rivers, streams and wetlands fall under federal jurisdiction has been a decades long struggle. In 2015, the Obama administration issued a regulation known as the Waters of the United States rule, or WOTUS, to define when a water body would be regulated by EPA and the Army Corps of Engineers or by local or state governments.

But the Obama rule sharply expanded federal jurisdiction, and several red states fought back, arguing in court that WOTUS was a major overreach and that more waters should be under state control.

After years of legal fighting, the rule now applies in some states but not others. As of Sept. 19, judges have blocked the Obama-era WOTUS rule in 28 states, mostly ones won by Trump, leaving it in effect in 22 others, mostly those Clinton won.gulp With multiple ongoing lawsuits across the U.S., the field of play might change again. Meanwhile, the Trump administration is furiously writing a replacement rule that is also expected to draw years of litigation—another rulemaking that may well one day make its way to the Supreme Court.

Print Citations

CMS: Guillen, Alex, Beatrice Jin, and Eric Wolff. "Trump's Environmental Policies Rule Only Part of America." In *The Reference Shelf: National Debate 2021-2022: Water Resources,* edited by Micah L. Issitt, 157-159. Amenia, NY: Grey House Publishing, 2021.

MLA: Guillen, Alex, Beatrice Jin, and Eric Wolff. "Trump's Environmental Policies Rule Only Part of America." *The Reference Shelf: National Debate 2021-2022: Water Resources,* edited by Micah L. Issitt, Grey House Publishing, 2021, pp. 157-159.

APA: Guillen, A., Jin, B., & Wolff, E. (2021). Trump's environmental policies rules only part of America. In Micah L. Issitt (Ed.), *The reference shelf: National debate 2021-2022: Water resources* (pp. 157-159). Amenia, NY: Grey House Publishing.

Why Farmers and Ranchers Think the EPA Clean Water Rules Goes Too Far

By Reagan Waskom and David J. Cooper
The Conversation, **February 27, 2017**

President Trump issued an executive order Feb. 28 directing federal agencies to revise the Clean Water Rule, a major regulation published by the Environmental Protection Agency and the Army Corps of Engineers in 2015. The rule's purpose is to clarify which water bodies and wetlands are federally protected under the Clean Water Act.

EPA Administrator Scott Pruitt led a multi-state lawsuit against the rule as Oklahoma attorney general, and has called it "the greatest blow to private property rights the modern era has seen."

At the Colorado Water Institute at Colorado State University, we work in partnership with the farm and ranch community to find solutions to difficult western water problems. Farmers and ranchers often express frustration with one-size-fits-all worker protection, food safety, animal welfare, immigration, endangered species and environmental regulations. So, we understand their concern that this rule may further constrain agricultural activities on their land.

In particular, they fear the Clean Water Rule could expand federal regulations that impact their private property rights. However, regulatory agencies and the regulated community need to know the limits of the Clean Water Act's reach so they can take appropriate measures to protect water resources. If the rule is scrapped, we still will need to know which water bodies require protection under the law.

Which Waters?

The Clean Water Act of 1972 protects the "waters of the United States" from unpermitted discharges that may harm water quality for humans and aquatic life. However, it leaves it up to EPA and the Army Corps of Engineers to define which waters the law covers.

Agencies and the courts agree that this term includes "navigable waters," such as rivers and lakes. It also covers waterways connected to them, such as marshes and wetlands. The central question is how closely connected a water body must be to navigable waters to fall under federal jurisdiction.

In 2001 and 2006, the Supreme Court handed down rulings that narrowed the

> Science shows that relatively minor effects at the edge of one field can aggregate across a watershed in cumulative impacts that are significant and sometimes serious.

definition of protected waters, but used confusing language. These opinions created regulatory uncertainty for farmers, ranchers and developers.

The Supreme Court wrote in the 2006 case, *Rapanos v. United States*, that if a water body had a "significant nexus" to a federally protected waterway–for example, if a wetland was some distance from a navigable stream but produced a relatively permanent flow to the stream–then it was connected and fell under federal jurisdiction. But it failed to clearly define the significant nexus test for other situations.

The Clean Water Rule seeks to clarify which types of waters are 1) protected categorically, 2) protected on a case-by-case basis or 3) not covered. Here are some of the key categories:

- Tributaries formerly were evaluated case by case. Now they are automatically covered if they have features of flowing water–a bed, a bank and a high water mark. Other types, such as open waters without beds and banks, will be evaluated case by case.

- "Adjacent waters," such as wetlands and ponds that are near covered waters, are protected if they lie within physical and measurable boundaries set out in the rule.

- "Isolated waters" are not connected to navigable waters but still can be ecologically important. The rule identifies specific types that are protected, such as prairie potholes and California vernal pools.

EPA estimated that the final Clean Water Rule expanded the types of water subject to Clean Water Act jurisdiction by about 3 percent, or 1,500 acres nationwide. Opponents clearly think it could be much broader–and until they see the rule implemented on the landscape, their fears may have some basis in fact.

Protecting Drainage Ditches?

Industry and agriculture groups believe the new rule defines tributaries more broadly. They see this change as unnecessary overreach that makes it difficult to know what is regulated on their lands.

Western farms are laced with canals that provide critical irrigation water during the growing season. These canals and ditches divert water from streams and return the excess through a downstream return loop, which is fed by gravity. Because they are open and unlined, they also serve as water sources for wildlife, ecosystems and underground aquifers. And because they are connected to other water bodies, farmers fear they could be subject to federal regulation.

The only way to surface-irrigate in western valleys without affecting local water systems would be to lay thousands of miles of pressurized pipes, like those that carry water in cities. This approach would be impractical in many situations and incredibly expensive.

More generally, farmers and ranchers want to be able to make decisions about managing their land and water resources without ambiguity or time-consuming and expensive red tape. In spite of EPA assurances, they worry the Clean Water Rule could include agricultural ditches, canals and drainages in the definition of "tributary."

They fear EPA will use vague language in the rule to expand its power to regulate these features and change the way they are currently operated. They also fear becoming targets for citizen-initiated lawsuits, which are allowed under the Clean Water Act. Moreover, they are skeptical the outcomes will significantly benefit the environment.

Former EPA Administrator Gina McCarthy argued that the rule would not unduly burden farmers. "We will protect clean water without getting in the way of farming and ranching," McCarthy told the National Farmers Union in 2015. "Normal agriculture practices like plowing, planting, and harvesting a field have always been exempt from Clean Water Act regulation; this rule won't change that at all."

All Waters Eventually Connect

Farmers and ranchers are independent by nature and believe they know what is best for the stewardship of their own land. They tend to be regulation-averse and believe voluntary approaches to water quality provide the flexibility needed to account for site-specific variations across the landscape. However, science shows that relatively minor effects at the edge of one field can aggregate across a watershed in cumulative impacts that are significant and sometimes serious.

From an ecological perspective, scientists have long understood that surface water bodies and tributary groundwater within a watershed are connected over time. Even if it takes years, water will move across and through the landscape. Determining which tributaries have a "significant nexus" to traditional navigable waters depends on how you define "significant."

Even small wetlands and intermittent ponds provide ecosystem services that benefit the larger watershed. Wetlands and small water bodies that are geographically isolated from the floodplain may still impact navigable waters as either groundwater flows or surface runoff during heavy or prolonged precipitation events.

In that sense, all water runs downhill to the stream eventually. As a dozen prominent wetland scientists wrote last month in an amicus brief to the Sixth U.S. Circuit Court of Appeals, which is reviewing the Clean Water Rule, "the best available science overwhelmingly demonstrates that the waters [protected] categorically in the Clean Water Rule have significant chemical, physical, and biological connections to primary waters."

Scientists and ecologists agree interpreting the degree and frequency of this kind of connectivity requires site-by-site analysis. We now understand more clearly how isolated water bodies function on the landscape as part of a larger complex, and our knowledge can help clarify how directly water bodies are connected. But deciding where to draw the bright line of regulatory certainty may lie beyond the realm of science.

If the Trump administration withdraws or weakens the Clean Water Rule, it is likely to leave regulators interpreting case by case whether tributaries and adjacent waters are covered, as they have been doing since 2006, and land and water owners guessing about what they can do with their resources. So, in the end, repealing the rule won't answer the underlying question: how far upstream federal protection extends.

Print Citations

CMS: Waskom, Reagan, and David J. Cooper. "Why Farmers and Ranchers Think the EPA Clean Water Rules Goes Too Far." In *The Reference Shelf: National Debate 2021-2022: Water Resources,* edited by Micah L. Issitt, 160-163. Amenia, NY: Grey House Publishing, 2021.

MLA: Waskom, Reagan, and David J. Cooper. "Why Farmers and Ranchers Think the EPA Clean Water Rules Goes Too Far." *The Reference Shelf: National Debate 2021-2022: Water Resources,* edited by Micah L. Issitt, Grey House Publishing, 2021, pp. 160-163.

APA: Waskom, R., & Cooper D. J. (2021). Why farmers and ranchers think the EPA clean water rules goes too far. In Micah L. Issitt (Ed.), *The reference shelf: National debate 2021-2022: Water resources* (pp. 160-163). Amenia, NY: Grey House Publishing.

The Green New Deal: What Does It Mean for Water?

By Marc Yaggi

Waterkeeper Alliance, March 7, 2019

With 2018 being the fourth-hottest year on record, and 18 of the 19 warmest years on record having occurred since 2001, there is no denying that we need bold action to stave off the worst impacts of climate change. On February 7, Rep. Alexandria Ocasio-Cortez (D-NY) and Sen. Ed. Markey (D-MA) unveiled to the House and Senate a Green New Deal (GND) resolution—a framework to address the climate crisis. The GND is a bold, ambitious plan to achieve net zero greenhouse gas emissions while creating economic prosperity for all Americans. While the GND may not pass Congress, it has spurred greater national conversation around climate change. And that national conversation might finally force some bipartisan action on climate change.

The GND is modeled after President Franklin D. Roosevelt's New Deal, which helped pull the U.S. out of the Great Depression and bring economic stability back to Americans. The proposed 10-year plan aims to achieve "net-zero greenhouse gas emissions" by moving America to 100 percent clean and renewable energy while creating jobs and "economic prosperity for all." The GND resolution's goals would be achieved by a number of projects such as building climate change-resilient infrastructure; meeting 100 percent of our energy needs from clean, renewable power; building a smart grid; overhauling our food systems; expanding electric vehicle manufacturing; building high-speed rail systems; increasing forested areas; and more. The 14 aspiring infrastructure and industrial projects identified in the resolution would, in turn, create a plethora of green jobs.

So, What Does This All Mean for the World's Waters?

Aside from the fact that clean water is included in the GND's goals, the answer to this question is simple when you realize that climate change and water are interconnected. Climate change is altering the chemistry of our oceans, the character of our coastlines, and the timing and intensity of rain and snow, wreaking havoc across the planet. The impacts can be understood by hearing from the Waterkeepers we work with both in the United States and around the world:

- Our Waterkeepers in Louisiana have seen the government remove more than 40 names from places on maps because those places no longer exist, except for in the memories of coastal residents who saw the land disappear.

> **The GND is a bold, ambitious plan to achieve net zero greenhouse gas emissions while creating economic prosperity for all Americans.**

- In Ladakh, India, our Himalayan Glacier Waterkeeper will tell you that over the past decade things have turned upside down. It snows when it shouldn't and it doesn't rain when it should. Some communities have relocated due to drought while others are forced to rebuild after devastating floods.

- In Mongolia, our Tuul River Waterkeeper reports how drought is forcing more and more people to migrate from the countryside into cities that aren't equipped to handle the population growth.

- Puget Soundkeeper in Seattle sees ocean acidification threatening a $270 million year shellfish industry.

- Our Waterkeepers in the Bahamas know there is a real risk that they will lose a majority of their land to sea level rise this century. They worry for the security of their culture, their heritage, and their existence.

Those are just a few examples of many that demonstrate how climate change and water are intertwined. The GND reflects that access to and availability of clean water is waning as a result of greenhouse gas emissions, whether it be through climate change or waterways polluted by fossil fuels, and that low-income communities, communities of color, and indigenous communities are disproportionately affected. The resolution would protect public lands, waters, and oceans and ensure "eminent domain is not abused," while restoring waterways and expanding sustainable farming and soil practices on agricultural land.

The framework for the Green New Deal is ambitious; it is a gigantic step toward combating climate change. While the current proposal is a non-binding resolution, it sends a powerful message that the United States needs to take bold, decisive action now to mitigate the climate crisis and create a better future for all. And at the end of the day, a Green New Deal also is a Blue New Deal for our waters.

Print Citations

CMS: Yaggi, Marc. "The Green New Deal: What Does It Mean for Water?" In *The Reference Shelf: National Debate 2021-2022: Water Resources,* edited by Micah L. Issitt, 164-166. Amenia, NY: Grey House Publishing, 2021.

MLA: Yaggi, Marc. "The Green New Deal: What Does It Mean for Water?" *The Reference Shelf: National Debate 2021-2022: Water Resources,* edited by Micah L. Issitt, Grey House Publishing, 2021, pp. 164-166.

APA: Yaggi, M. (2021). The green new deal: What does it mean for water? In Micah L. Issitt (Ed.), *The reference shelf: National debate 2021-2022: Water resources* (pp. 164-166). Amenia, NY: Grey House Publishing.

Green New Deal: Strengths and Weaknesses

By Rob Jordan
Stanford Woods Institute for the Environment, March 29, 2019

Eighty-six years ago this month, President Franklin Roosevelt delivered his first inaugural address to a nation mired in the Great Depression. Promising to "wage a war against the emergency," Roosevelt hinted at the New Deal to come: an unprecedented series of massive public programs and projects intended to put America back to work.

In an echo of the past, the Green New Deal resolution drafted by Rep. Alexandria Ocasio-Cortez of New York and Sen. Edward J. Markey of Massachusetts labels climate change a "direct threat to the national security of the United States" and calls for the conversion of all U.S. power to clean, renewable energy sources and the creation of millions of green jobs, among other objectives. Supporters enthusiastically embrace the idea of a 10-year mobilization to reduce carbon emissions in the United States. Still, critics deride the plan as hopeless government overreach short on details and financial realism.

Stanford Report spoke with Sally Benson, co-director of the Precourt Institute for Energy; Rob Jackson, chair of the Global Carbon Project; and Mark Jacobson, director of Stanford's Atmosphere/Energy Program, about the Green New Deal's strengths and weaknesses. Jacobson's research has provided state- and national-level roadmaps for transitioning all energy sectors to 100 percent clean, renewable energy and storage. Jackson published a recent op-ed in *The Hill* about the plan. Benson was co-author of a 2018 paper highlighting "particularly difficult to decarbonize" parts of the energy system. While the scholars have diverse opinions about the fastest, most likely to succeed and lowest cost pathway to deep decarbonization, they agree on the urgency and importance of the issue.

What Components/Details Would a Well Done Final Green New Deal (GND) Have?

Benson: Given the urgency of reducing emissions, we should pursue a strategy of "everything that works." Now is not the time to take solutions off the table. Specifically, carbon dioxide capture, utilization and storage, and nuclear power should be considered, in addition to renewable energy resources. In California, for example, decarbonizing the electricity sector with renewables only would cost about two times more than when you include CCS [carbon capture and storage] and nuclear power. Our results are consistent with many

> **Carbon dioxide capture, utilization and storage, and nuclear power should be considered, in addition to renewable energy resources.**

global studies, such as those described in the Intergovernmental Panel on Climate Change reports, showing that including some amount of CO_2 capture and storage reduces the overall costs of deep decarbonization. I would also like to see the U.S. reach out to and partner with other countries to share knowledge about cost-effective deep decarbonization strategies. We don't have time to waste with false starts and ineffective approaches to decarbonization.

Jackson: We'd set a national path to net-zero emissions in the electric-power sector and work hard to decarbonize the tougher transportation and industrial sectors. The GND should also reduce methane and nitrous oxide emissions from agriculture and industry. It doesn't need to pick winning technologies. Solar, wind, hydro, nuclear, even fossils with carbon capture and storage could play a role, with most of the gains coming from renewables.

Jacobson: A GND should be based on transitioning all energy to 100 percent clean, renewable and zero-carbon wind-water-solar energy. This includes not only electricity, transportation, heating and cooling, but industry, agriculture and other energy use. Wind-water-solar excludes new nuclear power plants, fossil fuels with carbon capture, biofuels and capturing CO_2 from the atmosphere aside from forestation. Such technologies increase air pollution, global warming, energy insecurity and other social costs compared with wind-water-solar. At least 37 papers among 11 independent research groups find that the electric grid can stay stable at low cost with at or near 100 percent wind-water-solar.

What Are the Most Important Reasons/Benefits of a GND?

Jackson: Is saving the planet reason enough? I hope so. If not, how about the tens of thousands of Americans who die unnecessarily each year from coal-fired power plants and our vehicles, the two deadliest sources of air pollution in the country?

Jacobson: Such a transition will eliminate 62,000 air pollution deaths per year in the U.S, saving taxpayers $600 billion a year. Climate costs savings to the world due to reducing U.S. emissions would be $3.3 trillion a year. These savings would continue for 100 years. The transition would create 2 million net jobs over those lost in the U.S.

Benson: The Green New Deal is sparking an important and necessary conversation around the urgency of climate change. It's a catalyst for a plan that will put us on an accelerated path to decarbonization. That starts with putting a price on carbon to incentivize industry to reduce emissions and unleash market forces to drive the best approaches to scale. Beyond these market forces, the government should step up funding of research, maintain regulations that drive energy efficiency and lead modernization of the electricity grid.

What Are the Biggest Potential Problems/Weaknesses of a GND?

Jacobson: There is no technical or economic weakness, but social and political opposition is formidable. The fossil fuel industry has a lot at stake, and they sow doubt and oppose all legislation that will phase them out. The intent of the GND as originally written is to "transition off of nuclear and fossil fuels as soon as possible," so the nuclear folks will try to oppose it as well. In addition, many people don't care one way or the other and just don't want to change their current lifestyle, so it is hard to encourage them to change.

Jackson: Trying to do too much and accomplishing too little. The GND is right to couple climate action to poverty because poorer people are already bearing the brunt of climate's costs. However, this coupling could make action more difficult. Many Democrats may see social change as necessary. Many Republicans may not. I don't want those differences to keep us from cleaner energy and improved energy efficiency.

Benson: The biggest potential problem would be broadly deploying technologies that aren't yet sufficiently developed. We need to move as quickly as we can with technologies that are ready to go, like wind and solar power, and continue to develop other critical components of a deeply decarbonized energy system like large-scale weekly to seasonal energy storage.

What Would Have to Happen in American Politics and Society for a GND to Pass?

Jackson: There's tremendous energy on the Hill for green energy and social change. Today's politics differ vastly from the first New Deal, though, when one party controlled both the White House and Congress. We aren't clawing our way out of a Great Depression, either. We do face a global climate crisis, and our youth understand the urgency. Because the first New Deal arrived in many bills, not one, the GND will too. I think we'll see narrower bills with bipartisan sponsors, such as a national clean energy standard for electric power. Heartland voters in states like Texas, Iowa and Oklahoma share a lot with coastal voters in embracing cheap wind and solar power. I suspect we'll see newer incentives for energy efficiency, electric vehicles, and carbon capture and storage technologies, as well.

Jacobson: People need to realize how financially and job-beneficial the GND is.

Approximately How Much Would It Cost to Institute a GND, and How Could We Pay for It?

Jacobson: Rather than increasing costs, the GND reduces costs substantially. The upfront capital cost of a 100 percent wind-water-solar electric power generation system is about $9.5 trillion. However, this cost is spread out over many years and will pay itself off over time through electricity sales.

Further, a wind-water-solar system uses half the energy as a fossil fuel system and also eliminates health and climate costs due to fossil fuels. As such, U.S. consumers will pay only $1 trillion per year in energy costs with the GND, whereas under a fossil fuel system, they will pay $2 trillion per year in energy costs and $600 billion per year in air pollution health costs, and will incur $3.3 trillion per year in global climate costs due to U.S. emissions, for a total economic cost of $5.9 trillion per year. Thus a wind-water-solar system costs society one-sixth that of a fossil fuel system.

Jackson: No one can answer what it would cost because no specific agenda exists. To pay for it, a price on carbon emissions would help. A fee and dividend would price pollution, giving companies financial incentives to cut emissions. To have much chance politically, though, it may need to be revenue neutral, redistributing the funds to taxpayers. That redistribution is where social change could occur, but then again it wouldn't pay for other aspects of the GND.

Benson: It depends on what the GND becomes. We can take many actions today with low or no cost. For example, in many cases it is less expensive to use natural gas instead of coal for producing electricity, and more efficient cars and appliances can actually save money for consumers when you consider the total cost of ownership. Adding renewable power to the grid can also be cost effective, such as all of the wind power added in the Midwest and Texas and solar power in the Southwest. Within the next decade, owning an electric car is likely to be cost-competitive with a gasoline-powered car. On the other hand, comprehensive approaches for completely decarbonizing transportation and industry are not available today. R&D is needed to drive down costs for decarbonization technologies.

Print Citations

CMS: Jordan, Rob, and Stanford Woods Institute for the Environment. "Green New Deal: Strengths and Weaknesses." http://woods.stanford.edu/news/green-new-deal-strengths-and-weaknesses. In *The Reference Shelf: National Debate 2021-2022: Water Resources,* edited by Micah L. Issitt, 167-171. Amenia, NY: Grey House Publishing, 2021.

MLA: Jordan, Rob, and Stanford Woods Institute for the Environment. "Green New Deal: Strengths and Weaknesses." http://woods.stanford.edu/news/green-new-deal-strengths-and-weaknesses. *The Reference Shelf: National Debate 2021-2022: Water Resources,* edited by Micah L. Issitt, Grey House Publishing, 2021, pp. 167-171.

APA: Jordan, R., & Stanford Woods Institute for the Environment. (2021). The green new deal: Strengths and weaknesses. http://woods.stanford.edu/news/green-new-deal-strengths-and-weaknesses. In Micah L. Issitt (Ed.), *The reference shelf: National debate 2021-2022: Water resources* (pp. 167-171). Amenia, NY: Grey House Publishing.

Lawmakers Open Groundwater Fight Against Bottled Water Companies

By Alex Brown

PEW Stateline, **February 12, 2020**

OLYMPIA, Wash.—Washington state, land of sprawling rainforests and glacier-fed rivers, might soon become the first in the nation to ban water bottling companies from tapping spring-fed sources.

The proposal is one of several efforts at the state and local level to fend off the fast-growing bottled water industry and protect local groundwater. Local activists throughout the country say bottling companies are taking their water virtually for free, depleting springs and aquifers, then packaging it in plastic bottles and shipping it elsewhere for sale.

"I was literally beyond shocked," said Washington state Sen. Reuven Carlyle, who sponsored the bill to ban bottling companies from extracting groundwater. It was advanced by a Senate committee last week.

"I was jolted to the core to realize the depth and breadth and magnitude of how they have lawyered up in these small towns to take advantage of water rights," the Democrat said. "The fact that we have incredibly loose, if virtually nonexistent, policy guidelines around this is shocking and a categorical failure."

Elsewhere, lawmakers in Michigan and Maine also have filed bills to restrict the bottling of groundwater or tax the industry. Local ballot measures have passed in Oregon and Montana to restrict the industry, though Flathead County, Montana's zoning change remains tied up in court.

"The Washington state bill is groundbreaking," said Mary Grant, a water policy specialist with the environmental group Food and Water Watch. "As water scarcity is becoming a deeper crisis, you want to protect your local water supply so it goes for local purposes. [Bottled water] is not an industry that needs to exist."

Though much of the controversy around the bottled water industry has concerned "bottled at the source" spring water sites, nearly two-thirds of the bottled water sold in the United States comes from municipal tap water, according to Food and Water Watch. The Washington state legislation would not keep companies from buying and reselling tap water.

Americans consumed nearly 14 billion gallons of bottled water in 2018, while sales reached $19 billion—more than doubling the industry's size in 2004. The bottled water industry is expected to grow to more than $24 billion in the next three years, according to *Beverage Industry* magazine.

Industry leaders have opposed sweeping legislation that would cut off resources, pointing out the potential hit to local employment and the importance of bottled water in disaster relief.

"This legislation would prevent any community from having these jobs or having a project in their area," said Brad Boswell, executive director of the Washington Beverage Association, who testified against the bill. "We think these issues are best dealt with on a project-by-project basis."

The International Bottled Water Association defended the track record of its members in an emailed statement. The bill in Washington and other legislation to limit the industry "are based on the false premise that the bottled water industry is harming the environment," wrote Jill Culora, the group's vice president of communications.

"All IBWA members," she wrote, "are good stewards of the environment. When a bottled water company decides to build a plant, it looks for a long-term, sustainable source of water and the ability to protect the land and environment around the source and bottling facility."

Culora did not address specific examples of community claims that bottling companies have damaged their watersheds and aquifers.

The American Beverage Association, which represents bottled water and soft drink companies, declined to take a stance on Washington's proposed ban, calling it a "local issue" that would be better addressed by in-state bottlers.

Local Fights

When residents in Randle, Washington, learned of a proposed Crystal Geyser operation last year, some worried about a large industrial plant in their quiet, rural valley near Mount Rainier.

Many feared that the company's plan to pump 400 gallons a minute from springs on the site would deplete the local aquifer and dry up their wells.

The worry turned to furor when a leaked email exposed the company's plan to sue the nearby subdivision in response to neighbor opposition, then conduct an underground public relations campaign to gain support for the project.

"Pumping water out of the ground, putting it in plastic bottles and exporting it out of the state of Washington is not in the public interest," said Craig Jasmer, a leader of the Lewis County Water Alliance, the group that sprung up to oppose the Randle plant and has pushed for the statewide ban.

Recent news increased the concerns: Last month, Crystal Geyser pled guilty to storing arsenic-contaminated wastewater at a California facility, and then illegally dumping the water into a sewer after being confronted by authorities. The company did not respond to a *Stateline* request for comment.

In 2016, Crystal Geyser paid a timber company for access to a spring that had historically provided the water for the city of Weed, California, forcing the town to find a new water supply.

Local activists in California, Oregon, Michigan and Florida say they've been targeted by big bottlers that damage the environment and provide scant economic benefit.

Nestle has drawn criticism for its bottling operation in California's San Bernardino National Forest, which federal officials have concluded is "drying up" creeks.

"[The creeks] are visibly different where the water is extracted and where it's not," said Michael O'Heaney, executive director of the Story of Stuff Project, a California-based group that makes films about waste, pollution and environmental issues.

During California's drought, he said, "Nestle wasn't being asked to curtail its water [in]take at the same time as Californians were being asked to significantly reduce the amount of water they were using."

Just across the Columbia River from Washington, the residents of Hood River County, Oregon, passed a ballot measure in 2016 to ban commercial water bottling after Nestle announced plans to build a plant that would extract more than 100 million gallons a year.

Aurora del Val, who helped lead the campaign for the ballot measure, said Nestle first made inroads with local officials, promising jobs for an area that had seen its economy suffer with the decline of the timber industry.

"This seemed like the golden ticket to having a boomtown again," she said. "But the more educated people became, the more opposition there was in the town."

In an emailed statement, Nestle noted its contributions to state economies—one study showed it provided 900 jobs and had an economic impact of $250 million in Florida in 2018. The company also defended its environmental record, without addressing specific claims that its operations are damaging watersheds.

"We have a proven track record of successful long-term management of water resources in states where we operate," wrote Nestle Waters North America spokesman Adam Gaber. "It would make absolutely NO sense for Nestle Waters to invest millions of dollars into local operations just to deplete the natural resources on which our business relies."

Michigan Melee

One of Nestle's most controversial projects is in Osceola Township, Michigan, where local officials are fighting the company's plan to nearly double the groundwater it extracts from the area.

Locals say that nearby trout streams have turned into mud flats since Nestle's arrival, and its promise of jobs did not materialize when it chose to build its bottling plant miles away.

"Streams are flooding all over Michigan, except for Twin and Chippewa creeks, which are not," said Peggy Case, president of the group Michigan Citizens for Water Conservation. "The city aquifer is down 14 feet now, and it's not recharging. There are people with wells in the area that are starting to run dry. They no longer are as happy with Nestle as they used to be."

Even if the company's operations had no environmental effect, Case said her group would still object.

"They are privatizing water," she said, "and we are opposed to that."

In a state where the Flint water crisis is still fresh in people's minds, and residents carry a fierce pride in their Great Lakes heritage, water resources are a charged issue, said state Rep. Yousef Rabhi, a Democrat. Rabhi is part of a group of lawmakers pushing a package of bills that would limit the bottled water industry.

Rabhi has filed a bill that would define water as a public trust, instead of a privately owned commodity. Another measure would prohibit shipping bottled water out of the Great Lakes watershed. A third bill would bolster the regulatory authority of the state Department of Natural Resources.

Rabhi has previously proposed a wholesale excise tax on corporations selling bottled water. He said another group of legislators is working on a similar tax bill this year.

A representative for Absopure, a Michigan-based company that bottles spring water, did not respond to a request for comment. The Michigan Retailers Association said it was not taking a position on the bill, while the Michigan Soft Drink Association and the Michigan Chamber of Commerce did not respond to requests for comment.

In an emailed response, Nestle said the Michigan bills unfairly "single out one industry, one type of water user, for such restrictions." The company noted that water bottling accounts for less than 0.01% of water use in the state and said its Michigan operations employ 280 workers.

Opponents counter that the industry's water use is wholly extractive, while other heavy users, such as agriculture, return much of the water they use to the watershed.

All Eyes on Washington

Carlyle's bill in Washington has eight co-sponsors, all Democrats except for state Sen. John Braun, the Republican who represents the Randle community that battled Crystal Geyser. Braun did not offer comment when reached by text message.

The bill moved through the Senate Agriculture, Water, Natural Resources & Parks Committee. Backers are waiting to see whether it will be added to the Senate voting calendar.

However, some lawmakers have expressed misgivings about taking statewide action against a specific business.

"We're looking at banning a certain industry," Republican state Sen. Judy Warnick said at a committee meeting on the measure, before voting against it. "I understand the need to protect water withdrawals in certain areas, but what we're doing is taking away the right of locals to decide that."

Nearly two-thirds of the bottled water sold in the United States comes from municipal tap water.

Warnick, as well as the other two GOP senators who voted against the bill in committee, received $2,000 each in campaign contributions from the Washington Beverage Association during the last campaign cycle. Warnick did not respond to a request for comment.

Print Citations

CMS: Brown, Alex. "Lawmakers Open Groundwater Fight Against Bottled Water Companies." In *The Reference Shelf: National Debate 2021-2022: Water Resources,* edited by Micah L. Issitt, 172-176. Amenia, NY: Grey House Publishing, 2021.

MLA: Brown, Alex. "Lawmakers Open Groundwater Fight Against Bottled Water Companies." *The Reference Shelf: National Debate 2021-2022: Water Resources,* edited by Micah L. Issitt, Grey House Publishing, 2021, pp. 172-176.

APA: Brown, A. (2021). Lawmakers open groundwater fight against bottled water companies. In Micah L. Issitt (Ed.), *The reference shelf: National debate 2021-2022: Water resources* (pp. 172-176). Amenia, NY: Grey House Publishing.

How States' Rights Became a Liberal Environmental Cause

By Amanda Paulson and Martin Kuz
The Christian Science Monitor, October 9, 2019

States' rights are sacred for many conservatives in the United States.

So how did liberal California become a poster child for states' rights in its esca-lating battle with the Trump administration on environmental regulation?

From fuel emissions to oil and gas drilling permits, California is at war with the Trump administration. And at the heart of the feud is the state's desire to set its own environmental regulations—an issue of states' rights, and also a continuation of the "cooperative federalist" model that has long been a backbone of American environ-mental policy. But in this case, as well as in environmental battles being fought in other states, it's the Republican administration arguing for the supremacy of federal rule.

"They're exercising what the Western Governors' Association executive director has called 'fair-weather federalism,'" says David Hayes, executive director of the State Energy & Environmental Impact Center at New York University School of Law and deputy interior secretary under President Barack Obama. "As long as states do what they want them to do, it's fine. If they exercise their rights in a way that the feds don't like because it's not consistent with their policy, then they're against it."

In California, as in some other liberal-leaning states, states' rights has become a rallying cry. "To those who claim to support states' rights—don't trample on ours," proclaimed California Attorney General Xavier Becerra last month, after the Trump administration revoked the state's long-standing waiver that allowed it to set its own vehicle emissions.

The idea of states' rights as a conservative principle is somewhat more nuanced: For decades, both liberals and conservatives have touted federalism when it suits them on some issues, and not on others.

"I often talk about selective federalism," says Barry Rabe, a public policy profes-sor at the University of Michigan. "For the party out of power there's often a kind of discovery of federalism because it gives a greater chance of getting what you want."

But, he notes, in the absence of significant environmental legislation from Con-gress in the past 30 years, creative engagement between state, federal, and some-times local authorities has allowed real advances to be made in cleaning up the nation's air and water. What's happening now, he says, seems to be dismantling that, and points to a starker division that's emerged on climate, in particular.

When President Obama issued the Clean Power Plan, 24 state attorneys general immediately filed suit. When the Trump administration removed the Clean Power Plan, 22 states went to court to protest that move. "There is a pattern here, and it shows a real deep divide," Professor Rabe says. This is "the next step in a process that's been intensifying for some period of time."

And the lack of federal action on climate, says Mr. Hayes, has meant that some states have tried to step into the void.

"Traditionally, states' rights are considered a conservative principle, but it's the more progressive states now that are showing the way to environmental protection in the climate area in particular, so it's kind of flipped the script a little bit," says Mr. Hayes.

Battle over Tailpipe Emissions

In California, the biggest shot across the bow came last month when the Trump administration announced it was revoking California's waiver that allows it to set its own auto emissions standards. The state has held this waiver since 1967, when Congress made the exception in recognition of the unusual pollution challenges that California faces. Since 2009, California's waiver has expanded to include greenhouse gases in its list of pollutants, affecting Corporate Average Fuel Economy (CAFE) standards. That was a more unusual move (and was denied by the Bush administration when the state first made the request in 2007), but several automakers voluntarily joined with California, pledging to raise CAFE standards to nearly 50 mpg by 2026. And 13 other states have joined with California's stricter tailpipe emissions.

> In the absence of significant environmental legislation from Congress in the past 30 years, creative engagement between state, federal, and sometimes local authorities has allowed real advances to be made in cleaning up the nation's air and water.

It's the impact those standards have on the rest of the country that acting Environmental Protection Agency Administrator Andrew Wheeler took issue with.

"To borrow from Louisiana Attorney General Jeff Landry, CAFE does not stand for California Assumes Federal Empowerment," Mr. Wheeler said in a September speech to the National Automobile Dealers Association. "We embrace federalism and the role of the states, but federalism does not mean that one state can dictate standards for the nation."

A week later, Mr. Wheeler sent letters to California officials charging that the state was failing to take enough action to clean up its air and water, and threatening to withhold some federal funds as a result.

And on Friday, the Trump administration announced it was opening up 720,000 acres of federal land in California for oil and gas development. There had previously been a five-year moratorium on leases in the state, following a court ruling that there was insufficient analysis of the environmental impacts of fracking.

Anticipating that decision, state lawmakers have been fighting back.

Assemblyman Al Muratsuchi, a Democrat who represents a Southern California district, authored legislation to ban building any new oil and gas infrastructure on state land that would be used to support oil and natural gas extraction on protected federal lands (which could impact some of the lands being opened for leasing). The bill passed last month, but has yet to be signed by Democratic Gov. Gavin Newsom.

"If there's anything that brings bipartisan outrage in California, it's when people start messing with our beaches and oceans," Mr. Muratsuchi says. Last year, he initiated a bill that prohibited the construction of new infrastructure in state coastal waters that would aid federal oil and gas development.

The legislator casts his latest bill as an extension of the state's ongoing efforts to be a world leader on climate change and renewable energy—even if that means bucking the Trump administration. "We're not looking for a fight," Mr. Muratsuchi says. "But if we need to stand up to protect our state, our people, and our beautiful lands, we will."

A Consistent Pattern

While California—and the emissions waiver, in particular—is a major example of the federal government breaking with tradition and revoking a state's power, it's only one of several, says Mr. Hayes. Also under attack, he says, have been states' right to approve or disapprove projects based on their water-quality standards, to petition the EPA to take action against upwind states that negatively impact their air quality, and to determine what kind of energy they want, as fossil fuels claim they're being unfairly pushed out by states that want clean energy.

It's a consistent enough pattern that last month, the Environmental Council of the States, a nonpartisan association of state environmental agency leaders, sent a letter to Administrator Wheeler raising their concerns. The organization is "seriously concerned," it stated, about unilateral actions "that run counter to the spirit of cooperative federalism and to the appropriate relationship between the federal government and the states who are delegated the authority to implement federal environmental statutes."

In California, the threats to revoke federal funding over failing to meet clean air and water standards seemed to some critics like a declaration of war on the state.

"It strikes me as a really special kind of hypocrisy that [Administrator Wheeler] attacks California over its air quality and the problems it's facing with air pollution a mere week before the administration opens three-quarters of a million acres for oil and gas drilling, which will invariably worsen the air pollution problems we have," says Clare Lakewood, a senior attorney at the Center for Biological Diversity, one of the groups that sued to get a moratorium on drilling leases in 2013.

And other Californians worry, primarily, about the effect that the federal actions will have on the state.

Several studies in recent years have found that the agricultural region that stretches between San Francisco and Los Angeles has the country's worst air quality, says Gustavo Aguirre Jr., a county director with the Central California Environmental Justice Network.

"We're already dealing with bad air and bad water in our area," he says. "With these policies, we risk making things even worse and undoing the small progress we've made in the last 20, 30, 40 years."

Print Citations

CMS: Paulson, Amanda, and Martin Kuz. "States' Rights Became a Liberal Environmental Cause." In *The Reference Shelf: National Debate 2021-2022: Water Resources,* edited by Micah L. Issitt, 177-180. Amenia, NY: Grey House Publishing, 2021.

MLA: Paulson, Amanda, and Martin Kuz. "States' Rights Became a Liberal Environmental Cause." *The Reference Shelf: National Debate 2021-2022: Water Resources,* edited by Micah L. Issitt, Grey House Publishing, 2021, pp. 177-180.

APA: Paulson, A., & Kuz, M. (2021). States' rights became a liberal environmental cause. In Micah L. Issitt (Ed.), *The reference shelf: National debate 2021-2022: Water resources* (pp. 177-180). Amenia, NY: Grey House Publishing.

This Is How the Government Should Define Waters of the United States

By Daren Bakst

The Hill, August 13, 2019

How should the term "Waters of the United States" be defined under the Clean Water Act? For decades, the Environmental Protection Agency and the Army Corps of Engineers have struggled to define this term, primarily because they have consistently sought to go beyond what is legally authorized. The Trump administration has proposed a new definition that does something different by seeking to stay within the law.

Even if the Trump administration develops a clear, reasonable, and legally defensible rule, a future administration can always try to undo it. Rather than leave the matter iffy, Congress should step in and properly define the term itself in statute. Fortunately, there are some proposed legislative solutions. Senators Mike Braun and Joni Ernst have introduced the Define Waters of the United States Act, which is similar to legislation introduced in the lower chamber by Representative Jaime Herrera Beutler.

These proposals would, for the first time, expressly clarify in statute that the regulatory reach of the Clean Water Act goes well beyond traditional navigable waters, extending to their tributaries and adjacent wetlands as well. The legislation though would bring some common sense to discussions of what the act does not cover. For example, it would not regulate what most people would consider to be dry land, such as depressions that hold water a few days a year after heavy rainfall.

Nor would it regulate waters that cannot be seen by the naked eye or may no longer even exist. It also would not include a catch all category of waters so that the federal government can retroactively, on a case-by-case basis, determine that specific waters are regulated under the law. The proposed legislation would address two of the biggest problems of the definition, which are the complete disrespect for the states under the Clean Water Act and the lack of clarity as to what is even regulated.

The Environmental Protection Agency and the Army Corps of Engineers have failed to follow the plain language of the Clean Water Act regarding the state role in addressing pollution. In fact, they have acted more like a local zoning board than a responsible federal agency. The Clean Water Act, right at the start of the statute, makes it perfectly clear that the states should take the lead on water pollution. The proposed legislation respects this position by not trampling on the role of state and local governments.

The Environmental Protection Agency and the Army Corps of Engineers have also adopted subjective and vague definitions, while inconsistently enforcing the law. These problems have gotten worse since the General Accounting Office highlighted them in 2004. Owners may simply decide to forgo certain ordinary activities on their property, such as farming, out of fear that they could be subject to civil and criminal penalties. The legislation would provide much needed clarity for property owners, detailing what is regulated and what is expressly excluded.

> **The Clean Water Act, right at the start of the statute, makes it perfectly clear that states should take the lead on water pollution.**

This is important because a vague and subjective "Waters of the United States" definition can impact almost anyone. If people are merely engaged in dirt moving activities, they might be affected, depending on the scope of the definition. It can impact anyone from farmers plowing land and families seeking to build their dream homes to cities and counties trying to build public safety ditches to help prevent flooding.

Legal and practical considerations too often get ignored because some assume that to have clean water, the federal government must regulate almost every water imaginable. Yet, Congress expressly disagreed with such a mindset in the Clean Water Act. Instead, Congress looked to the states, a choice that makes perfect sense since states know how best to address their specific environmental needs, as opposed to the federal government using a centralized "one size fits all" approach.

The bill keeps the legal and practical considerations in mind, helping to protect private property rights and respect the rule of law. By creating objective and clear definitions, the Environmental Protection Agency and the Army Corps of Engineers would be able to spend less time guessing on what is regulated, thereby generating fewer horror stories born of trying to regulate tire ruts in dirt roads, and more time focusing their attention and resources on those waters that must clearly be considered "Waters of the United States." This approach is ultimately a win for the environment and for achieving the objectives of the Clean Water Act.

Print Citations

CMS: Bakst, Daren. "This Is How the Government Should Define Waters of the United States." In *The Reference Shelf: National Debate 2021-2022: Water Resources*, edited by Micah L. Issitt, 181-183. Amenia, NY: Grey House Publishing, 2021.

MLA: Bakst, Daren. "This Is How the Government Should Define Waters of the United States." *The Reference Shelf: National Debate 2021-2022: Water Resources*, edited by Micah L. Issitt, Grey House Publishing, 2021, pp. 181-183.

APA: Bakst, D. (2021). This is how the government should define waters of the United States. In Micah L. Issitt (Ed.), *The reference shelf: National debate 2021-2022: Water resources* (pp. 181-183). Amenia, NY: Grey House Publishing.

Why Shifting Regulatory Power to the States Won't Improve the Environment

By Michael A. Livermore
The Conversation, **August 2, 2017**

Trump and his appointees, particularly Environmental Protection Agency Administrator Scott Pruitt, have made federalism a theme of their efforts to scale back environmental regulation. They argue that the federal government has become too intrusive and that states should be returned to a position of "regulatory primacy" on environmental matters.

"We have to let the states compete to see who has the best solutions. They know the best how to spend their dollars and how to take care of the people within each state," Trump said in a speech to the National Governors Association last February.

Some liberal-leaning states have responded by adopting more aggressive regulations. California has positioned itself as a leader in the fight to curb climate change. New York is restructuring its electricity market to facilitate clean energy. And Virginia's Democratic governor, Terry McAuliffe, has ordered state environmental regulators to design a rule to cap carbon emissions from power plants.

State experimentation may be the only way to break the gridlock on environmental issues that now overwhelms our national political institutions. However, without a broad mandate from the federal government to address urgent environmental problems, few red and purple states will follow California's lead. In my view, giving too much power to the states will likely result in many states doing less, not more.

What's So Great about the States?

Politicians are happy to praise states' rights, but they rarely say much about what federalism is supposed to accomplish. Granting more power to the states should not be an end unto itself. Rather, it's a way to promote goals such as political responsiveness, experimentation and policy diversity.

Many U.S. environmental laws include roles for states and the federal government to work cooperatively to achieve shared objectives. Often, this involves the federal government setting strict goals, with states taking the lead on implementation and enforcement. This careful balance of federal and state power has been implemented by Republican and Democratic administrations alike.

In recent years, scholars have expanded on Justice Brandeis' famous "laboratories of democracy" model of federalism with the notion of "democratic experimentation." Brandeis' core insight, updated for contemporary society, is that decentralization lets state and local governments experiment with different policies to generate

> **Granting more power to the states should not be an end unto itself. Rather, it's a way to promote goals such as political responsiveness, experimentation and policy diversity.**

information about what works and what doesn't. Other states and the national government can use those insights to generate better policy outcomes.

But as I have shown in recent work, there is no guarantee that state experimentation will produce neutral technical information. It also can generate political information that can be put to good or bad uses.

For example, state experimentation with pollution controls may allow regulators to identify cheap ways to reduce emissions. On the other hand, big polluters may use the opportunity to figure out clever ways to avoid their obligations.

This happened in the 1970s and '80's after the Clean Air Act was enacted. State experimentation allowed polluters to learn that by building very tall smokestacks at electric power plants, they could send pollution downwind while keeping local officials happy. Experimentation resulted in information on how to push pollution around instead of cleaning it up, and utilities in midwest states used this knowledge to shift pollutants to states downwind in the Northeast.

An Elusive Balance

It makes rhetorical sense for the Trump administration to wrap its environmental agenda in federalism. Air and water pollution are unpopular, and conservation groups have called out Trump's policies and budget for undoing "environmental safeguards."

Reframing deregulation as federalism turns the issue into a debate about how to allocate power between the national government and the states. But striking the right balance between federal and state power requires careful attention to context and the costs and benefits of decentralization.

For example, Pruitt has formally proposed to rescind the Clean Water Rule, an Obama administration regulation that clarifies the jurisdiction of EPA and the Army Corps of Engineers to regulate smaller water bodies and wetlands under the Clean Water Act. One might think that without EPA on the beat, states will take a more central role in water pollution control. But in fact, many states have passed laws banning any clean water regulation that is more stringent than federal standards. Shifting responsibility in this area back to states will create a policy vacuum instead of space for experimentation.

Less Creativity, not More

There is even more need for a federal role in addressing problems that have global impacts, such as climate change. Once greenhouse gases are emitted, they do not just cause warming in the place where they were released. Instead, they mix in the atmosphere and contribute to climate change around the world. This means that no given jurisdiction pays the full cost of its emissions. Instead, in the language of economics, these impacts are externalities that are felt elsewhere.

This is why a global agreement is needed to effectively slow climate change. The United States has already withdrawn from the Paris climate accord. If we pull back on regulating greenhouse gases nationally as well, many states will have little incentive to take action.

Under the Obama administration's Clean Power Plan, which Pruitt is reviewing and has told states to ignore, every state was required to figure out how to meet a carbon reduction goal. However, it did not dictate how they should do it.

This approach would have produced valuable political information from red and purple states, which tend to rely more heavily than blue states on fossil fuels. By forcing Republican leaders to craft state climate policies and sell them to their constituents, the Clean Power Plan promoted what I consider truly useful experimentation that could have helped break the national gridlock on climate policy.

Now, without a prod from the federal government, those experiments are unlikely to occur. EPA's retreat will mean that we have less, not more, insight into smart and politically viable ways of cutting carbon emissions.

Any regulation can be improved on, and the Trump administration could have risen to that challenge. Instead, the leadership at EPA is abdicating the agency's traditional leadership role. In doing so, it is promoting stagnation and backsliding rather than innovation.

Print Citations

CMS: Livermore, Michael A. "Why Shifting Regulatory Power to the States Won't Improve the Environment." In *The Reference Shelf: National Debate 2021-2022: Water Resources,* edited by Micah L. Issitt, 184-186. Amenia, NY: Grey House Publishing, 2021.

MLA: Livermore, Michael A. "Why Shifting Regulatory Power to the States Won't Improve the Environment." *The Reference Shelf: National Debate 2021-2022: Water Resources,* edited by Micah L. Issitt, Grey House Publishing, 2021, pp. 184-186.

APA: Livermore, M. A. (2021). Why shifting regulatory power to the states won't improve the environment. In Micah L. Issitt (Ed.), *The reference shelf: National debate 2021-2022: Water resources* (pp. 184-186). Amenia, NY: Grey House Publishing.

Relax: Gutting the EPA Won't Make Your Air Dirtier and Water More Polluted

By Ronald Bailey
Reason, March 21, 2017

President Donald Trump's proposed cuts in the Environmental Protection Agency's budget "will not 'Make America Great Again', " asserted Conrad Schneider, the advocacy director at Clean Air Task Force activist group. "It will 'Make America Gag Again.'" Schneider and other alarmed activists are conjuring the bad old days of the mid-20th century when America's cities were blanketed with smog and its streams clotted with filth. In his new budget blueprint, Trump wants to cut back Environmental Protection Agency funding by 31 percent and fire 3,200 of agency's bureaucrats.

But would such steep EPA budget cuts really unleash polluters to pump out more smoke and sewage? To get a handle on this question, let's take an amble down memory lane to assess the evolution of pollution trends in the United States since President Richard Nixon cobbled together the Environmental Protection Agency in 1970.

First, with regard to air pollution, air pollution in most American cities had been declining over the course of the 20th century. Why? Many American cities had recognized the problem of air pollution in the late 19th century. Consequently, they passed ordinances that aimed to abate and control the clouds of smoke emitted from burning coal in industry, heating, and cooking. For example, Chicago and Cincinnati adopted smoke abatement ordinances in 1881.

American Enterprise Institute scholars Joel Schwartz and Steven Hayward document in their 2007 book, *Air Quality in America*, that emissions of smoke, soot, ozone and sulfur dioxide had been falling for decades before the creation the EPA and the adoption of the Clean Air Act. For example, ambient sulfur dioxide had fallen by 58 percent in New York City during the seven years preceding the adoption of the Clean Air Act. "Air quality has indeed improved since the 1970 passage of the" Clean Air Act, they claim. "But it was improving at about the same pace for decades before the act was passed, and without the unnecessary collateral damage caused by our modern regulatory system."

They attribute a lot of the pre-EPA improvement in air quality to market-driven technological progress and increases in wealth that enabled households to switch from coal to cleaner natural gas for heating and cooking; railroads to replace coal-fired locomotives with diesels; more efficient industrial combustion that reduced the emissions of particulates; and improvements in the electrical grid that allowed power plants to be situated closer to coal mines and further from cities.

Even if the Clean Air Act did not noticeably speed up the rate of air pollution abatement, the air is nevertheless much cleaner than it used to be. How clean? Since 1980 the index for six major pollutants, carbon monoxide, ozone, particulates, sulfur dioxide, nitrogen dioxide and lead has dropped by 65 percent since 1980. In the meantime, the economy grew more than 150 percent, vehicle miles increased by more 100 percent, population grew by more than 40 percent and energy consumption rose by 25 percent. And yet, a 2016 Gallup poll found that 43 percent of Americans say that they worry about air pollution a great deal.

Schwartz and Hayward persuasively argue, "The public's interest lies in sufficiently clean air, achieved at the lowest possible cost. But federal air quality regulation suffers from incentives to create requirements that are unnecessarily stringent, intrusive, bureaucratic, and costly." Basically, the costs of ever tightening federal air pollution controls are now exceeding their benefits. Since most remaining air pollution (except for greenhouse gases which we will set aside for a discussion at another time) is now concentrated in discrete regions rather than crossing jurisdictional lines, cities, counties and states can be reasonably expected to monitor and regulate those pollutants without much federal oversight.

The EPA also regulates water pollution under the Clean Water Act of 1972. That act prohibits anybody from discharging "pollutants" through a "point source" into a "water of the United States" unless they have a permit issued by the EPA that specifies limits on what may be discharged and sets up monitoring and reporting requirements. In addition, the Clean Water Act requires that each state develop a list of impaired surface waters including rivers, lakes, and estuaries. The states also set limits on the maximum amount of each pollutant that can be present in a body of water called Total Maximum Daily Loads (TMDLs).

The EPA under the Obama administration issued regulations that more broadly defined the waters of the United States to include farm ponds, irrigation ditches, intermittent streams, and prairie potholes. At least 32 states had filed lawsuits seeking to block the implementation of Obama administration's new waters of the United States regulations. In February, President Trump signed an executive order instructing the EPA to begin the process of revising the regulations in line with former Supreme Court Justice Antonin Scalia's plurality opinion in the 2006 *Rapanos vs. United States* case that would limit EPA regulation of ephemeral and minor sources of water.

Regulation of non-point source water pollution in the form of runoff from agricultural fields and stormwater drainage from city streets is largely accomplished through setting TMDLs by the states. In many ways, this is just the sort of "cooperative federalism" policy that new EPA administrator Scott Pruitt says he intends to pursue. In the past EPA has provided categorical grants to state environmental agencies to help them devise water quality standards and set up scientific monitoring. The new Trump budget cuts such categorical grants to states and localities by

45 percent, falling from $1.1 billion to $597 million. Since the budget document is basically a hortatory wish list, it is not clear to what the claim that "this funding level eliminates or substantially reduces Federal investment in State environmental activities that go beyond EPA's statutory requirements" is referring. Presumably states and localities would be expected to pay more for their own standard-setting and monitoring.

According to most recent water quality data reported by the states to EPA, about 55 percent of the 1,124,000 miles of rivers and streams assessed are considered impaired due to the presence of pollutants like pathogens, excessive sediments, nutrients, and oxygen depletion. Nearly 72 percent of the assessed 18.3 million acres of lakes, reservoirs, and ponds are impaired and nearly 49 percent of the 1.7 million square miles of the assessed estuaries and bays are impaired. The National River and Streams Assessment 2008/2009 reported that 28 percent of the nation's river and stream length is in good biological condition, 25 percent in fair condition, and 46 percent in poor condition. A U.S. Geological cal Survey report that assessed nitrogen fertilizer runoff trends in the Mississippi River watershed found that they generally increased between 1980 and 2010. Excess nitrogen fertilizer can cause algal blooms that deplete streams, lakes, and estuaries of oxygen producing dead zones.

> **The costs of ever tightening federal air pollution controls are now exceeding their benefits.**

The sources of water pollutants are always local, but by flowing downstream they become someone else's problem as they cross state, county, and municipal boundaries. Just last week, a federal judge dismissed a lawsuit filed by Des Moines Water Works against three upstream drainage districts in three northwest Iowa counties. The Water Works utility that supplies drinking water to 500,000 Iowans claimed that the drainage districts were responsible for loading up the Raccoon River with nitrate runoff from farmers' fields in their counties. The utility was seeking $80 million to upgrade its nitrate removal equipment from the drainage districts.

A fascinating study just published in January by Iowa State University economist David Keiser and Yale University economist David Shapiro seeks to evaluate the benefits and the costs of the Clean Water Act. Specifically, did the benefits of the 35,000 federal government grants amounting to nearly $1 trillion (2014 real dollars) given to municipalities to improve wastewater treatment plants exceed their costs? To get at this question, the researchers compiled what they claim to be the most comprehensive database on U.S. water pollution trends ever. They find that pollution measures like dissolved oxygen deficits, the share of waters that are not fishable or swimmable, the presence of fecal coliform bacteria, and the amount of sediments in streams had all been improving since 1962 and then flattened out after 1990. Overall, they find that during the "period 1972- 2001, the share of waters that are not fishable and the share not swimmable each fell by 11 percentage points."

They do, however, note that "the rate of decrease in pollution slowed after 1972" when the Clean Water Act was adopted. For example, oxygen levels in streams and lakes were improving at a rate of 3 percent per year before 1972 and fell to 1.5 percent thereafter. They suggest that the slow-down could have resulted from the fact that lots of relatively cheap water pollution abatement had been implemented before 1972 and/or that increases in harder to regulate non-point source pollution counterbalanced the improvements achieved through better wastewater treatment.

Keiser and Shapiro try to get a handle on the benefits of the $1 trillion in federal grants spent on wastewater treatment plants by parsing the trends in housing values up to 25 miles downstream. Without going into the details, they calculate based on housing values that the costs of the Clean Water Act wastewater treatment grants were about three times greater than their benefits. They suspect that people value water pollution abatement considerably less than they do reductions in air pollution due to differences in the health consequences of breathing unfiltered air versus drinking water generally filtered through treatment plants. In addition, it is harder to relocate from a polluted airshed than it is to substitute between nearby clean and dirty rivers for recreation.

Nevertheless, the researchers suggest that other amenity values might justify the costs of the grants. For instance, while on a high school band trip from Southwest Virginia in 1970 I recall vividly walking down to the Potomac River at Mount Vernon to see a sign bobbing in the water warning against coming in contact with the water as it was dangerous to one's health. I have now enjoyed many pleasant days boating and sailing on the cleaned up river. In addition, as pollution has abated American cities that once turned inward from their polluted waterfronts have transformed those areas into high rent neighborhoods and entertainment districts.

In addition, to the reductions in the EPA's air and water pollution programs, the Trump budget would cut by $330 million the Superfund program that is supposed to clean up specific hazardous waste sites like abandoned dumps and industrial plants. The program sparks a great deal of litigation that boosts costs and slows clean up. One 1999 study estimated that Superfund remediation would on average avert less than 0.1 case of cancer per site and that the cost per cancer case averted is over $100 million. As Case Western Reserve University law professor Jonathan Adler has argued, "Contamination of soil and groundwater are site-specific, rarely crossing state lines. Due to the local nature of hazardous waste problems, state governments should be given the opportunity to assume leadership of hazardous waste regulation and cleanup." In line with that recommendation, the Trump budget document, instructs the EPA to "look for ways to remove some of the barriers that have delayed the program's ability to return sites to the community."

One other observation: The Trump budget would eliminate the EPA's Endocrine Disruptor Screening Program. Good riddance. Billions of dollars have been spent pursuing the so-called endocrine disruption hypothesis in which trace exposures synthetic chemicals are supposedly causing hormone havoc in people. Two decades of research has comprehensively debunked it. "Taking into account the large resources spent on this topic, one should expect that, in the meantime, some endocrine disruptors that cause actual human injury or disease should have been identified," a group of European toxicologists assert in 2013 review article. "However, this is not the case. To date, with the exception of natural or synthetic hormones, not a single, man-made chemical endocrine disruptor has been identified that poses an identifiable, measurable risk to human health."

Of course, state and local governments will decry the proposed cuts in the EPA grants they expected to receive. Federal dollars are generally treated as "free money" enabling local officials to avoid having to make hard tradeoffs between various programs and amenities and raise state and municipal taxes to pay them. Whatever the achievements of EPA programs in the past—don't forget that rates of air and water pollution abatement didn't actually speed up after the creation of the agency in 1970—we are well past the point of rapidly diminishing returns when it comes to additional pollution abatement. It is the right moment to make states and municipalities more responsible and responsive to their local citizens when it comes to handling environmental concerns and issues.

Print Citations

CMS: Bailey, Ronald. "Relax: Gutting the EPA Won't Make Your Air Dirtier and Water More Polluted." In *The Reference Shelf: National Debate 2021-2022: Water Resources,* edited by Micah L. Issitt, 187-191. Amenia, NY: Grey House Publishing, 2021.

MLA: Bailey, Ronald. "Relax: Gutting the EPA Won't Make Your Air Dirtier and Water More Polluted." *The Reference Shelf: National Debate 2021-2022: Water Resources,* edited by Micah L. Issitt, Grey House Publishing, 2021, pp. 187-191.

APA: Bailey, R. (2021). Relax: Gutting the EPA won't make your air dirtier and water more polluted. In Micah L. Issitt (Ed.), *The reference shelf: National debate 2021-2022: Water resources* (pp. 187-191). Amenia, NY: Grey House Publishing.

Water and U.S. National Security

By Peter Gleick

War Room–U.S. Army War College, June 15, 2017

Around 2500 BC, Urlama, the King of the city-state of Lagash, diverted water from boundary irrigation canals between the Tigris and Euphrates rivers to deprive a neighboring region, Umma, of water. This act, in a region corresponding to parts of modern day Iraq, Syria, and southern Turkey, was the first recorded political and military dispute over water resources. Four and a half millennia later, water remains an instrument of coercion and a source of tensions and conflict. The Islamic State has reportedly used water as a weapon, depriving communities in Mosul of access to a water supply, and control over water facilities has been used repeatedly, worsening access to safe water for civilian populations.

Fresh water has long been a vital and necessary natural resource, and it has long been a source of tension, a military tool, and a target during war. The links between water and conflict have been the subject of extensive analysis for several decades, beginning with the development of the literature on "environmental security" and water conflicts in the late 1980s and early 1990s. In coming years, new factors, including rising populations, industrial and agricultural demand for water, human-induced climate change, and political uncertainties make it increasingly urgent that solutions to water tensions be found and implemented. The failure to address water problems through diplomacy will lead to new and growing security risks, including for the U.S. The U.S. and its allies must develop and employ a wide variety of instruments to reduce instability and the risk of conflict related to growing water problems, before military intervention is needed.

Global and Regional Water Challenges

Fresh water is vital for all human economic and social activities, from the production of food and energy, to support for industrial development, to the maintenance of natural ecosystems. Yet freshwater resources are limited, unevenly distributed in space and time, increasingly contaminated or overused, and poorly managed. These constraints, coupled with growing populations and economies, are putting more and more pressure on natural water resources, even in regions where they were previously considered abundant. Such pressures have the potential to explode into violent conflict.

In the late 1970s and early 1980s, military and academic experts concerned about international security and conflict began to shift their focus from *realpolitik* and superpower politics to an evaluation of other threats to national and international stability. These included environmental threats such as energy security and oil transfers, transboundary environmental pollution, conflicts over water resources, and the potential impacts of climate change.

The fundamental concept, now widely accepted, is that political instability and violence, especially at the local or regional level, are extensively *influenced* by economic, demographic, and social factors that are themselves sensitive to resource and environmental conditions.

Even in a static world, conditions and challenges in major international river basins would persist. Yet the world is not static, but experiencing dynamic and often rapid changes in demographics and environmental conditions. Populations are growing rapidly, economies are expanding or changing focus, and the climate is undergoing increasingly rapid shifts due to rising concentrations of greenhouse gases.

The links between resources and security concerns include direct and indirect impacts. Direct conflicts over access to water are uncommon and almost always local–related to water scarcity and access. But there is also a rise in direct attacks on water systems, such as dams, water treatment and distribution plants, and hydroelectric facilities, in conflicts that start for other (non-resource-related) reasons. In recent years, major dams and water infrastructure have been both used as weapons of war and directly attacked by different sides in the wars in Iraq and Syria, as well as in Ukraine.

Indirect effects include cases in which water resources lead to changes in food production or other economic factors, which in turn contribute to state instability and conflict. In Syria, for example, the civil war is a complicated mix of ethnic, religious, and ideological disputes, but there are also

> **Modern technologies such as precision irrigation, soil-moisture monitors, desalination, distributed wastewater treatments, smart metering, and more can also reduce the difficulties associated with sustainable water management.**

documented links between social unrest and violent conflict related to influences of regional long-term drought, climate change, agricultural crop failures, rising rural unemployment and migration to cities.

It is no accident that water is especially politically controversial in the Middle East: it is an arid, water-short region; every significant river and watershed is shared by two or more countries, including the Nile, Jordan, Tigris, Euphrates, and Orontes. As a result, international agreements about sustainable river management are critical, yet there have been very few successful inter-basin treaties signed for the region.

In recent decades, the lack of adequate international agreements has contributed to a series of political and potentially violent water-related disputes in the region. In 1974, Iraq threatened to bomb the al-Thawra (Tabqa) Dam in Syria and massed troops along the Syrian-Iraq border, alleging that the dam reduced flows of Euphrates water to Iraq. In 1990, the flow of the Euphrates was temporarily interrupted when Turkey finished construction on the massive Ataturk Dam. Both Syria and Iraq protested the interruption. The political situation was worsened when Turkish President Turgut Özal threatened to restrict water flow to Syria to force it to withdraw support for Kurdish rebels. In June 2015, Islamic State militants shut off and redirected water flows below Ramadi Dam on the Euphrates River in order to facilitate military movements. Two months later, Syrian rebel groups cut off water from a spring in Ain al-Fijah, reducing water output to Damascus by 90 percent for three days and leading to water shortages and rationing. In December 2015, Russian Federation forces reportedly bombed the al-Khafsa water treatment facility in the city of Aleppo cutting off water for millions of people.

According to *Global Water Security*, a recent report produced by the U.S. intelligence community, such threats are increasingly relevant to decisions about conflict resolution and national security policy and strategy. Analyzing global and regional water security issues, the report concludes that water problems along with social tensions, poverty, environmental degradation, weak governments, and other factors will contribute to political instability in regions and countries important to U.S. national security. The intelligence report also identified competition between nations over water, weak economies, and limited technical ability as destabilizing factors in some countries. It concluded that these issues would grow over the next decade.

Similarly, the U.S. Department of Defense and the U.S. intelligence community have acknowledged the reality of environmental disruptions and the risks they pose to U.S. global interests as "threat multipliers" that contribute to destabilizing political and security impacts. The Center for Naval Analysis Military Advisory Board raised this point in the context of the growing likelihood that climate change would worsen drought, famine, flood, and refugee problems.

The 2014 U.S. Quadrennial Defense Review also considered resource issues as threat multipliers that pose significant challenges for the United States and the world at large. The 2014 Review argued that these threats "can enable terrorist activities and other forms of violence." A March 2017 North Atlantic Treaty Organization Parliamentary Assembly assessment identified food and water problems as special challenges for security in the Middle East and North Africa, noting, "[d]eteriorating food and water security can lead to domestic unrest, potentially destabilising countries" and "[f]ood and water resources and infrastructure can also be targeted or used as coercive tools in times of conflict." The May 11, 2017 statement of the Director of National Intelligence to the U.S. Senate Select Committee on Intelligence noted, "[h]eightened tensions over shared water resources are likely in some regions."

Recent security concerns in Europe have been related to the massive population dislocation and refugee flows driven by the civil war in Syria, as well as by the continued economic and political unrest in Iraq and North Africa. The European Commission has linked the refugee crisis to both the overall political situation in the conflict region as well as to climate change and water problems.

National and international leaders must take steps to reduce the risks and threats associated with water insecurity. Options include: improvements and modifications in water supply and use; reduction in inefficient water practices; agricultural reform; economic strategies to strengthen resilience to climate and water variability; improved resource management; broader political stabilization; diplomatic approaches; and direct military strategies.

For water resources, combinations of these approaches have been synthesized in descriptions of a more integrated management approach, or a "soft path for water." An application of these kinds of strategies could have reduced the role that water played in the recent Syrian civil war: more efficient agricultural water use would have permitted greater food production and the retention of rural jobs. Policies to more effectively manage variable supplies could have lessened the economic costs of the drought. Modern technologies such as precision irrigation, soil-moisture monitors, desalination, distributed wastewater treatment, smart metering, and more can also reduce the difficulties associated with sustainable water management.

A long history of political tensions and violence associated with poor water policies and management, combined with new threats associated with growing populations, new ideological challenges, and a changing climate make it urgent that we better understand—and work to reduce—the risks of water-related conflict. Solutions to water tensions exist but the failure to address these issues greatly increases the risks that violence and conflict over water will grow and that military and intelligence resources will be called into action. The British politician, Tony Benn, said, "War represents a failure of diplomacy." If we fail to manage water sustainably, strategically, and effectively, water will be an increasing source of conflict. The good news is that smart solutions exist if we have the foresight and initiative to pursue them.

Print Citations

CMS: Gleick, Peter. "Water and U.S. National Security." In *The Reference Shelf: National Debate 2021-2022: Water Resources,* edited by Micah L. Issitt, 192-195. Amenia, NY: Grey House Publishing, 2021.

MLA: Gleick, Peter. "Water and U.S. National Security." *The Reference Shelf: National Debate 2021-2022: Water Resources,* edited by Micah L. Issitt, Grey House Publishing, 2021, pp. 192-195.

APA: Gleick, P. (2021). Water and U.S. national security. In Micah L. Issitt (Ed.), *The reference shelf: National debate 2021-2022: Water resources* (pp. 192-195). Amenia, NY: Grey House Publishing.

A Military View on Climate Change, It's Eroding Our National Security and We Should Prepare for It

By David Titley

The Conversation, October 6, 2016

In this presidential election year we have heard much about some issues, such as immigration and trade, and less about others. For example, climate change was discussed for an estimated 82 seconds in the first presidential debate last week, and for just 37 minutes in all presidential and vice presidential debates since the year 2000.

Many observers think climate change deserves more attention. They might be surprised to learn that U.S. military leaders and defense planners agree. The armed forces have been studying climate change for years from a perspective that rarely is mentioned in the news: as a national security threat. And they agree that it poses serious risks.

I spent 32 years as a meteorologist in the U.S. Navy, where I initiated and led the Navy's Task Force on Climate Change. Here is how military planners see this issue: We know that the climate is changing, we know why it's changing and we understand that change will have large impacts on our national security. Yet as a nation we still only begrudgingly take precautions.

The Obama administration recently announced several actions that create a framework for addressing climate-driven security threats. But much of the hard work lies ahead—assuming that our next president understands the risks and chooses to act on them.

Climate-Related Disruptions

Climate change affects our security in two ways. First, it causes stresses such as water shortages and crop failures, which can exacerbate or inflame existing tensions within or between states. These problems can lead to state failure, uncontrolled migration and ungoverned spaces.

On Sept. 21 the National Intelligence Council issued its most recent report on implications of climate change for U.S. national security. This document represents the U.S. intelligence community's strategic-level view. It does not come from the Intergovernmental Panel on Climate Change, politicians of either party or an advocacy group, but from nonpartisan, senior U.S. intelligence professionals.

The NIC report emphasizes that the problem is not simply climate change, but the interaction of climate with other large-scale demographic and migration trends; its impacts on food, energy and health; and the stresses it will place on societies, especially fragile ones.

> **The more ability we have to adapt to and manage changes and the rate of change in our climate, the greater our chances are to avoid catastrophic chaos and instability.**

As examples the report cites diverse events, ranging from mass protests and violence triggered by water shortages in Mauritania to the possibility that thawing in the Arctic could threaten Russian oil pipelines in the region. Other studies have identified climate change as a contributing factor to events including the civil war in Syria and the Arab Spring uprisings.

Second, climate change is putting our military bases and associated domestic infrastructure in the United States under growing pressure from rising sea levels, "nuisance flooding," increasingly destructive storm surges, intense rainfalls and droughts, and indirect impacts from wildfires. All of these trends make it harder to train our soldiers, sailors, airmen and marines to deploy and fight the "away" game and to keep our forces ready to deploy.

These changes are not hypothetical. Consider Hurricane Matthew: although we cannot directly attribute this storm to climate change, scientists tell us that as climate change worsens, major hurricanes will become more severe. As Matthew moves up the Atlantic coast, the armed forces are evacuating thousands of service members and dependents out of its path, and the Navy is moving ships out to sea. Other units are preparing to deliver hurricane relief to hard-hit areas.

Many of us who work in this field have written and talked about risks like these for years. Along with 24 other retired senior officers, civilian defense officials from Republican and Democratic administrations, and well-respected academics, I recently signed a consensus statement that calls climate change a strategically significant risk to our national security and international stability. We called for "a robust agenda to both prevent and prepare for climate change risks," and warned that "inaction is not an option."

The "change" part of climate change is critical: The more ability we have to adapt to and manage changes and the rate of change in our climate, the greater our chances are to avoid catastrophic chaos and instability.

Meeting the Challenge

Simultaneously with the NIC report on Sept. 21, the White House released a Presidential Memorandum, or PM, on climate change and national security. This document formally states the administration's position that climate change impacts national security.

Building on past executive orders and policies, it directs senior climate officials at 20 federal agencies to form a working group on climate change and national security, cochaired by the president's national security adviser and science adviser. This working group will analyze questions such as which countries and regions are most vulnerable to climate change impacts in the near, medium and long term.

That's high-level attention! In the words of a senior administration official, the PM "gives permission" for career civil servants and military professionals to work on this challenge, just as they address myriad other security challenges daily.

But we need to do much more. I am a member of the Climate and Security Advisory Group – a voluntary, nonpartisan group of 43 U.S.-based military, national security, homeland security, intelligence and foreign policy experts from a broad range of institutions. We have produced a comprehensive briefing book for the next administration that makes detailed recommendations about how to expand our efforts to address security risks associated with climate change.

Our top-line recommendation is to "mainstream" this issue by ensuring that U.S. leaders consider climate change on an equal basis with more traditional security issues, such as changing demographics, economics, political dynamics and other indicators of instability–as well as with low-probability, high-consequence threats like nuclear proliferation. We also recommend that the next president should designate senior officials in key departments, the intelligence community, the National Security Council and within the Executive Office of the President itself to ensure this intent is carried out.

What's next? As a retired naval officer, I find myself drawing on the words of American naval heroes like Admiral Chester Nimitz. In 1945, while he was commander in chief of the U.S. Pacific Fleet, Nimitz wrote about a devastating storm near the Philippines that had sunk three ships and seriously damaged more than 20 others, killing and injuring hundreds of sailors. He concluded by observing that:

"The time for taking all measures for a ship's safety is while still able to do so. Nothing is more dangerous than for a seaman to be grudging in taking precautions lest they turn out to have been unnecessary. Safety at sea for a thousand years has depended on exactly the opposite philosophy."

The next president will have a choice to make. One option is to continue down the path that the Obama administration has defined and develop policies, budgets, plans and programs that flesh out the institutional framework now in place. Alternatively, he or she can call climate change a hoax manufactured by foreign governments and ignore the flashing red lights of increasing risk.

The world's ice caps will not care who is elected or what is said. They will simply continue to melt, as dictated by laws of physics. But Americans will care deeply about our policy response. Our nation's security is at stake.

Print Citations

CMS: Titley, David. "A Military View on Climate Change, It's Eroding Our National Security and We Should Prepare for It." In *The Reference Shelf: National Debate 2021-2022: Water Resources,* edited by Micah L. Issitt, 196-199. Amenia, NY: Grey House Publishing, 2021.

MLA: Titley, David. "A Military View on Climate Change, It's Eroding Our National Security and We Should Prepare for It." *The Reference Shelf: National Debate 2021-2022: Water Resources,* edited by Micah L. Issitt, Grey House Publishing, 2021, pp. 196-199.

APA: Titley, D. (2021). A military view on climate change, it's eroding our national security and we should prepare for it. In Micah L. Issitt (Ed.), *The reference shelf: National debate 2021-2022: Water resources* (pp. 196-199). Amenia, NY: Grey House Publishing.

What Does Water Have to Do with National Security?

By Charles Iceland and Betsy Otto
World Resources Institute, **February 27 2017**

When thinking of national security issues, rivers, lakes and glaciers are not usually what come to mind. But water stress is, in fact, an often-overlooked and increasing threat to national security for many countries.

Water security is an important issue driving state stability and safety in many regions of the world. The direct and indirect effects of water stress—such as migration, food shortages and general destabilization—transcend national boundaries. As water stress increases in the coming years, prioritization of water resources in domestic and global security policies will become even more essential.

World's Water Is Increasingly Stressed

A given location experiences "water stress" when its water demand is high relative to its water supply. Water demand is growing in many places, driven by population and economic growth. At the same time, climate change is beginning to deprive mid-latitude areas of their usual rainfall, which reduces water supply and exacerbates stress. In a new paper, the Council on Foreign Relations (CFR) used WRI's Aqueduct global water risk tool to show water stress levels in 2030, under one plausible global scenario. This scenario shows that many regions in the world—such as the Middle East and the western United States—will experience increased water stress in 2030.

Water stress increases the likelihood of disputes over water, as people and countries compete for scarce resources. In CFR's "Water and U.S. National Security," author Joshua Busby argues that this risk is maximized when water stress and weak governance intersect. Water stress has played a key role in a number of recent conflicts, including the war in Darfur and fighting in the Lake Chad Basin, where the Boko Haram insurgency has taken place. In these instances, diminishing water supply has been a contributing factor to conflict, as groups fought for access to this increasingly precious resource.

A Troubling Case Study from the Middle East

Water has been a hidden player in the current conflict in Syria. From 2006 through

2011, Syria experienced its worst drought in recorded history. NASA satellite data from that time period showed that water in the Tigris and Euphrates river basins decreased at an alarming rate, as demand for freshwater contin-

> **The direct and indirect effects of water stress—such as migration, food shortages and general destabilization—transcend national boundaries.**

ued to rise. This drought, combined with water mismanagement, resulted in crop failures and food insecurity, which were some of the many catalysts for the civil war.

Water has also been used as a weapon during the war itself. During fighting between the government and rebel forces in December 2016, water supply was cut off to the city of Damascus. Each side blamed the other for the disruption, which left more than 5.5 million people with only minimal access to water. This led the UN to declare that depriving Damascus of water constituted a war crime if done intentionally.

What Do We Do?

With water stress projected to rise in so many of the world's highly populated and strategically important areas, countries should include studying and mitigating water risks in their national security strategies. The United States, for example, began to do so by evaluating the implications of global water stress for national security. In 2012, at the direction of the Secretary of State, the National Intelligence Council (NIC) prepared a report on global water security. The NIC concluded that over the next 10 years, freshwater availability worldwide would not be able to keep up with demand, hindering food production, economic growth and security. The council predicted that water will increasingly be used as leverage between nations and even as a "weapon to further terrorist objectives."

The solution to these problems, according to the NIC, lies in improving water management through water pricing, more efficient water allocation, and virtually trading water from water-rich countries to water-scarce ones. National, state and local governments, the private sector and NGOs all have a role to play in improving water management worldwide.

Improved water management also requires better data and effective early-warning systems. A new High Level Panel on Water, led by the UN, World Bank and several heads of state, sees better data as a crucial element to water security. Water risk and early-warning tools such as Aqueduct and the Famine Early Warning Systems Network (FEWS NET) can help decision-makers prioritize action, both in the short- and long-terms.

Busby writes that, "the failure to invest in water and security now could mean that the United States and other international actors will pay billions later to respond to crises, whether they be humanitarian emergencies, disease outbreaks, or conflicts within or between states." We know how to identify water-related risks to national security, and we are beginning to identify best practices for reducing them. Will governments muster the political will to tackle the issue?

Print Citations

CMS: Iceland, Charles, and Betsy Otto. "What Does Water Have to Do with National Security?" In *The Reference Shelf: National Debate 2021-2022: Water Resources,* edited by Micah L. Issitt, 200-202. Amenia, NY: Grey House Publishing, 2021.

MLA: Iceland, Charles, and Betsy Otto. "What Does Water Have to Do with National Security?" *The Reference Shelf: National Debate 2021-2022: Water Resources,* edited by Micah L. Issitt, Grey House Publishing, 2021, pp. 200-202.

APA: Iceland, C., & Otto, B. (2021). What does water have to do with national security? In Micah L. Issitt (Ed.), *The reference shelf: National debate 2021-2022: Water resources* (pp. 200-202). Amenia, NY: Grey House Publishing.

Climate Change, Water Security, and U.S. National Security

By Carolyn Kenney
Center for American Progress, March 22, 2017

The first months of Donald Trump's presidency have raised serious concerns about the new administration's understanding of climate change and the associated security risks. President Trump's vocal skepticism of climate change and his appointment of several prominent climate deniers to his Cabinet, along with deep proposed budget cuts to government activities aimed at slowing or adapting to climate change, could see the new administration do untold damage to the environment, human health and security, economic development, and international peace and stability.

The Trump administration's disengagement comes at a time when severe weather conditions spurred on by climate change are having devastating effects in the United States and around the world. In California, for example, despite a recent respite, the state's long-running drought cost the state's agricultural sector an estimated $2.7 billion in 2015 alone, and the state is expected to experience chronic water shortages in the future.[1] In southern Africa, for example, millions are at risk of starvation following a two-year drought and above-average temperatures.[2] And in Sri Lanka, the worst drought in 40 years has left more than 1 million people affected by acute water shortages.[3]

These worrying signs early in the Trump administration contrast sharply with the legacy of former President Barack Obama. Before leaving office, President Obama signed a Presidential Memorandum on Climate Change and National Security designed to elevate and address the national security implications of climate change. Hailed as an historic step, the memorandum directed federal departments and agencies to "ensure that climate change-related impacts are fully considered in the development of national security doctrine, policies, and plans."[4] Released alongside a National Intelligence Council, or NIC, report, "Implications for US National Security of Anticipated Climate Change," the memorandum reflected the consensus among U.S. national security experts that climate change is a core national security concern and should be addressed as such.[5] Indeed, even some within the Trump administration agree with this consensus: Trump's Secretary of Defense James Mattis, in his written testimony following his confirmation hearing, noted that climate change poses a serious threat to American interests abroad.[6]

Both Obama's presidential memorandum and the NIC report argue that extreme and more frequent weather events, droughts, heat waves, rising sea levels, and ocean acidification—all driven or exacerbated by climate change—will increasingly threaten food and water security, energy and transportation infrastructure, and other crucial systems in the decades to come. These disruptions can seriously stress or overwhelm affected governments' ability to respond to crises, threatening human security and eroding state legitimacy. Deteriorating conditions or severe crises can undermine economic livelihoods and contribute to decisions to migrate. Taken in the aggregate, these stresses can create political instability and amplify conditions that lead to conflict, especially in already fragile or unstable regions.[7] And, as many recent crises have demonstrated, instability and violence in one country often do not remain confined solely within that country's borders. Both reports therefore conclude that it is in the United States' national interest to try and address the underlying drivers of crises abroad to prevent future instability and avoid more expensive crisis interventions.

While the Trump administration's approach to the issues outlined in the memorandum and the NIC report are shaping up to be hostile, the fact that such challenges exist is unequivocal.[8] The administration would do well to heed the advice of climate and national security experts and ensure that the United States continues to address these issues.

Climate Change and Water Security

Perhaps the most pressing area of concern at the nexus of climate change and national security is that of water security. As outlined clearly in a recent World Bank report, the effects of climate change will come through the water cycle—affecting food, energy, urban, and environmental systems as populations, cities, and economies continue to grow and strain increasingly limited water resources.[9] According to the World Bank, roughly 1.6 billion people already live in countries with water scarcity, and that number could double in just two decades.[10] The continued impacts of climate change on water supplies, if not properly managed, will have far-reaching consequences for national and international security. Indeed, these consequences are already visible.

In recent years, there have been regular reports of heightened social tensions and even violent conflict, partially as a result of climate-induced disasters related to water security, such as prolonged droughts and increased desertification. One of the more notable cases demonstrating this has been that of Syria, where prolonged drought linked to climate change and the Syrian government's poor response to it—while not a direct cause of the conflict in the country—played a role in exacerbating the social, economic, and political conditions that led to the outbreak of conflict in 2011 and the resulting refugee crisis, in which more than 4.9 million Syrians have fled the country as of March 2017.[11] A more recent example is that of Tunisia, where there have been concerns that the country might be heading toward a "thirst uprising."[12] Since July 2016, there have been several protests in regions across the country sparked by water scarcity from prolonged drought and years of poor resource management.[13]

Some of the most critical questions that come next include how and where serious climate-related national security concerns might manifest in the future, and what the United States and the international community are doing to try to prevent, respond to, and mitigate them.

Water Supply and Demand

At the most basic level, the greatest challenges regarding water security and climate change come back to issues of supply and demand. According to U.N. predictions, the world population will reach 8.5 billion by 2030 and 9.7 billion by 2050, with Africa expected to account for half of this growth.[14] As populations grow, so do economies, both of which require increased water resources. For instance, it takes about 4,000 gallons of water to produce roughly two pounds of beef; 240 gallons of water to manufacture one cell phone; and three to six gallons of water to produce one gallon of gasoline.[15] Additionally, as countries become more prosperous and incomes rise, water use increases dramatically—and often unsustainably.[16] As a result of these pressures, the United Nations projects that by 2050, global water demand will increase by 55 percent, with the greatest demands coming from manufacturing, thermal electricity generation, and domestic use.[17]

On the supply side, the amount of total surface water around the world is expected to remain fixed in the coming decades.[18] However, the distribution of this water varies greatly and could become more uneven, with many already water-stressed regions becoming more so in the future, as snowmelt and precipitation patterns become more variable around the world due to climate change.[19] The decline in surface water is projected to hit hardest in the least developed countries, where water availability is most critical for agriculture, energy production, and economic development.[20] Also of note

> **The United Nations projects that by 2050, global water demand will increase by 55 percent, with the greatest demands coming from manufacturing, thermal electricity generation, and domestic use.**

is the fact that there are currently 150 million people who reside in cities with perennial water shortages, and as demographics shift, this number is projected to increase to almost 1 billion people by 2050—with much of this growth happening in the developing world.[21]

Climate change will also affect groundwater found in aquifers, which contain roughly 30 percent of the world's available freshwater.[22] Groundwater reservoirs will be directly affected by climate change through recharge patterns—in areas where total surface water declines, groundwater resources are also likely to decline.[23] And as temperatures rise, the risk of increased groundwater salinity grows, meaning the quality and usability of water resources will decline in some areas.[24]

If nothing is done to increase water efficiency and better manage and protect both surface water and groundwater in the face of a changing climate, demand could exceed current sustainable water supplies by 40 percent by 2030.[25]

Effects of Water Scarcity

The consequences of water scarcity, as with the distribution of water supplies, vary greatly around the world as a result of a number of factors, including political, social, and economic conditions; existing infrastructure—or lack thereof; and policy decisions. Of particular concern are the impacts of water scarcity on human livelihoods and social tensions, which can contribute to cycles of poverty and violence.

If not appropriately addressed, water scarcity has the potential to negatively affect economic performance at all levels, as economic growth requires greater water resources. This in turn inhibits poverty alleviation, which is highly dependent on economic growth. Water scarcity also adversely affects agricultural production, food security, and commodity prices, all of which directly affect human livelihoods and contribute to cycles of poverty. This is especially true for the almost 78 percent of the world's poor who rely on agriculture, livestock, or aquaculture to survive.[26]

Additionally, as water supplies become constrained, social tensions over access to available resources can escalate and even turn violent. This is especially likely in fragile states that have a history of conflict and in areas where access to water resources has been politicized. The United Nations has found that while disputes over natural resources are rarely the sole driver of violent conflict, they certainly can be a contributing factor when other drivers are present, such as poverty, ethnic polarization, and poor governance.[27]

The case of Darfur in Sudan highlights some of the consequences of water scarcity when combined with complex political, social, and economic conditions. As with most conflicts, the origins of the violence in Darfur are highly complex and driven by many forces; any discussion of environmental drivers should in no way exculpate those who have carried out violent acts or enacted destructive policies. However, as highlighted by the United Nations, "regional climate variability, water scarcity and the steady loss of fertile land" in the country played an important underlying role in the conflict that broke out in 2003.[28] These underlying environmental factors combined with increased population and livestock density to help foster violent competition among various groups in the region, 75 percent of whose livelihoods were directly dependent on natural resources.[29] While these environmental and demographic shifts were taking place, the Sudanese national government in Khartoum took steps to undermine and eventually eliminate local governance systems that had evolved to prevent resource conflicts.[30] With few mechanisms to resolve disputes, the region was left vulnerable to violent conflict driven in part by competition for resources—competition propelled, in turn, by environmental and demographic trends. The United Nations estimates that between 2004 and 2008, as many as 300,000 people died and 2.7 million people were displaced as a result of the conflict.[31]

Main Areas of Concern

To determine where water scarcity may drive security risks, it is critical to understand both future water constraints and a particular state's ability to cope with such stresses in the context of the other social, economic, and political challenges it might face. One way to identify these areas of concern is by cross-referencing indices that track water constraints and state fragility around the world. Projecting the effects of climate change, shifting and expanding demographics, and economic changes is extremely difficult and subject to countless variables, but there are a number of tools that can provide a general picture of where these factors are likely to strain water supplies in the future.

One such tool, developed by the World Resources Institute, or WRI, is the Aqueduct Projected Water Stress Country Rankings.[32] To develop the data set, WRI used a number of climate models and socioeconomic scenarios to project future water stress under three different scenarios—"business-as-usual," "optimistic," and "pessimistic"—in 167 countries in 2020, 2030, and 2040.

Examining the top 50 countries in Aqueduct's business as usual scenario across all three time spans gives a sense of which regions will experience the most severe water stress if action is not taken to improve water efficiency and resource management. Not surprisingly, the Middle East and North Africa account for the highest proportion of high-risk countries across all three time spans, with 18 countries likely to face high water stress in each period. Europe accounts for the next highest proportion with 12 countries facing water stress in 2020 and 14 countries in both 2030 and 2040. Next is Asia with 11 countries in 2020 and 2030 and 12 countries in 2040. Also of note here is the United States' presence on the list for each time span.

But projecting future water stress does not account for a state's ability to respond to these trends. While it is difficult to predict a state's ability to cope with future stress, there are several indices that highlight current state fragility and coping abilities, which can help pinpoint areas of concern. One index that captures these elements is the Fragile States Index 2016 by the Fund for Peace.[33] Using their own analytical platform, the Fund for Peace analyzes millions of documents from three primary sources each year to inform scores on 12 social, economic, and political indicators, which then allows them to rank 178 states by their own measurement of fragility.

Looking at the Fragile States Index and the Aqueduct index together, eight countries stand out: Afghanistan, Iran, Iraq, Lebanon, Libya, Pakistan, Syria, and Yemen. These countries appear in the top 50 on Aqueduct's business as usual list of the most water-stressed countries in 2020, 2030, and 2040 and also appear in the top 50 on the Fragile States Index rankings for 2016. In addition, of the top 50 fragile states, Eritrea appears as one of the top water-stressed countries in 2020 and 2030; Timor Leste in 2020; and both Haiti and Sri Lanka in 2040. Some countries not included in this cross-reference still warrant concern given historical tensions over water, such as Palestine and Israel, as well as India and Pakistan.[34]

It is clear from these various lists that some of the greatest areas of concern with regard to water security will continue to be the Middle East, North Africa, and

South Asia, and mostly in countries that have experienced or continue to experience protracted conflicts.

U. S. and International Community Responses

The United States has undertaken a number of efforts in recent years to address climate change and water security, such as through President Obama's executive orders directing agencies to integrate various dimensions of climate change into their planning, including national security, and through their leadership role in negotiating the Paris Agreement. Under a Trump administration, however, many of these efforts remain vulnerable to attack. Although there are still some measures which are not as easy to dismiss.

As mandated by the Senator Paul Simon Water for the World Act of 2014, President Trump—with the help of the U.S. Agency for International Development, the State Department, and other federal departments and agencies—must submit to Congress a Global Water Strategy by October 1, 2017 outlining how the United States plans to "increase access to safe water, sanitation and hygiene in high priority countries; improve the management of water resources and watersheds in such countries; and work to prevent and resolve intra- and trans-boundary conflicts over water resources in such countries."[35] Presumably, government agencies have been working on contributions to this strategy since this law was enacted, and hopefully a Trump administration will come to see the necessity of continuing to provide resources for completing and eventually implementing such a strategy, as mandated. In the process of doing so, the administration will have the opportunity to see the evidence, including the conviction of many in the military and intelligence community, that climate change is indeed a critical factor in maintaining national and international security.

Absent U.S. leadership in this area, there are a number of other multilateral organizations and individual countries that have shown a desire to act on these issues. For example, in addition to the historic Paris Agreement on combatting climate change, which has been ratified by 134 parties and passed the threshold for entry into force, the United Nations' Sustainable Development Agenda includes two goals which directly address climate change and water security: SDG number six on ensuring "the availability and sustainable management of water and sanitation for all" and SDG number 13 on taking "urgent action to combat climate change and its impacts."[36] Furthermore, Germany has now taken over the G-20 leadership and has identified the implementation of the Paris Agreement and the Sustainable Development Goals as their main priorities, both of which are critical to addressing issues of water security.[37]

Conclusion

As consistently argued by the U.S. military and intelligence community, scientific and academic experts, the United Nations, the World Bank, and America's closest allies, climate change is a threat multiplier; it has the potential to exacerbate existing social, political, and economic tensions to devastating effect. If humans continue to ignore climate change and its impacts, such as on the world's critical water supply, the consequences will only grow more dire. In a world of increasing uncertainty, it is essential to not only change behaviors that lead to further climate change but also to work to prevent and mitigate the now unavoidable impacts the world will face as a result of it.

Endnotes

1. Richard Howitt and others, "Economic Analysis of the 2015 Drought For California Agriculture" (Davis, CA: UC Davis Center for Watershed Sciences, ERA Economics, UC Agricultural Issues Center, 2015), available at https://watershed.ucdavis.edu/files/biblio/Final_Drought%20Report_08182015_Full_Report_WithAppendices.pdf; Jay Famigliette and Michelle Miro, "Our Wild, Wet Winter Doesn't Change This Reality—California Will Be Short of Water Forever," *Los Angeles Times*, March 2, 2017, available at http://www.latimes.com/opinion/op-ed/la-oe-famiglietti-miro-after-the-drought-20170307-story.html.

2. Kevin Corriveau, "Food Security Crisis in Southern Africa after Drought," *Al Jazeera*, January 5, 2017, available at http://www.aljazeera.com/news/2017/01/food-security-crisis-southern-africa-drought-170105094830319.html?utm_source=Review+for+January+6%2C+2017&utm_campaign=DMR-+EN+-+1%2F6%2F2017&utm_medium=email.

3. Dominique Mosbergen, "Sri Lanka Is Suffering Its Worst Drought In 40 Years," The Huffington Post, January 25, 2017, available at http://www.huffingtonpost.com/entry/sri-lanka-drought_us_5885bcb4e4b0e3a7356a1160.

4. White House Office of the Press Secretary, "Presidential Memorandum—Climate Change and National Security," Press release, September 21, 2016, available at https://www.whitehouse.gov/the-press-office/2016/09/21/presidential-memorandum-climate-change-and-national-security.

5. National Intelligence Council, *Implications for US National Security of Anticipated Climate Change* (Office of the Director of National Intelligence, 2016), available at https://www.dni.gov/files/documents/Newsroom/Reports%20and%20Pubs/Implications_for_US_National_Security_of_Anticipated_Climate_Change.pdf; For example, see the Climate and Security Advisory Group, "Briefing Book for a New Administration: Recommended Policies and Practices for Addressing the Security Risks of a Changing Climate" (Washington: The Center for Climate and Security, 2016), available at https://climateandsecurity.files.wordpress.com/2016/09/climate-and-security-advisory-group_briefing-book-for-a-new-administration_2016_091.pdf.

6. Andrew Revkin, "Trump's Defense Secretary Cites Climate Change as National Security Challenge," ProPublica, March 14, 2017, available at https://www.propublica.org/article/trumps-defense-secretary-cites-climate-change-national-security-challenge.

7. National Intelligence Council, *Implications for US National Security of Antici- pated Climate Change.*

8. As highlighted in several pieces written by the Center for American Progress over the years. For a list of publications, see the Center for American Progress, "Climate-Migration-Security," available at https://www.americanprogress.org/ projects/climate-migration-security/view/ (last accessed March 2017).

9. World Bank Group, "High and Dry: Climate Change, Water, and the Econo- my." Working Paper (2016), available at http://hdl.handle.net/10986/23665.

10. Ibid.

11. Francesco Femia and Caitlin Werrell, "Climate Change Before and After the Arab Awakening: The Cases of Syria and Libya." In Werrell and Femia, eds., "The Arab Spring and Climate Change: A Climate and Security Correlations Series (Washington: Center for American Progress, 2013), available at https:// www.americanprogress.org/issues/security/reports/2013/02/28/54579/the-ar- ab-spring-and-climate-change/; United Nations High Commissioner for Refu- gees, "Syrian Regional Refugee Response: Inter-agency Information Sharing Portal," available at http://data.unhcr.org/syrianrefugees/regional.php (last ac- cessed March 2017).

12. Perrine Massy, "Is Tunisia Heading toward a 'Thirst Uprising'?", Al-Monitor, September 16, 2016, available at http://www.al-monitor.com/pulse/origi- nals/2016/09/tunisia-water-scarcity-crisis-protests.html.

13. Bouazza Ben Bouazza and Mehdi El Alem, "'We Are Thirsty' Say Tunisians as Drought Creates Tensions," Associated Press, September 24, 2016, avail- able at http://www.stripes.com/news/middle-east/2.1198/we-are-thirsty- say-tunisians-as-drought-creates-tensions-1.430751?utm_source=Media +Review+for+September+26%2C+2016&utm_campaign=DMR-+EN+- +09%2F26%2F2016&utm_medium=email.

14. United Nations Department of Economic and Social Affairs, "World Popula- tion Projected to Reach 9.7 Billion by 2050," July 29, 2015, available at http:// www.un.org/en/development/desa/news/population/2015-report.html.

15. *The Guardian*, "How Much Water Is Needed to Produce Food and How Much Do We Waste?", January 10, 2013, available at https://www.theguardian.com/ news/datablog/2013/jan/10/how-much-water-food-production-waste; Wa- ter Footprint Network, "GRACE launches new Water Footprint Calculator," available at http://waterfootprint.org/en/about-us/news/news/grace-launches- new-water-footprint-calculator/ (last accessed March 2017).

16. United Nations World Water Assessment Programme, "The United Nations World Water Development Report 2015: Water for a Sustainable World" (Par- is: United Nations Educational, Scientific and Cultural Organization, 2015), available at https://www.unesco-ihe.org/sites/default/files/wwdr_2015.pdf.

17. Ibid.

18. World Bank Group, "High and Dry."

19. Ibid.

20. Ibid.

21. Robert I. McDonald and others, "Urban Growth, Climate Change, and Freshwater Availability," *PNAS* 108 (15) (2011): 6312–6317, available at http://www.pnas.org/content/108/15/6312.full.

22. World Bank Group, "High and Dry."

23. Ibid.

24. Ibid.

25. Ibid.

26. Ibid.

27. The United Nations Interagency Framework Team for Preventive Action, "Renewable Resources and Conflict: Toolkit and Guidance for Preventing and Managing Land and Natural Resources Conflict" (2012), available at http://www.un.org/en/land-natural-resources-conflict/renewable-resources.shtml.

28. Ibid.

29. Ibid.

30. Schulyer Null and Lauren Herzer Risi, "Navigating Complexity: Climate, Migration, and Conflict in a Changing World" (Washington: USAID and Woodrow Wilson International Center for Scholars, 2016), available at https://www.wilsoncenter.org/publication/navigating-complexity-climate-migration-and-conflict-changing-world.

31. UNICEF, "Darfur – Overview," available at https://www.unicef.org/infobycountry/sudan_darfuroverview.html (last accessed March 2017).

32. Tianyi Luo, Robert Samuel Young, and Paul Reig, "Aqueduct Projected Water Stress Country Rankings" (Washington: World Resources Institute, 2015), available at http://www.wri.org/publication/aqueduct-projected-water-stress-country-rankings.

33. Fund for Peace, "Fragile States Index 2016," available at http://fsi.fundforpeace.org/ (last accessed March 2017).

34. James Fergusson, "The World Will Soon Be at War Over Water," *Newsweek*, April 24, 2015, available at http://www.newsweek.com/2015/05/01/world-will-soon-be-war-over-water-324328.html.

35. *Senator Paul Simon Water for the World Act of 2014*, Public Law 113-289, 113th Cong. (December 19, 2014), available at https://www.congress.gov/bill/113th-congress/house-bill/2901.

36. United Nations Framework Convention on Climate Change, "The Paris Agreement," available at http://unfccc.int/paris_agreement/items/9485.php (last accessed March 2017); United Nations, "Sustainable Development Goals," available at http://www.un.org/sustainabledevelopment/sustainable-development-goals/ (last accessed March 2017).

37. G20, "The G20 Presidency 2017 at a Glance," available at https://www.g20.org/Webs/G20/EN/G20/Agenda/agenda_node.html (last accessed March 2017).

Print Citations

CMS: Kenney, Carolyn. "Climate Change, Water Security, and U.S. National Security." In *The Reference Shelf: National Debate 2021-2022: Water Resources,* edited by Micah L. Issitt, 203-212. Amenia, NY: Grey House Publishing, 2021.

MLA: Kenney, Carolyn. "Climate Change, Water Security, and U.S. National Security." *The Reference Shelf: National Debate 2021-2022: Water Resources,* edited by Micah L. Issitt, Grey House Publishing, 2021, pp. 203-212.

APA: Kenney, C. (2021). Climate change, water security, and U.S. national security. In Micah L. Issitt (Ed.), *The reference shelf: National debate 2021-2022: Water resources* (pp. 203-212). Amenia, NY: Grey House Publishing.

Bibliography

Black, Matt. "America's Clean Water Crisis Goes Far Beyond Flint: There's No Relief in Sight." *Time*. Feb 20, 2020. https://pulitzercenter.org/stories/americas-clean-water-crisis-goes-far-beyond-flint-theres-no-relief-sight.

Borja-Vega, Christian, and Eva Kloeve. "Why a Human Rights Based Approach to Water and Sanitation Is Essential for the Poor." *World Bank*. Sep 28, 2018. https://blogs.worldbank.org/water/why-human-rights-based-approach-water-and-sanitation-essential-poor.

"The Business Opportunity in Water Conservation." *McKinsey Quarterly*. Dec 1, 2009. https://www.mckinsey.com/business-functions/sustainability/our-insights/the-business-opportunity-in-water-conservation.

"Climate Change and Water—Warmer Oceans, Flooding and Droughts." *EEA*. European Environment Agency. Nov 23, 2020. https://www.eea.europa.eu/signals/signals-2018-content-list/articles/climate-change-and-water-2014.

Cohen, Steve. "The Human and Financial Cost of Pollution." *State of the Planet*. Columbia University. Oct 23, 2017. https://blogs.ei.columbia.edu/2017/10/23/the-human-and-financial-cost-of-pollution/.

"Combined Sewer Overflows (CSOs)." *EPA*. National Pollutant Discharge Elimination System. Aug 13, 2020. https://www.epa.gov/npdes/combined-sewer-over-flows-csos.

De Feo, Giovanni, et al. "The Historical Development of Sewers Worldwide." *Sustainability*. Vol 6. 2014. file:///Users/micahissitt/Downloads/sustainability-06-03936.pdf.

Denchak, Melissa. "Flint Water Crisis: Everything You Need to Know." *NRDC*. Nov 8, 2018. https://www.nrdc.org/stories/flint-water-crisis-everything-you-need-know.

Dickstein, Corey. "GAO: 102 Military Bases Face Water Shortage Risk; Pentagon Must Track Issue Better." *Stars and Stripes*. Dec 3, 2019. https://www.stripes.com/news/us/gao-102-military-bases-face-water-shortage-risk-pentagon-must-track-issue-better-1.609642.

"Drought." *World Health Organization*. 2021. https://www.who.int/health-topics/drought#tab=tab_1.

Evans, Mary Anna. "Flushing the Toilet Has Never Been Riskier." *The Atlantic*. Sep 17, 2015. https://www.theatlantic.com/technology/archive/2015/09/americas-sewage-crisis-public-health/405541/.

Fong, Joss, and Dion Lee. "How Antony van Leeuwenhoek Discovered Bacteria in the 1970s." *Vox*. Oct 24, 2016. https://www.vox.com/2016/8/9/12405306/antoni-van-leeuwenhoek.

"Future Widespread Water Shortage Likely in U.S." *SITN*. Science in the News.

Mar 20, 2019. https://sitn.hms.harvard.edu/flash/2019/widespread-water-short-age-likely-in-u-s-caused-by-population-growth-and-climate-change/.

Gaynes, Robert P. *Germ Theory*. Washington, D.C.: ASM Press, 2011.

Goldenberg, Suzanne. "The Worst of Times: Bush's Environmental Legacy Examined." *The Guardian*. Jan 16, 2009. https://www.theguardian.com/politics/2009/jan/16/greenpolitics-georgebush.

Grandoni, Dino, and Scott Clement. "Americans like Green New Deal's Goals, but They Reject Paying Trillions to Reach Them." *Washington Post*. Nov 27 2019. https://www.washingtonpost.com/climate-environment/2019/11/27/americans-like-green-new-deals-goals-they-reject-paying-trillions-reach-them/.

Hampton, Liz. "Factbox: U.S. Oil and Gas Regulatory Rollbacks under Trump." *Reuters*. Aug 29, 2019. https://www.reuters.com/article/us-usa-climate-regulations-factbox/factbox-u-s-oil-and-gas-regulatory-rollbacks-under-trump-idUSKC-N1VJ2BP.

Harrington, Samantha. "Causes of Global Warming: How Scientists Know That Humans Are Responsible." *Yale Climate Connections*. Mar 27, 2020. https://yaleclimateconnections.org/2020/03/causes-of-global-warming/.

Hayes, Jared, and Scott Faber. "UPDATED MAP: Suspected and Confirmed PFAS Pollution at U.S. Military Bases." *EWG*. Apr 2, 2020. https://www.ewg.org/news-and-analysis/2020/04/updated-map-suspected-and-confirmed-pfas-pollution-us-military-bases.

"History of the Clean Water Act." *EPA*. https://www.epa.gov/laws-regulations/history-clean-water-act.

"How Sewage Pollution Ends Up in Rivers." *American Rivers*. 2019. https://www.americanrivers.org/threats-solutions/clean-water/sewage-pollution/.

"How Technology Is Providing Solutions for Clean Water." *Ohio University*. Mar 2, 2021. https://onlinemasters.ohio.edu/blog/how-technology-is-providing-solutions-for-clean-water/.

"How We Use Water." *EPA*. https://www.epa.gov/watersense/how-we-use-water.

"Implementation of the Federal Water Pollution Control Act (Regulation and Monitoring of Toxic and Hazardous Chemicals)." Hearings before the Subcommittee on Oversights and Review of the Committee on Public Works and Transportation U.S. House of Representatives. *U.S. Government Printing Office*, 1980, p. 1904.

Jackson, Brooks. "Bush as Businessman." *CNN*. May 13, 1999. https://www.cnn.com/ALLPOLITICS/stories/1999/05/13/president.2000/jackson.bush/.

James, Kirsten. "Report: How the Biggest Companies Score on Water Sustainability." *Water Deeply*. The New Humanitarian. Mar 22, 2018. https://deeply.thenewhumanitarian.org/water/community/2018/03/22/report-how-the-biggest-companies-score-on-water-sustainability.

Kennedy, Merrit. "Lead-Laced Water in Flint: A Step-By-Step Look at the Makings of a Crisis." *NPR*. Apr 20, 2016. https://www.npr.org/sections/thetwo-way/2016/04/20/465545378/lead-laced-water-in-flint-a-step-by-step-look-at-the-makings-of-a-crisis.

Kenney, Carolyn. "Climate Change, Water Security, and U.S. National Security." *Center for American Progress*. Mar 22, 2017. https://www.americanprogress.org/issues/security/reports/2017/03/22/428918/climate-change-water-security-u-s-national-security/.

"'Killer' Trees? Not Exactly." *Earth Observatory*. Sep 30, 2013. https://earthobservatory.nasa.gov/images/84021/killer-trees-not-exactly.

Lakhani, Nina. "Revealed: Millions of Americans Can't Afford Water as Bills Rise 80% in a Decade." *The Guardian*. Jun 23, 2020. https://www.theguardian.com/us-news/2020/jun/23/millions-of-americans-cant-afford-water-bills-rise.

Lindwall, Courtney. "Industrial Agricultural Pollution 101." *NRDC*. Jul 31, 2019. https://www.nrdc.org/stories/industrial-agricultural-pollution-101.

Madrigal, Alexis C. "A Short Masterpiece on the History of Sewers." *The Atlantic*. Oct 5, 2010. https://www.theatlantic.com/technology/archive/2010/10/a-short-masterpiece-on-the-history-of-sewers/64076/.

Manke, Kara. "Clean Water Act Dramatically Cut Pollution in U.S. Waterways." *Berkeley News*. Oct 8, 2018. https://news.berkeley.edu/2018/10/08/clean-water-act-dramatically-cut-pollution-in-u-s-waterways/.

McGraw, George, and Radhika Fox. "Closing the Water Access Gap in the United States." *US Water Alliance*. 2019. http://uswateralliance.org/sites/uswateralliance.org/files/publications/Closing%20the%20Water%20Access%20Gap%20in%20the%20United%20States_DIGITAL.pdf.

McSweeney, Robert. "Explainer: 'Desertification' and the Role of Climate Change." *Carbon Brief*. Aug 6, 2019. https://www.carbonbrief.org/explainer-desertification-and-the-role-of-climate-change.

Pechet, Tamin. "Turning Water Problems into Business Opportunities." *Tech Crunch*. Jun 22, 2015. https://techcrunch.com/2015/06/22/turning-water-problems-into-business-opportunities/.

Pimental, David, et al. "Water Resources: Agricultural and Environmental Issues." *BioScience*. Vol. 54, No. 10. Oct 2004.

"Resolution Adopted by the General Assembly on 28 July 2010." *United Nations*. Sixty Fourth Session. Aug 3, 2010. https://documents-dds-ny.un.org/doc/UNDOC/GEN/N09/479/35/PDF/N0947935.pdf?OpenElement.

Richards, Ryan. "Debunking the Trump Administration's New Water Rule." *Center for American Progress*. Mar 27, 2019. https://www.americanprogress.org/issues/green/news/2019/03/27/467697/debunking-trump-administrations-new-water-rule/.

Robertson, Derek. "Flint Has Clean Water Now: Why Won't People Drink It?" *Politico*. Dec 23, 2020. https://www.politico.com/news/magazine/2020/12/23/flint-water-crisis-2020-post-coronavirus-america-445459.

Rotman, Michael. "Cuyahoga River Fire." *Cleveland Historical*. 2021. Oct 5, 2019. https://clevelandhistorical.org/items/show/63.

Royte, Elizabeth. "The Simple River-Cleaning Tactics That Big Farms Ignore." *National Geographic*. Dec 7, 2017. https://www.nationalgeographic.com/science/article/iowa-agriculture-runoff-water-pollution-environment.

Shabecoff, Philip. "Reagan and Environment: To Many, a Stalemate." *New York Times*. Jan 2, 1989. https://www.nytimes.com/1989/01/02/us/reagan-and-environment-to-many-a-stalemate.html.

Simon, Matt. "Desalination Is Booming: But What About All That Toxic Brine?" *Wired*. Jan 14, 2019. https://www.wired.com/story/desalination-is-booming-but-what-about-all-that-toxic-brine/.

Tamvada, Jagannadha Pawan, and Mili Shrivastava. "Going Green Dramatically Benefits Businesses—It Should Be Central to Their Coronavirus Recovery Strategy." *The Conversation*. Aug 17, 2020. https://theconversation.com/going-green-dramatically-benefits-businesses-it-should-be-central-to-their-coronavirus-recovery-strategy-143855.

Tortajada, Cecilia, and Pierre van Rensburg. "Drink More Recycled Wastewater." *Nature*. Dec 31, 2019. https://www.nature.com/articles/d41586-019-03913-6.

"Total Water Use in the United States." *USGS*. https://www.usgs.gov/special-topic/water-science-school/science/total-water-use-united-states?qt-science_center_objects=0#qt-science_center_objects.

Verhoeven, Harry. "Climate Change, Conflict and Development in Sudan: Global Neo-Malthusian Narratives and Local Power Struggles." *Development and Change*. Vol 42, No 3, 2011.

"Water." *World Bank*. Understanding Poverty. Mar 01, 2021. https://www.worldbank.org/en/topic/water/overview.

"The Water Crisis." *Water.org*. 2021. https://water.org/our-impact/water-crisis/.

"Water Public Opinion Polls and Data." *Water Polls*. 2021. https://waterpolls.org/.

"Water Recycling." *CASA*. California Association of Sanitation Agencies. 2021. https://casaweb.org/renewable-resources/water-recycling/.

"Watersheds, Flooding, and Pollution." *NOAA*. National Oceanic and Atmospheric Administration. 2021. https://www.noaa.gov/education/resource-collections/freshwater/watersheds-flooding-and-pollution.

Weisskopf, Michael. "Auto-Pollution Debate Has Ring of the Past." *Washington Post*. Mar 26, 1990. https://www.washingtonpost.com/archive/politics/1990/03/26/auto-pollution-debate-has-ring-of-the-past/d1650ba3-2896-44fa-ac1b-4e28aca78674/.

"What Communities Are Doing." *EPA*. Urban Waters. Aug 11, 2020. https://www.epa.gov/urbanwaters/what-communities-are-doing.

"What Is a Harmful Algal Bloom?" *NOAA*. Apr 27, 2016. https://www.noaa.gov/what-is-harmful-algal-bloom.

"What Is a Watershed?" *NOAA*. National Oceanic and Atmospheric Administration. Feb 26, 2021. https://oceanservice.noaa.gov/facts/watershed.html.

Willis, Jay. "The Hidden Racial Inequities of Access to Water in America." *GQ*. Nov 25, 2019. https://www.gq.com/story/hidden-racial-inequities-water-access.

Websites

American Geosciences Institute (AGI)

Americangeosciences.org

The AGI is a political organization dedicated to providing support and data for federal legislators involved in crafting policy for federal legislation. The organization also works with state-level member groups and supports programs for geophysics, earth science, and geology. Founded in 1948, the organization also publishes *Nautilus* magazine, which provides articles on issues involving water preservation and natural resource conservation.

American Water Resources Association

Awra.org

Established in 1964, the American Water Resources Association (AWRA) is a nonprofit professional organization open to individuals working in various water resources-related professions. AWRA operates and maintains resources for hydrologic engineers, hydrologists, forestry and biological conservation professionals, educators, and legal professionals. The organization also publishes the *Journal of the American Water Association* and a trade magazine that covers employment, new technology and development, and the economic dimension of the industry. The AWRA also publishes digital articles, through the organization's website, that provide resources for educators, professionals, and students interested in various water resource issues.

National Water Resources Association

Nwra.org

First established in the 1890s, the National Water Resources Association (NWRA) supports research into water resources preservation and management. The organization sponsors and publishes data and studies, holds conferences of water resource professionals and acts as a federation of local and regional water resources institutions and associations. The organization is also involved in federal lobbying, and has been active in campaigns to reauthorize and to enhance the Clean Water Act, Endangered Species Act, and the Safe Drinking Water Act.

Soil and Water Conservation Society (SWCS)

Swcs.org

The Soil and Water Conservation Society is a professional and scientific association dedicated to promoting and supporting natural resources management and sustainable development. Founded in 1945 by Hugh Bennett, often called the "Father of American Soil Conservation," the SWCS funds research, education, and advocacy programs and partners with a variety of regional and local conservation organizations to promote local conservation efforts. The SWCS operates a large scale program, through Iowa State University, to study and develop methods for the preservation of watersheds and is also involved in Wetland conservation. With the National Resources Conservation Service, the SWCS also operates one of the nation's largest media resource banks focused on conservation history and other issues.

U.S. Environmental Protection Agency (EPA)
www.epa.org

The Environmental Protection Agency (EPA) is the branch of the federal government responsible for protecting environmental resources, enforcing federal regulations on pollution, and addressing public health issues involving environmental agents and pollution. The EPA provides a variety of free information available to the general public, as well as specific publications for students and educators. In addition, the EPA supports a large number of research and education initiatives aimed at raising awareness about environmental threats and supporting federal regulations on environmental protection and conservation.

U.S. Geological Survey (USGS)
www.usgs.gov

The U.S. Geological Survey is the official branch of the U.S. government designated to support scientists in the geological and natural resources management. Founded in 1879, under the auspices of the U.S. Department of the Interior, the organization supports resources and produces data that has been used for more than a century to guide federal and state decisions on resources management. Subdivisions within the USGS handle specific types of resources, including water. The USGS also publishes fact sheets, press releases, and articles for students, teachers, and the general public that explain the organization's current and future goals and the various challenges facing the United States in terms of resource management.

World Resources Institute (WRI)
Wri.org

The World Resources Institute is an international nonprofit established in 1982 under a grant from the MacArthur Foundation. WRI supports research and programs in the areas of water conservation, sustainable energy, forest and ecosystem preservation, climate change, oceanic biodiversity, food production, and urban development. The WRI website contains a number of articles summarizing major studies in the realm of resource management and provides a large amount of information about the global effort to protect the oceans and natural water reservoirs.

Index